DAVID McDOWALL

BRITAIN
IN CLOSE-UP

Longman

Pearson Education Limited
Edinburgh Gate
Harlow
Essex CM20 2JE
England
and Associated Companies throughout the world.

www.longman.com

© Pearson Education Limited 1999

Ninth impression 2007

ISBN 978-0-582-32826-6

Printed in China
SWTC/09

Acknowledgements

We are grateful to the following for permission to reproduce copyright photographs:
Ace for 106/Roger Howard, 112/Berry Bingel, 135 right/Ronald Toms; Action Images for 113; Andes Press/Carlos Reyes-Manzo for 97 bottom, 173, 174; Arcaid/Mark Fennes for 76; BBC for 163, 164; J.Allan Cash for 85, 122; Circa Photo Library/John Smith for 171 bottom, 172, 177; Ecoscene for 15 bottom, 71 & 187 top/Eric Schaffer; Environmental Images/V Miles for 186; Format for 83 top & 91 top/Judy Harrison, 87 & 190/Jacky Chapman, 92 & 191/Lisa Woolett, 156/Maggie Murray, 197/Sally Lancaster; Ronald Grant Archive/Keith Hamshere for 144; Sally & Richard Greenhill for 16 top, 23, 57, 59, 66, 67, 94 middle, 103, 192, 199, 200; Robert Harding Picture Library for 176/David Beatty, 180 top/Rolf Richardson, 11 bottom, 83 bottom; David Hockney for 115; David Hoffman for 69, 99; Hutchison Library for 175/Liba Taylor, 182; Impact Photos for 138/Roger Scrutton, 153/Caroline Penn, 160/Alex Macnaughton, 195/Peter Arkell, 196/Ben Edwards; The Independent/Brian Harris for 124; Katz Pictures/Richard Baker for 123 bottom, 166; Paul Mulcahy for 161 top; Network for 15 top & 17/Michael Abrahams, 18, 20 & 75/John Sturrock; PA News for 9/Rebecca Naden, 27/Michael Stephens, 28, 41, 50 & 63/Fiona Hanson, 31 middle & 52/Neil Munns, 31 top/Sean Dempsey, 38/Dave Kendall, 42 & 43/John Stillwell, 44/Adam Butler, 62/Justin Williams, 81/Owen Humphreys, 82/John Giles, 126 top right & 127/Brian Little,

129/David Jones, 141 &143/Chris Bacon,180 bottom/David Giles, 35, 105 bottom; Photofusion fo 148/Christa Stadtler, 150/Crispin Hughes, 151/Peter Olive, 154/Giles Barnard; Pictor International for 22, 94 bottom left, 104 top, 135 left, 152, 162; Popperfoto for 30 & 78/Kevin Lamarque/REUTERS, 131 top/Dave Joiner, 26, 181; Rex Features for 8 & 126 bottom right/Peter Brooker, 31 bottom/Today, 96/The Times, 123 top/Paul Darrah, 142 top/Sipa, 161 bottom/Graham Trott, 171 top/Chris Harris, 188/David Hartley, 33, 34, 40, 126 top left, 126 bottom left, 128, 139, 179; Science Photo Library/Jim Selby for 194; Scottish Exhibition Centre/George Mahoney for 118; Shakespeares Globe/John Tramper for 117; Skyscan for 189; Sporting Pictures for 114; Stockwave for 29, 32; Tony Stone for 11 top left/John Lamb, 16 bottom/Doug Armand, 90/Martin Salter, 91 bottom/Bob Thomas, 94 top right/Frank Siteman, 104 bottom/Chris Haigh, 111/Joe McBride, 134 & 155/David H Endersbee, 187 bottom/Michael Busselle, 12, 84 right, 86, 94 bottom right, 97 top; Telegraph Colour Library for 11 top right & 107/V.C.L, 21/Stewart Bonney, 60/Neil Setchfield, 108/Keith MacGregor, 109/Michael Nischke, 116/Ben Rector, 203/P Thurston, 19; Topham Picturepoint for 119; TRIP for 46, 70, 77 & 105 top/H.Rogers, 110/N.Price; Universal Pictorial Press for 142 bottom; John Walmsley fo 94 top left, 131 bottom, 147, 157; Janine Wiedel for 84 left, 98.

Illustrations by Dave Green, Graham Humphries and Celia Witchard.

Cover photo © Tony Stone Images/Joe Cornish

Cover design by Michele Ashby

Text design by Jennifer Coles

Picture research by Louise Edgeworth

Project Management by Matthew Duffy and Judith King

Contents

Author's acknowledgements

No book of this kind can possibly be written without substantial help from the work of other writers who have written either about Britain generally or about a particular aspect of it. These books are listed among the study materials at the end of each chapter. In addition, I am greatly indebted to those who kindly read particular chapters or advised me on particular points: Pat Gordon, John Neil, Caroline Nolan, and Nuala and Siobhan Savage. Finally, I am particularly grateful to my editor, Brigit Viney, for the way in which her diligence brought significantly sharper focus to the text.

A note on study tools

At the end of each chapter are lists of printed materials and Internet websites with primary material for research, reading and classroom discussion. Websites are usually current, but often lack the depth of analysis of printed sources. Printed sources, on the other hand, can seem dated, but they are usually more considered. However, media websites (see Chapter 12), particularly those for the BBC and the broadsheet press, can be invaluable for political, economic and social commentary.

Some websites listed here are official government ones, others are not. The Central Office of Information and www.open.gov.uk offer official departmental information.

Northern Ireland has an extensive listing which is intended to cover the range of political views.

Relief map of Great Britain, Northern Ireland and the Republic of Ireland

Key

Height in metres

400

200

0

0   150km

0°

Orkney Islands

Shetland Islands

Outer Hebrides

Inverness

Aberdeen

SCOTLAND

NORTH SEA

River Tay

56°   Stirling   Firth of Forth   56°

Glasgow

Edinburgh

River Tweed

Firth of Clyde

Derry   River Tyne   Newcastle upon Tyne

NORTHERN IRELAND   Carlisle   Durham

Belfast   ENGLAND

REPUBLIC OF IRELAND   Isle of Man

Dublin   IRISH SEA   York

Leeds   Hull

Preston

Liverpool   Manchester

Sheffield

Anglesey   Lincoln

Caenarvon   Chester

Nottingham

River Severn   Stafford

Leicester   Norwich

Peterborough

Birmingham   Great Ouse   Cambridge

WALES   Warwick   Ipswich

Milton Keynes

Carmarthen   Gloucester   Colchester

Swansea   Oxford

Cardiff   Bristol   Reading   London

Bristol Channel   River Thames

Dover

Brighton   Calais

Exeter   Portsmouth

Isle of Wight

Plymouth

Truro   ENGLISH CHANNEL

FRANCE

Reproduced with the kind permission of Brepols

Introduction

This book aims to describe Britain as it is today, and to go beyond popular and stereotyped images to examine the more complex realities of modern Britain and its people. It also attempts to assess the changes taking place in Britain today and to indicate the direction in which the country is travelling as it enters the twenty-first century.

The political background

It is impossible to do so without reviewing, in very broad outline, what has been happening to Britain in recent years. In general terms, Britain has experienced three major phases of government since 1945: 1945–79, 1979–97 and the period since 1997. In 1945 a Labour government under Prime Minister Clement Attlee established what was later called 'the post-war consensus' between the two main parties, the Conservative and Labour Parties. This consensus referred to fundamental economic and social matters, so that Britain could rebuild itself economically and socially following the Second World War.

Despite ideological differences, both Conservative and Labour governments followed the principles for the national economy formulated by the great pre-war economist J.M. Keynes, which stated that capitalist society could only survive if government controlled, managed and even planned much of the general shape of its economy. The requirements of war (1939–45) had increased the belief in, and practice of, government planning. Labour nationalised those industries and services considered central to the national economy: notably coal and steel production, gas and electricity supply, and the railways.

Labour also established virtually full employment and a 'welfare state', which guaranteed free health and education, pensions and benefits for the old, disabled, sick or unemployed. The maintenance of the welfare state and full employment were accepted by the Conservatives as fundamental responsibilities of government. However, neither principle could be ensured without an expanding economy. As the Conservative Prime Minister Harold Macmillan (1957–63) remarked, managing the post-war economy was like juggling four balls in the air: an expanding economy, full employment, stable prices and a strong pound. It was only in the question of full employment that post-war governments were truly successful.

Regardless of which party was in power, Britain's economy became characterised by a 'stop–go' cycle: periods of inflation followed by crises in the balance of payments, the difference between the value of total imports and exports. By its own standards Britain seemed to be doing reasonably well, but it was doing only half as well as other industrialised countries, and Britain's share of world trade fell from 13.9 per cent in 1964 to 10.8 per cent in 1970. This poor comparative performance was reflected in the decline of the manufacturing industry, once Britain's proudest asset. By 1980, manufacturing productivity per head in Britain was two-thirds that in Italy, half that in France and less than half that in West Germany.

By 1975 the post-war consensus was beginning to collapse, with growing economic difficulties, most notably the doubling of the number of unemployed in the two years 1974–75, to exceed one million. In the winter of 1978–79, nicknamed 'the Winter of Discontent', the trade unions refused to accept the pay restraint demanded by the Labour government's economic strategy. Largely as a result of this refusal, Labour lost the election of 1979, which was fought on two issues: the question of union strength and the broader question of national economic decline. While Labour proposed continuing with the same economic policies, the victorious Conservatives, under their new leader Margaret Thatcher, offered a radical alternative.

Thatcher's ideas and values, marking the second major phase of post-war government, dominated government policies until the defeat of the Conservatives in 1997. She brought an entirely new tone to government. 'I am not a consensus politician,' she announced in one of her most famous remarks. 'I am a conviction politician.' Having taken over the party leadership in 1975, she became convinced that the Conservatives had implemented basically socialist-type policies since 1945. She decided to establish a genuinely free-market economy unconstrained by government, which she regarded as true Conservatism, and to destroy socialism, which she blamed for the country's ills. Her targets were the Labour strongholds: council estates (public housing rented by local government to people on low incomes); the trade unions; the local authorities; and the nationalised industries.

Margaret Thatcher, Prime Minister 1979-1990, polarised the country with her 'conviction' politics.

Mrs Thatcher believed that Keynesian economics were fundamentally wrong-headed and that all controls and regulation of the economy, except regulation of money supply, should be removed. She would limit government borrowing by reducing expenditure in the public sector, and she would set high interest rates to discourage everyone from borrowing. This, according to her philosophy, would create a stable economic climate with low rates of inflation and taxation. This in turn would allow a market economy to recover. The government role in economic revival would be minimal beyond securing these stable conditions and cutting public expenditure.

Mrs Thatcher pressed on with a free-market agenda where her Conservative predecessors had retreated and had little time for differing views. As she herself said, 'I have no time for arguments' – even with her colleagues. High interest rates made it impossible for many manufacturers to borrow money. Her refusal to assist struggling industries led to dramatic changes. By its second anniversary

in 1981 the Thatcher government had presided over the greatest decline in total output in one year since the Depression of 1931, and the biggest collapse in industrial production in one year since 1921. Britain's balance of payments began to deteriorate. Its share of world trade fell by 15 per cent between 1979 and 1986, a larger fall than in any other industrialised country during that period. In 1983 the import of manufactured goods exceeded exports for the first time in 200 years. There were social consequences, too. In May 1979 there had been 1.2 million unemployed. By May 1983 it was 3 million, over 13 per cent of the workforce.

Furthermore, the stress created by government policies began to divide the nation. Growth in the south of the country was three times as fast as in the rest of the country during most of the decade. The divide was not purely geographical. The policies led to a growing gulf between the richest and poorest all over the country.

Mrs Thatcher was determined to break with the past and did not look back. She began to sell into private hands many publicly-owned production and service companies, and even the regional water authorities. She had two basic interests: to free these areas from government control and to persuade ordinary individuals to buy a stake in these enterprises. In both aims, she was largely successful. Government largely gave up its traditional intervention in the economy and began to turn Britain into a 'share-owning democracy'. Between 1979 and 1992 the proportion of the population owning shares rose from 7 to 24 per cent, powerfully emphasising that the accepted philosophy of the 1980s was personal wealth rather than public ownership. Such was the attraction of this philosophy that even the Labour Party, traditionally the party of public ownership, felt compelled to accept the new realities.

Mrs Thatcher also set about controlling government spending. In central government her success was limited. While she successfully reduced the size of the Civil Service, she failed to reduce government expenditure significantly.

She had greater success with local government. She abolished the metropolitan authorities – created to coordinate the affairs of London and six other large conurbations – all of which had been Labour-controlled. She also undermined local authorities (or councils) by limiting their ability to raise money, by forcing them to allow occupants of council-owned rented accommodation to purchase their homes at attractive prices, by reducing their authority in areas like education, and by breaking up local authority bus services. Margaret Thatcher resigned in 1990, when she lost the confidence of over one-third of her party colleagues in Parliament. Her measures largely failed to achieve what they had been intended to do. Whilst trying to cut public expenditure, she faced major increases in costs: pensioners were living longer; unemployment figures stayed high; and the cost of the health service and the armed forces rose rapidly. Her economic solution proved simplistic. Britain continued to be outperformed by its competitors. By the early 1990s Britain's share of world trade had fallen to 6 per cent.

Fundamentally Mrs Thatcher faced the same dilemma her predecessors had all faced since the war. The commitment to reduce government spending conflicted with the need for investment in education, training, research and development, in order to produce long-term improvements in the economy.

Thatcher's successor, John Major, had a softer manner. It soon became clear he valued the idea of consensus more highly than Mrs Thatcher had done. But he won the fourth consecutive Conservative election victory in 1992 just as Britain entered its worst period of recession since the 1930s. Recession was followed by a dramatic day of speculation on the pound sterling in 1993, which forced Britain out of the European Exchange Rate Mechanism, the structure intended as a preparation for Europe's single currency. The Major administration never recovered. It raised taxes having promised not to, and many of its MPs were caught acting in ways that were perceived as corrupt. A deep split emerged between the growing right wing and the centre left of the party. The prime issue of disagreement was British commitment to the European Union, with the right refusing further integration and expressing implacable hostility to the European Monetary Union. The government's majority in Parliament was so reduced that it had to depend on the vote of Ulster Unionist Members of Parliament (MPs), and this in turn undermined its ability to resolve the conflict in Northern Ireland. Thus the Conservatives were heavily defeated in May 1997, because they were widely perceived to be unfit to govern.

Tony Blair's Labour Party came to power with a 'landslide' victory, and the promise of an entirely new beginning. It had dissociated itself from old-style Labour by rejecting the ideology of state-owned industry, and by reducing trade union influence on the party. It also portrayed itself as

filled with youthful vigour, in vivid contrast with the Conservatives who seemed old and tired. It made long-term issues its priority, in particular raising educational standards in order to achieve a workforce fit for the twenty-first century. It also laid emphasis on the compassionate values of socialism, but without the old ideology. It was happy to pursue the new capitalism as long as it

'Glad Morning': Tony Blair greets well-wishers following his electoral triumph in May 1997.

could be made inclusive of 'the many, not the few', as its central campaign slogan put it. It believed Britain had no choice but to join the European Monetary Union, and so worked towards the necessary 'economic convergence'. Finally, it argued for constitutional reform. It would decentralise power and be more openly accountable than any previous government. Above all, Labour promised to rejuvenate Britain. No one could doubt that it had a real job on its hands.

Further information

PRINTED MATERIAL

Blair, Tony 1996 *New Britain: My Vision of a Young Country* Fourth Estate

Coxall, Bill and Robins, Lynton 1994 *Contemporary British Politics* Chapters 1–5, 32, 33 Macmillan

Davies, A.J. 1995 *The Conservative Party and the Pursuit of Power* Abacus

Davies, A.J. 1996 *To Build a New Jerusalem: The British Labour Party from Keir Hardie to Tony Blair* Abacus

Young, Hugo 1989 *One of Us: A Biography of Margaret Thatcher* Macmillan

1 *Snapshots of Britain*

A sense of identity

The United Kingdom of Great Britain and Northern Ireland, to give it its formal title, is a highly centralised and unitary state, and its largest component, England, has been so for almost 1,000 years, longer than any other European country. By the sixteenth century Wales was fully incorporated into English administration and law but Britain as a political entity did not emerge until 1707, when the ancient kingdoms of Scotland and England were united. Ireland, which fell completely under English rule in the sixteenth century, became formally part of the United Kingdom in 1801 when, like Scotland a century earlier, it lost its own parliament. Ireland achieved independence in 1921, with the exception of six northern counties which remained part of the United Kingdom. Yet Northern Ireland is not part of Britain, although the term 'Britain' is often used loosely to mean the United Kingdom.

It is widely assumed that the British form a relatively homogeneous society with a strong sense of identity, but it is an assumption that requires considerable qualification. Even after 300 years the terms 'British' and 'Britain', which are used for official purposes, can seem very artificial. In his famous *Dictionary of Modern English Usage*, first published in 1926, Fowler wrote:

It must be remembered that no Englishman, or perhaps no Scotsman, calls himself a Briton without a sneaking sense of the ludicrous, or hears himself referred to as a BRITISHER without squirming. How should an Englishman utter the words Great Britain *with the glow of emotion that for him goes with* England*? His Sovereign may be Her* Britannic *Majesty to outsiders, but to him is Queen of* England.

For centuries it has been the idea of England (or Scotland, or Wales), rather than of Britain, which has been charged with patriotic emotion, particularly at times of national crisis. For example,

at the Battle of Trafalgar in 1805, Admiral Lord Nelson's famous order to the British fleet read, 'England expects that every man will do his duty'. In 1939, during Parliament's emergency debate on the eve of war, one MP called across the chamber to another who was rising to speak: 'Come on, Arthur, speak for England.'

One should not be surprised, either, that Fowler wrote the words quoted above under the entry for 'England'. If you look up 'Britain', 'British' and 'Briton', you will find 'See England'. Many people call Britain 'England', and the British 'English', as if Wales, Northern Ireland and Scotland were merely outer additions to England. Nothing, it should be said, infuriates the Scots, Welsh or Irish more than ignorantly to be called English, or for all Britain to be referred to as England. They have their own distinctive identities (see Chapter 9).

Moreover, the idea of England evokes images of the Queen, the Houses of Parliament, Westminster Abbey, the Tower of London and the soft landscape of the southern counties of England. This is not so surprising since almost one quarter of the British people live within 25 miles (40 km) of London's Trafalgar Square. But it also reveals that England as well as Britain is dominated by the south, and particularly the south east.

These popular images of England are very misleading. The United Kingdom is a land of great diversity, partly in its landscape, but more importantly in the human sphere. In addition to Scotland, Wales and Northern Ireland, the regions of England also have their special identities, which tend to be stronger the further one travels from London and the south east. In Cornwall, in the far south west, there is a reviving sense of Celtic identity, and a romantic affinity with their cousins, the people of Brittany in north-west France, persists. In the north of England, in the words of one MP, people are 'warm, friendly, quick-tempered and insular'. Communities in the north often have a strong sense of loyalty and identity. As one moves closer to London, community loyalties weaken and society is both more

Westminster Abbey: the present building, one of Britain's most famous buildings, was erected in the early thirteenth century. It is the royal church where coronations and other state ceremonies take place.

The White Tower, built 900 years ago, within the Tower of London, Britain's most famous tourist attraction.

The Houses of Parliament, the site of Britain's democratic development. The present buildings were built between 1840 and 1860.

homogeneous and yet also more individualistic, the twin characteristics of a highly integrated modern society.

Each shire or 'county', the administrative divisions of England created over 1,000 years ago, still commands its own local loyalties, expressed in that most English of games, cricket. Even in the most homogeneous part of Britain, the 'Home Counties' around London (Middlesex, Hertfordshire, Essex, Kent, Surrey), people can still feel strongly about their county identity. The sense of local difference may be partly a matter of history, but it is also to do with the subtle changes in landscape, architecture or the way English is spoken.

England, unlike the largely mountainous countries of Wales and Scotland, is mainly lowland, except for six major hilly regions: the Pennines, called the 'backbone of England' dividing the north west of England from the north east; the scenic Lake District in the north west; the Yorkshire Dales, running to the east coast of Yorkshire; the moorlands of Cornwall and Devon in the south west; and the border areas with Scotland and Wales respectively. Elsewhere the ranges of hills are relatively low, while the East Midlands and East Anglia are notably flat and featureless. In Scotland and Wales the greater part of the population is concentrated in the more lowland areas, particularly the area between Glasgow and Edinburgh, and in the eastern and south-eastern parts of Wales.

The core and the periphery

There is another way of looking at the country. Throughout history the centre of economic and political power, and therefore the largest population concentration, has been in the south of the country. By the seventeenth century London already contained at least 10 per cent of England's population. The only partial exception was in the two centuries following Britain's industrial revolution, approximately 1775–1975, when the availability of water and coal led to the growth of large industrial towns and cities in the north and Midlands of England. But as Britain leaves its industrial age behind, it is possible to recognise the older dominance of the south – a result of climate, agricultural wealth, and proximity to the European mainland.

One may draw a series of arcs outwards from London, marking an inner and outer 'core' to the country, and an inner and outer 'periphery' (see map). The pattern may seem crude, but it roughly describes the measure of authority and prosperity radiating from London since the days of Roman

The Yorkshire Dales, one of the hilly areas of England.

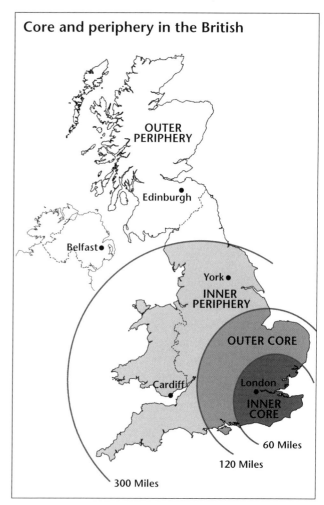

Core and periphery in the British

OUTER PERIPHERY

Edinburgh

Belfast

York
INNER PERIPHERY

OUTER CORE

Cardiff

London
INNER CORE

60 Miles

120 Miles

300 Miles

Population density by county, 1995

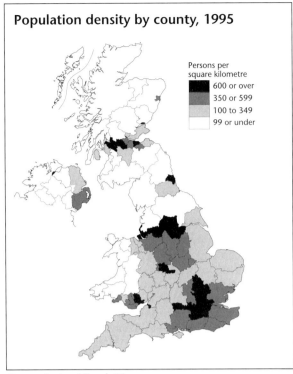

Persons per
square kilometre
- 600 or over
- 350 or 599
- 100 to 349
- 99 or under

Source: Regional Trends 32

Britain. The periphery, particularly Scotland, Wales and the north of England, has always resented the power of the south and periodically has challenged it. During the years of Conservative government, 1979–97, these were the areas of Labour Party strength, and of vehement rejection of the dominant Conservative political culture of the south.

Looking at Britain, region by region, one can see the continuing evidence of this core–periphery theory. Overall population density reveals the enduring concentration in the south east where over one-third of Britain's population lives, and also in areas of the Midlands and north of England as a result of the industrial age.

By 1997 Britain's total population was just over 58 million, but although barely increasing, the demographic distribution is changing. During the period 1980–95 there was a steady stream of young people, mainly aged between 18 and 35, who moved southwards to the core in order to improve their economic prospects. Between 1981

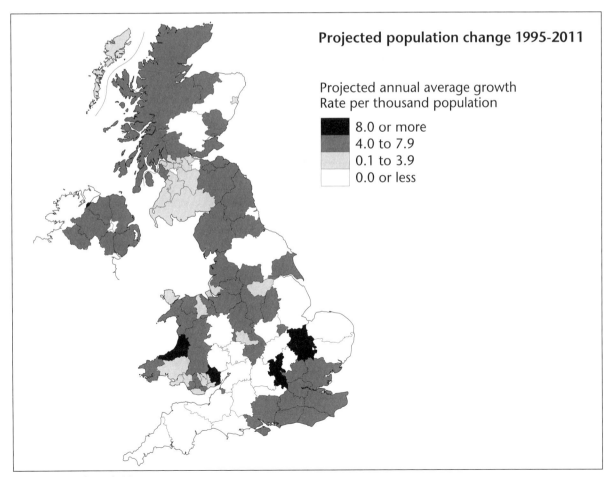

Projected population change 1995-2011

Projected annual average growth
Rate per thousand population
- 8.0 or more
- 4.0 to 7.9
- 0.1 to 3.9
- 0.0 or less

Source: Regional Trends 32

and 1987, Scotland, the north and north west of England all lost 1.3 per cent of their populations. There was a drift from Cornwall in the far south west and from western Wales towards the core also. The forecast up to the year 2016 reveals that population growth will be in the outer core and inner periphery, areas where the greatest economic growth is expected. Wales, Scotland and Northern Ireland will be virtually static or even slightly decline.

The north–south divide

If one looks at living standards and expectations in recent years, they clearly show that the south east, south, south west, East Anglia and the East Midlands tend to do much better than the peripheral areas. Over a century ago, the novelist Mrs Gaskell wrote a book entitled *North and South*, about a heroine from a soft southern village forced to move to the fictitious county of Darkshire, who confessed 'a detestation for all she had ever heard of the north of England, the manufacturers, the people, the wild and bleak country'. Mutual prejudice between a complacent population in the south and a proud but aggrieved one in the north persists. Precisely where the dividing line between north and south runs is a matter of opinion, but probably few would argue with a line from the Humber across to the Severn Estuary (the border between South Wales and England).

The divide goes well beyond mere prejudice. A survey of comparative prosperity in the 280 towns of Britain in 1990 showed the divide very clearly (see below). The most northerly of the ten most prosperous towns was Stratford-on-Avon in the Midlands. The most southerly of the poorest towns was still north of Nottingham. By 1995 male unemployment in Glasgow had risen to 25 per cent. Men in the south east earn the most and work the shortest week. The south east accounts for more than one-third of the Gross Domestic Product (GDP) of the United Kingdom. The average earnings in the south east in the mid-1990s were 14 per cent above the national average. Those in Northern Ireland, Wales and the north of England were 10 per cent below the average. The north of England had the lowest average weekly wages, and the second highest regional unemployment level. Northern Ireland had the highest. From time to time the divide seems less clear, but it has always been there.

The divide is noticeable in other ways, for example in health. Death rates are highest in Scotland, followed by the north and north-west regions of England, and are lowest in the south east and East Anglia. The northern population generally is more subject to heart disease and cancer. People in the north tend to smoke and drink more heavily than in the south. The Scots, for example, spend about one-third more on smoking than the national

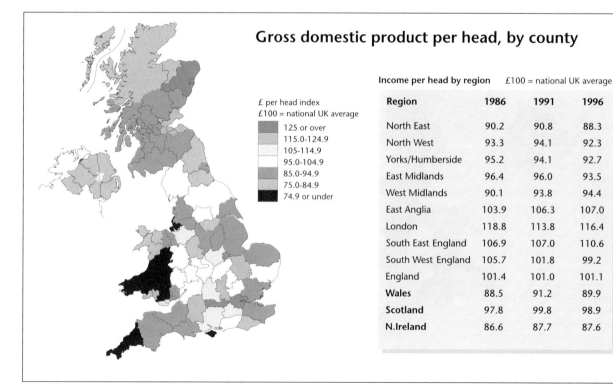

Gross domestic product per head, by county

£ per head index
£100 = national UK average
- 125 or over
- 115.0-124.9
- 105-114.9
- 95.0-104.9
- 85.0-94.9
- 75.0-84.9
- 74.9 or under

Income per head by region   £100 = national UK average

Region	1986	1991	1996
North East	90.2	90.8	88.3
North West	93.3	94.1	92.3
Yorks/Humberside	95.2	94.1	92.7
East Midlands	96.4	96.0	93.5
West Midlands	90.1	93.8	94.4
East Anglia	103.9	106.3	107.0
London	118.8	113.8	116.4
South East England	106.9	107.0	110.6
South West England	105.7	101.8	99.2
England	101.4	101.0	101.1
Wales	88.5	91.2	89.9
Scotland	97.8	99.8	98.9
N.Ireland	86.6	87.7	87.6

Source: Cambridge Econometrics

The dispiriting prospect for many who live in poor public housing on the edge of cities, and who have little prospect of employment.

average. The north west is the only English region where women outnumber men smokers. Such things are symptomatic of the greater stress and harder social conditions of life in the north. The difference is also seen in the rates of unemployment. The average rate of unemployment in 1996 was 7.5 per cent, but it varied between 5.8 per cent in East Anglia and 11.3 per cent in Northern Ireland.

Inevitably, the existence of greater employment opportunities encouraged many in the north to seek work in the south. On the whole those most successful in their search were also the best qualified. Although this may relieve short-term unemployment, it also drains depressed areas of their most talented people. Take for example Stranraer, the main town in the far south-west part of Scotland. It has no higher education facility within 50 miles (80 km). Those who go on to any form of further education after secondary school are unlikely to return. In other words, the whole district is annually stripped of its brightest young people. Without their talent it is difficult to see how the depressed periphery can be revived.

Why do not more people move in search of work? Apart from personal reasons, there is a significant economic barrier. Housing and rents are much more expensive in the south, and there are long waiting lists for public sector housing there. Generally, only young single people feel free to take the risks involved.

There are plenty of exceptions to the view of prosperity in the south and of depression in the north, where many firms are making a great success in unpromising circumstances. The largest shopping centre in Europe in 1990 was the Metrocentre in Gateshead, Newcastle, the achievement of a proud Northerner, John Hall. It is a symbol of the regional regeneration and rebirth of provincial pride that he and many other northern businessmen believe in. It is not only Northerners who believe in the north. In the 1990s Newcastle University was among the most popular for students. Newcastle was viewed as a 'cool' city. Leading Japanese firms have chosen periphery areas for major investment, for example Toyota in Wales, and Nissan in Sunderland. There are also

The north west of England may be one of Britain's most depressed regions, but as Lord Street in Southport indicates, there are also plenty of bustling and prosperous areas.

plenty of prosperous localities within an overall depressed region. Leeds, for example, boasted the fastest growing economy in England in 1990, with 50 major projects generating 12,000 jobs. The showpiece of Leeds's revival is its old shopping arcades, now revamped and renamed the Victoria Quarter.

However, there are not enough successes to reverse the overall trend. The impression of a more impoverished north persists. In the mid-1990s Yorkshire and Humberside had the worst rate of absenteeism, or truanting, from school. The north of England had the worst school examination results in Britain. The north west of England had the highest rate of births outside marriage, and the lowest proportion of 16-year-olds still in school. In Wales over 20 per cent of the population depended upon some form of state benefit. All these facts indicate profound social and economic problems. Indeed, by the year 2000 the north west will have lost 222,000 jobs, representing a fall in its share of national employment from 10.1 per cent to 8.8 per cent since 1985. Unemployment in the north generally is likely to remain three times higher than in the south for some time to come. People will continue to 'vote with their feet' by moving to more prosperous areas.

Petticoat Lane market in a low income area of London.

The theory that businesses will relocate in the north because of cheaper labour and site costs is not borne out by experience. In practice, businesses fear they will have difficulties in recruiting qualified people, a reasonable expectation if almost half of all 16-year-olds in the north leave school without seeking further training. There is great reluctance among most employees working in the south to move to the north. If their business relocates they are more likely to resign than move. Businesses prefer to seek a cheap site somewhere else in the south. Because Britain's financial sector is concentrated in London, businesses in the north find it difficult to obtain capital. It is much harder to persuade a banker of the merits of a venture by fax or e-mail than over lunch. Many northern businessmen would argue there is an urgent need for the decentralisation of the local financial sector to encourage local business. In the meantime, of those companies in the north which chose to relocate, over half have tended to move to the south.

It is questionable whether even the south really benefits from the growing regional imbalance, since in return for economic prosperity the environment is degraded by very high population concentrations, heavy air pollution and road traffic, and urban development. It will only change if government returns to the policy generally applied up to 1979 of providing incentives for economic growth in the underdeveloped areas, and discouragements from further concentration in the south.

Castle Combe, one of England's prettiest villages. There is an uneasy tension between the beauty of such places and their potential sterility.

Yet if one measures the quality of life to include other factors, for example neighbourliness, schools, cultural facilities, crowding, crime levels, tranquillity and a pleasant environment, a different pattern emerges. One must modify ideas of a north–south divide, or of core and periphery. Arguably the most attractive 'quality of life' regions are southern Britain, with the notable exception of Greater London, and also the south west, Scotland and Wales, three of the 'periphery' areas.

However, Greater London remains a magnet and has a character of its own. It is home to 7 million people, and the workplace for at least another million who commute to the capital every day. Because of its sprawling suburbs of small houses with gardens, Greater London stretches for 25 miles (40 km) from one side to the other. It is a thriving cultural capital not only because it is home to some of the most exciting music, theatre and art in Europe, but also because of the enriching contribution of its many ethnic minority communities which form a crucial part of London's hybrid vibrancy. Furthermore, London has all the architectural splendour of a once imperial capital. And it is rich, with an economy the size of Saudi Arabia. The City, London's finance centre, employs over 800,000 people, more than the population of Frankfurt. Yet 7 of its 32 boroughs are among the poorest 10 boroughs in the whole of Britain. Perhaps because of its size, and because in many respects the London suburbs remain a highly urbanised network of villages, one will search in vain for the kind of loyalty or civic pride to be found in most northern cities. Greater London is too large and too varied to evoke such feelings.

Cities and towns

Eighty per cent of the British people live in towns or cities of 100,000 inhabitants or more. Most of these town dwellers would prefer to live in the countryside if it were possible. This has a lot to do with a national state of mind, discussed in Chapter 8. People are moving out of larger cities, some going to the countryside (discussed below), and others to smaller towns. In the 1960s London had a population of 8.5 million. By 1981 this had fallen to only 6.7 million but is now very slowly increasing again. Other cities however, continue to decline numerically. Liverpool, in the north west, has suffered especially, as its location has compounded its decline. In 1961 its population was 745,000, but fell to 474,000 in 1991, and has continued to fall.

A scene of urban deprivation in Glasgow. The windows of the lower floor in this tenement (apartment) building have been boarded up to frustrate vandals entering the house.

In fact there has been a flight from the great cities by those who could afford to leave ever since the middle of the nineteenth century, when industrialisation made them such unpleasant places to live and when the invention of the railway made it possible to commute to the city from more pleasant areas. Take London, for example. By 1914 most of the middle classes and a smaller 'service' class had already moved to new suburbs which were engulfing the countryside within a 25-mile (40 km) radius. These suburbs were characterised by houses with front and back gardens. The British take this allusion to a rural existence for granted (see Chapter 8).

A typical suburban street of houses built sometime between 1900 and 1930. It intentionally gives the air of orderly tranquillity and conventionality.

During the middle years of the twentieth century, the 1920s to the 1970s, mainly professional middle-class people started to move out beyond 'suburbia' into the towns and villages of the Home Counties. They could either afford a motor car or the rail fares, and so could live in what were still quiet country towns. Places like Tunbridge Wells, Sevenoaks, Reigate and Redhill, Guildford and Dorking all acquired a new population of professional people who commuted daily to work in the City. Much of the countryside between these towns and Greater London was designated a protected 'Green Belt' in 1938. Other cities did the same, in order to protect their hinterland from uncontrolled urban sprawl.

In the late 1970s and 1980s the pressure to move out of London and its suburbs intensified. There were two main reasons for this. The most important was the steep rise in house prices in the London area. The other reason for moving was to escape a marked decline in the quality of life in Britain's larger cities. In London, for example, traffic congestion and pollution made life much less attractive than it had been in the 1960s. Yet people still had to remain close to their place of employment. Since house prices in the Home Counties had risen to virtually the same level as those in London itself, people began to look further afield. For those prepared to spend up to two hours travelling to work by rail each day, it was possible to buy a larger house perhaps 160 miles (250 km) or more from London, in areas around Brighton, Salisbury, Bristol, Oxford, Northampton, Cambridge, Peterborough and Norwich. Similar, though less pronounced, effects have become evident around other large cities, particularly the more depressed ones. Finally there was another smaller, but growing, category of people who, thanks to new information technology, no longer needed to work in central offices, and were either 'outposted' to lower cost locations away from London or, in many cases, even able to work from home, linked by computer and fax facilities to their employer.

The danger for Britain's large cities is that they will have impoverished inner areas, in which only the poorest live, while everyone who is able to will try to live on the edge of the city or outside it, shopping by car at large shopping centres sited on city ring roads. The growth of such large shopping centres spells danger for the old-fashioned high streets of city suburbs. If people find it more attractive to shop by car, they will find that high-street shops will close and local economic decline will set in, just as it has already done in some inner-city areas. Thus, unplanned free-market growth may strike at the roots of that local community coherence which still strongly exists in many city suburbs, particularly those based on old villages long since swallowed up by city growth. Since 1996 government has generally frowned upon out-of-town superstores for this reason.

Some towns are prospering and growing, usually because they have a higher quality of life, good transport links to London and a diversified economy. Most have populations under 150,000 and are in the southern half of England, for example Banbury, Bury St Edmunds, Cambridge, Colchester, Huntingdon, Milton Keynes, Reading, Swindon, Warwick and Worcester. Exeter represents the most western of these boom towns.

Commuters on their way to work. Many spend over one hour travelling both to and from their place of work.

One or two are significantly further north, for example Warrington and Harrogate, and Wrexham in North Wales. Warrington benefited from its relatively small size at a strategic location on the axis between the main north–south motorway, the M6, and the west–east network linking Blackpool and Manchester with the industrial areas of West and South Yorkshire. It also had a workforce able to prove its skill and productivity to foreign owned companies, such as McDonald Douglas, Volvo and Crane Freuhauf. Staff turnover is lower in Warrington than anywhere else in the United Kingdom. Wrexham's fortunes changed when two large Japanese electronics companies, Sharp and Brother, both established factories there, attracted by low labour costs and improved road access to Manchester. It is hard to exaggerate the psychological effect of Japanese and other Asian investment on local prosperity, for their confidence draws in British investors who would otherwise have had little confidence in a small market town in a low income area.

Yet, it is still within the south east that the greatest small town growth is taking place. The population of Milton Keynes in Bedfordshire was only 43,500 in 1981, but had grown to 168,000 by 1998, an almost fourfold increase. In terms of economic growth, Horsham, in West Sussex, overtook nearby Crawley in 1990 as one of the fastest-growing towns in the country. Both continue to grow

rapidly, combining a pleasant environment with proximity to Gatwick, Britain's second largest airport. Traditionally a quiet market town, Horsham became a busy and prosperous shopping centre for the area during the 1990s, with a large commuter population but also with a high level of business in the town itself. Its biggest employer is a large insurance company. As happens in most growing towns, the emphasis is on service industry rather than manufacturing and the job vacancies are for those with skills and educational qualifications. Few unskilled workers are wanted in these boom towns. The growth of these towns, however, puts intolerable pressure on 'the Green Belt'.

'Sunset' and 'sunrise' areas

The pattern of prosperity, or lack of it, is evident in the areas of development and stagnation in the country. The sunset areas are broadly those where traditional industries have collapsed during the past 30 years, for example cotton goods in Lancashire, car production in the West Midlands, coal and steel production in South Wales, Durham and parts of Yorkshire, and shipbuilding in Tyne and Wear, Clydeside and Belfast. That sense of economic collapse with its social implications was humorously and sensitively portrayed in the 1997 film, *The Full Monty*. Yet the north has its 'sunrise' areas, where significant new economic activity is occurring, for example between Manchester and Leeds, but unlike the large areas in the south, prosperous parts are far more patchy in the north.

The most sensational sunrise areas are in the outer core of Britain. Of these, the most notable is the 'M4 Corridor', the band of once lovely countryside stretching westwards from London to Swindon and beyond. Easy access to London's Heathrow airport, and to the M25 (London's orbital motorway), M3 and M4 motorways has made the towns west of London highly attractive to the new high-technology industries which grew rapidly during the 1980s. As a result, development and employment growth has been intensive. The town of Bracknell is a good example. It was a small town of barely 40,000 inhabitants when it was designated a new town in the early 1960s. By 1996 it had grown to about 110,000. Reading, Newbury, Hungerford, Basingstoke and Swindon, all west of London, have also grown rapidly. However, as each becomes densely populated and house prices rise, some companies and employees move further afield to avoid the overdevelopment to which they have contributed.

Another major area of development is around Cambridge and in East Anglia. Access to London, to the excellent scientific and technical resources of Cambridge, and to low-cost industrial areas and housing have made this area particularly attractive to high-technology and service industries. As a result, East Anglia, the most sparsely populated part of England in 1981, but with excellent seafreight facilities for Europe, had experienced a population growth of 8 per cent by 1995, twice the UK average.

Town and country

It is obvious that, especially in the south and south east, the pressure created by the growth of towns along the M4 Corridor and other development areas, and by the increasing departure of people from the cities, has been particularly felt in the countryside. In fact, it would be true to say that almost all of rural England has been affected. Large numbers of mainly middle-class families have bought cottages in the country, either to live in or to use as holiday homes.

A derelict factory, a familiar site in many areas of industrial decline since 1980.

This migration into the countryside has changed the nature of village life. Many villages today have a substantial proportion of commuters, people whose home is in the village but who earn their living elsewhere. This is in complete contrast with only half a century ago, when villages were much smaller and were populated by those who made their living from the country, primarily farmers and farm labourers. In Hampshire, for example, there is not a single village left which is not almost entirely commuter-based, its inhabitants travelling to work as far as Southampton in the south, Salisbury, Bath, or Bristol in the west, the M4 Corridor towns and London to the north and north east.

Apart from traffic congestion, this migration has transformed the occupancy of the villages. Pretty old cottages have been bought at higher prices than most local people can afford. Local people on low incomes have been steadily squeezed out, particularly during the past 30 years, into low-cost or publicly-owned rented housing on the edge of the village. A commuter-based village society has also led to the decline of village facilities. Forty per cent of villages no longer have a permanent shop

or post office, 30 per cent no longer have a pub and 13 per cent have lost their bus service.

Village geography has also changed. The pressure for housing has led to intensive infilling and expansion onto open land in and around villages. The county of Berkshire, for example, has more than doubled its housing stock since 1960. Reading, Wokingham and Bracknell have all expanded so that they almost form one single conurbation. Pressure has been particularly acute around London, with successive governments trying to infringe the 1947 Town and Country Planning Act which protects the Green Belt. According to government estimates, some 4.4 million new homes will be needed by 2016, around 175,000 yearly. But the pressure for new housing will be uneven, and will be felt more acutely in the countryside. Between 1971 and 1995 the rural population has increased by 21 per cent while the urban population has remained static. It will also be felt more in the southern counties. East Anglia, the south east and south west have all enjoyed population growth at twice the national average of 4 per cent, or more, in the

Victorian terrace houses with mid-twentieth century housing in the background. Virtually every town and city in England has houses like these.

period 1981–95. This has already been reflected in an average increase in dwellings in these regions of 18 per cent, compared with a national average of 13 per cent during the same period. The threat to the Green Belt causes widespread concern. It is inevitable that some Green Belt land will now be 'urbanised'. Labour promised, however, to build 60 per cent of the new housing requirement on 'brownfield' (reclaimed derelict urban land) sites. It also promised to designate more land as protected Green Belt, to offset land it now intended to build upon.

The pressure of people is also felt through tourism, in areas which receive large numbers of visitors during the summer. Two notable areas in danger are the Lake District, first made famous in the nineteenth century by the great romantic poet William Wordsworth, and the Peak District in the Pennines, which runs between Lancashire, Derbyshire and Yorkshire. National parks in Britain are significantly different from those in most of Europe, because they are already man-modified landscapes. Many of the landscapes now run the risk of development as leisure facilities. By 1990 there were a dozen major leisure complexes in the Lake District. The more people use or interfere with these national parks the more they will be degraded. Britain faces a major crisis in tourist damage both in its cities and countryside. The sheer numbers of people wishing to visit Canterbury Cathedral (1.7 million visitors in 1996) or to walk the Pennine Way (approximately 350,000 people spent one or more days on it in 1996) are literally wearing these facilities away.

The countryside probably also faces more systematic exploitation than in any other country in Western Europe. The English countryside has changed more in the past 40 years than in the previous 400 years. The main threat comes from farming. The pressure to improve yields, which rose from 4.37 tons per hectare in 1973 to 7.35 tons by 1994, has had a damaging effect on the countryside and the structure of farming. This pressure has led to increased capitalisation and

A party of walkers in the Lake District, in the north west, arguably England's most popular place for hill-walking.

mechanisation, and this in turn has led to the disappearance of smaller, less profitable farms in favour of much larger enterprises. The concentration of farmland in a few wealthy hands is a particularly British phenomenon. The average farm in Britain is much larger than in any other Western European country.

Intensive large-scale farming has changed the traditional landscape in many parts of England. In order to make maximum use of mechanisation many farmers have torn up thousands of the hedgerows that characterised the English landscape. Well over 100,000 miles of hedges – enough to encircle the world four times – have been removed since 1947. Some East Anglian fields are now 500 acres in size. Half the country's ancient lowland woods have been cleared for farmland since 1945. In addition the intensive use of chemical fertilisers has led to substantial pollution of rivers, and the destruction of fish and other wildlife. By the late 1980s there was growing concern at the degradation of the countryside. A vigorous nature conservation lobby, rivalled possibly only by that in Holland, is now actively challenging those responsible for the progressive degradation of the countryside.

Modern agricultural methods have also led to a sharp decline in the farming population. In 1946 there were 739,000 full-time agricultural workers. Only 190,000 are left. One Cambridgeshire farmer, for example, today employs only six people where his father employed 85, yet manages to produce twice as much. It is unlikely that farmers will return to previous methods, either by restoring hedgerows or by reducing the use of chemical fertilisers.

Rich and poor

What happened to half a million farm labourers? Many sought other unskilled or semiskilled work, some in nearby towns. Because of their very low income many found it almost impossible to move to town. Others have found it impossible to find work. The countryside remains an area of high unemployment, and over one-quarter of all rural households live in comparative poverty. The desire of the rural poor for better economic prospects, even at the cost of new housing estates in the village, contrasts sharply with the views of newly arrived middle-class people who do not want picturesque villages spoilt.

However, rural poverty is overshadowed by the far larger problem of urban poverty. Although there is a higher proportion of both rural and urban poor

on the periphery, particularly in the depressed areas of the north, the most casual tourist in London can easily find signs of desperate poverty among the homeless who sleep rough in the centre of the city. Most of Britain's poor live in the run-down areas which exist in almost every large town or city.

A beggar. Urban poverty poses a moral and practical challenge to the rest of society.

Between 1945 and 1979, the gap between the poorest and richest narrowed, but after 1979 it widened significantly. In 1979 the poorest tenth of the population received 4.1 per cent of the national income. By 1994 this had fallen to 2.5 per cent of the national income. Over the same period the share of national income taken by the richest tenth increased from 20 to 26 per cent. In fact, according to the Joseph Rowntree Foundation, which has a long record of concern for poverty-related issues, the average income of the poorest 10 per cent of the population fell, after taking into account housing costs, by 13 per cent in the period 1979–94. During the same period the income of the richest 10 per cent rose by 60 per cent. This was a direct result of economic policy and of changes to the tax system which intentionally rewarded the richest most, on the assumption that the highest-income earners were the most productive members of society.

The total number of those living in poverty has also grown. During the period from 1979 to 1994 the number of people living on less than half the national average income increased from roughly one-tenth to one-quarter of the whole population. In fact poverty seems to have increased more rapidly than elsewhere in the European Community. While the number of seriously poor people has undoubtedly increased, the remaining 75 per cent of the population are substantially wealthier than they were in 1979. The real problem is the gap which is now greater than at any point since 1939 and is continuing to grow. There is now a growing belief that society as a whole would benefit both economically and socially from the elimination of acute poverty.

Britain's diversity is, therefore, a good deal more complex than the range of pleasures of touristic London, the variety of the landscape, or quaint cultural features like Scottish bagpipes, Welsh harps and northern brass bands. During the closing years of the twentieth century the physical landscape has changed rapidly as a result of economic and social change. So have the people. Although these have been discussed in contrasting terms, north and south, town and country, rich and poor and so forth, it will be clear that these themes interact. It is not possible to look at the comparative prosperity of the south without considering its implications for the countryside, or for the decaying cores of its cities. Nor is it possible to consider, for example, the unfortunate impact of modern farming without seeing it in the context of a highly integrated modern society. In many respects the British people find themselves caught between their idealised view of Britain and its institutions and the less comfortable realities at the threshold of the twenty-first century. But in facing these dilemmas a more dynamic and cohesive society seems to be emerging after more than thirty years of self-doubt. These themes are explored further in the following chapters.

Further information

WEBSITES

Aspects of Britain	www.buckinghamgate.cc
British Tourist Authority	www.visitbritain.com
Central Office of Information	www.coi.gov.uk/coi
Countryside Commission	www.countryside.gov.uk

PRINTED MATERIAL

Central Office of Information (CoI) 1997 *Britain 1998* The Stationery Office
McDowall, David 1989 *An Illustrated History of Britain* Longman
Sted, A. and Cook, C. 1990 *Post-war Britain: A Political History* Penguin

QUESTIONS

Section analysis

1 A sense of identity What is the difference in usage between the words 'British' and 'English'?

2 Core and periphery Which is the 'core' area of Britain, and which is the 'periphery'? Give reasons why the core continues to be dominant.

3 The north–south divide Which of these two images, core–periphery or north–south divide, do you think best describes the social–economic differences in Britain? Explain your choice.

4 Cities and market towns Why have cities declined in population while towns and villages outside cities have increased? Is there a similar development in your country?

5 'Sunset' and 'sunrise' areas What does the author mean by 'sunset' and 'sunrise' areas? Find examples of each from the text.

6 Town and country In Britain there is a popular desire to move into the countryside. What social and environmental problems does this movement cause?

7 Rich and poor What happened to the gap between rich and poor during the period 1979 to 1994, and what were the main causes?

Chapter analysis and discussion

1 Which of the following statements is the best summary of Chapter 1?
a Britain is a highly homogeneous country in which suggestions of a north–south divide, or of great disparity between rich and poor, are exaggerated.
b The idea that British society is homogeneous must be qualified by cultural, social and economic variations.
c Britain is a dynamic country with picturesque and charming regional variations.
2 Find evidence in the text to support the following statements:
a During the 1980s and early 1990s there was an increasing proportion of the population that could be described as poor.

b The English countryside is suffering serious degradation.
c The regional pattern of health problems reflects variations in economic conditions.

3 Are there marked regional differences in your country? If so, are they similar to those in Britain? Are there other kinds of divisions in your country which do not apply in Britain?

Visual interpretation

1 Consider the following map indicating regional average weekly earnings by area in 1997. What does the map indicate? Does it confirm or qualify ideas such as the north–south divide, and core–periphery?

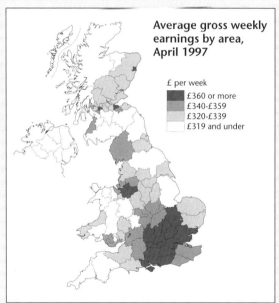

Source: Regional Trends 32

2 Consider this comparative index of inequality. Does it confirm what the author says or not?

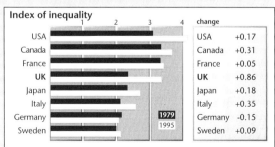

Source: OECD Economic Outlook July 1996

2 The system of government

Britain is a democracy, yet its people are not, as one might expect in a democracy, constitutionally in control of the state. The constitutional situation is an apparently contradictory one. As a result of an historical process, the people of Britain are subjects of the Crown, accepting the Queen as the head of the state. Yet even the Queen is not sovereign in any substantial sense since she receives her authority from Parliament, and is subject to its direction in almost all matters. In short, she 'reigns' but does not rule. Technically, if confusingly, British sovereignty collectively resides in the three elements of Parliament: the Crown, and Parliament's two chambers, the House of Lords and the House of Commons.

This curious situation came about as a result of a long struggle for power between the Crown and Parliament during the sixteenth and seventeenth centuries. In 1689 Parliament won that struggle, because it controlled most of the national wealth. It agreed to allow the Crown to continue to function within certain limits, and subject to Parliament's control. No constitution was written down either then or since, and the relationship between Crown, government, Parliament and people – and their respective constitutional powers – has been one of gradual development in three vital respects:
parliamentary 'sovereignty'; an independent judiciary; and consolidation of the rule of law. Various elements of what is usually considered 'the constitution' appear in different laws and conventions, but they are not specified as such. The state – itself sometimes called the Crown – operates on precedent, custom and conventions, and on unwritten rules and assumptions. Operating on precedent, custom and common sense is a very British arrangement, and the British have traditionally felt uncomfortable with a constitution based either on logic or theory.

The Crown

The reigning monarch is not only the head of state but also a symbol of the unity of the nation. The monarchy is Britain's oldest secular institution, its continuity for over 1,000 years broken only once by a republic that lasted a mere 11 years (1649–60). The monarchy is hereditary, the succession passing automatically to the oldest male child, or in the absence of males, to the oldest female offspring of the monarch. By Act (or law) of Parliament, the monarch must be a Protestant. Succession is automatic on the death of the monarch, confirmed later by a formal coronation ceremony. The coronation of Queen Elizabeth II in 1953, for example, took place over a year after she became queen.

The Coronation of Queen Elizabeth II in 1953 thrilled the nation. This pageantry is unlikely to be taken as seriously at the next coronation.

In law the monarch is head of the executive and of the judiciary, head of the Church of England, and commander-in-chief of the armed forces. However, since 1689, the monarch's sovereign powers have been formally limited by the idea that national sovereignty resides in 'the Crown in Parliament' – the idea that the Crown is only sovereign by the will of Parliament.

The remaining powers of the monarch are basically to summon, suspend until the next session and dissolve Parliament; to give royal assent to legislation passed by Parliament; to appoint government ministers, judges, officers of the armed forces, governors, diplomats and bishops of the Church; to confer honours, such as peerages and knighthoods; to remit sentences passed on convicted criminals; and finally to declare war on or make peace with an enemy power. In practice, of course, with the exception of a few honours she is free to decide herself, the monarch discharges all these functions on the direction of the government. In most matters of state, the refusal of the Queen to exercise her power according to the direction of her Prime Minister would risk a serious constitutional crisis.

Nevertheless, the function of the monarch is politically important. For as someone who reigns but does not rule, the sovereign separates the 'magic' of sovereignty, publicly visible in many ceremonies, from the power of the executive head of state. This contrasts with executive presidential systems of government. Away from the public gaze, the monarch plays a more practical role. The Queen is visited regularly by her Prime Minister to receive an account of Cabinet decisions and to be consulted on matters of national life. Since 1952 the Queen has given weekly audience, as it is called, to 11 Prime Ministers, some of whom have highly valued these meetings.

Whitehall – the seat of government

'Her Majesty's Government' governs in the name of the Queen, and its hub, Downing Street, lies in Whitehall, a short walk from Parliament. Following a general election, the Queen invites the leader of the majority (or largest, in the absence of an overall majority) party represented in the Commons, to form a government on her behalf. Government ministers are almost invariably members of the House of Commons, but infrequently members of the House of Lords are appointed. These are at a disadvantage since it is in the Commons that the government is expected to explain its conduct of affairs. All government ministers, even the Prime Minister, who are members of the Commons, continue to represent the parliamentary 'constituencies' which elected them. Unless the government is a coalition – the last of these was formed during the war years 1939–45 – governments today are drawn solely from one political party. But this has not always been so. During the nineteenth century leading politicians were far freer to follow their own convictions or ambitions rather than party discipline.

Most governments consist of about 100 ministers, but the essential core is the Cabinet, the 20 or so most senior ministers invited by the Prime Minister to belong to it. Cabinet government demands collective responsibility and confidentiality. Within the Cabinet the Prime Minister is meant to be first among equals. In theory this encourages balance and prudence in both policy and action. In practice the Cabinet principle can give rise to tension. While a Prime Minister must give strong leadership, he or she must allow for each minister to exercise responsibility within their field and should encourage collective decision-making on controversial issues, particularly ones beyond the responsibility of one ministry.

Prime Minister Tony Blair embracing his wife, Cherie. Cherie Blair is a practising QC (see p. 59).

(see p. 59)

In fact Prime Ministers have much more power than first among equals. They enjoy undisputed political leadership. Ministers must obey their will, or persuade the Prime Minister of their own point of view. If a clash of wills cannot be resolved, the minister must resign. In 1989 the Chancellor of the Exchequer (responsible for finance) suddenly resigned after persistent rumours about the Prime Minister's overbearing manner in Cabinet. In explaining his resignation, he gave a classic definition of the Cabinet principle: 'For our system of Cabinet government to work effectively, the Prime Minister of the day must appoint ministers that he or she trusts and then leave them to carry out the policy. When differences of view emerge, as they are bound to do from time to time, they should be resolved privately and, wherever appropriate, collectively.' The ex-Chancellor made this statement to the House of Commons, for all ministers are accountable to it. Although not the case on this occasion, once the confidence of a majority of his or her colleagues has been lost, a Cabinet minister has no choice but to resign. Because of the enormous increase in government business, all senior government ministers – most of whom have the title of Secretary of State – have junior ministers (Ministers of State or Parliamentary undersecretaries) to help with the workload. They are all subject to the rules of collective responsibility and must not disagree publicly with government policy.

Although government is essentially political, it depends upon a permanent body of officials, the Civil Service, to administer the decisions of ministers, and to keep the wheels of government – in its broadest sense – turning. The Civil Service, employing almost 500,000 people, is expected to discharge its responsibilities in a politically impartial way. Civil servants must be as loyal to an incoming government as to the outgoing one, however much as private individuals they may be pleased or dismayed at the change of government. Those civil servants wishing to stand for Parliament must first resign from the Civil Service.

The heart of the Civil Service is the Cabinet Office, whose Secretary is the most senior civil servant at any given time. The responsibilities are considerable, including the proper and smooth running of the whole Civil Service as well as serving ministers collectively in the conduct of Cabinet business and ensuring the coordination of policy at the highest level. In each ministry or department the senior official, or Permanent Secretary, and his or her immediate subordinates, undersecretaries and assistant secretaries, remain responsible for assisting their minister in the implementation of government policy. The Permanent Secretary does not really have a counterpart either in Europe or the United States.

In practice the implementation of policy is a two-way process – cleverly portrayed in the 1980s in two famous satirical television series, *Yes, Minister* and *Yes, Prime Minister* – in which alongside genuine cooperation there is also a permanent trial of strength between the political will of the minister and the concern of civil servants to minimise departures from known and trusted methods of government. Both sides are tempted to view the other as a potential obstacle to good government, but both also moderate the dangers implicit in one or other party enjoying unchallenged powers. In the words of one ex-minister, the Civil Service is 'a beautifully designed and effective braking mechanism. It produces a hundred well-argued answers against initiative and change.'

Members of the new Labour Cabinet meeting a week after their election victory in 1997. Tony Blair is discussing a point with the Cabinet Secretary, Sir Robin Butler.

There is a strong tradition of loyalty on the part of civil servants towards their ministers. A good example is recalled by a minister, who having rejected very strong advice from his (unusually) female permanent secretary, instructed her to draft the policy paper he wished to put to Cabinet. She produced a paper that was 'terse, clear, strongly argued and very convincing' for a policy with which she did not agree. As he recalled, 'She had had her say, the internal argument was over ... from now on it was her job to help me persuade my colleagues of its wisdom.' A minister and his or her senior civil servants will be the strongest of allies in fighting for the interests of their department, or ministry, against competing ones, particularly in the allocation of the financial budget.

Westminster – the seat of Parliament

Her Majesty's Government, in spite of its name, derives its authority and power from its party representation in Parliament. While the government machinery is frequently referred to as 'Whitehall', Parliament is known as 'Westminster',

since it is housed in the Palace of Westminster, once a home of the monarchy. Like the monarchy, Parliament is an ancient institution, dating from the middle of the thirteenth century.

Parliament is the seat of British democracy, but it is perhaps valuable to remember that while the House of Lords was created in order to provide a council of the nobility for the king, the Commons were summoned originally in order to provide the king with money. The more money a king demanded, the more the Commons questioned its use. Because of its growing financial power, its ability to raise or withhold money, the House of Commons eventually – from the seventeenth century onwards – gained power not only in matters of finance but also of legislation over both the monarch and also the Lords. Parliament is the supreme legislative body of the state. Free from the constraints of a written constitution it may make any laws it pleases. It could even prolong its own life without consulting the electorate, if it chose to do so. Thus Parliament, rather than the will of the people, is clearly the real sovereign power in the state. The only guarantee against

The House of Commons in session during John Major's administration, 1992-97. John Major is sitting opposite the Despatch Box on the Front Bench.

parliamentary tyranny is the sense of tradition and reasonableness of its members.

Furthermore, in practice it is not Parliament as a whole which is sovereign, but the government of the day and its supporters, since they almost invariably form a majority in the Commons. For the duration of its normal term, five years, the government of the day may enact or implement its policies, so long as it can ensure party support in the Commons. In the words of one distinguished and long-serving parliamentarian who has sat in both the Commons and the Lords, Britain's parliamentary system is in practice a form of 'elective dictatorship', an important qualification on the idea of Britain as a democracy.

Parliament's functions today are to pass laws, to raise enough money through taxation to enable the government to function, to examine government policy and administration, particularly its financial programme, and to debate or discuss important political issues.

The life of a Parliament is not fixed, and the government of the day may call for a general election at any time during its five-year term. Each Parliament is divided into annual sessions, running normally from October to October with breaks for public holidays and for a long summer 'recess' (usually late July until October).

The electoral system

For electoral purposes the United Kingdom is divided into constituencies, each one of which elects a Member of Parliament to sit in the House of Commons. To ensure equitable representation four permanent Boundary Commissions (for England, Wales, Scotland and Northern Ireland), make periodic reviews to adjust electoral boundaries and redistribute seats. Today there are 659 seats in the Commons, one seat on average for every 65,000 electors.

All British citizens (and also citizens of the Irish Republic resident in the UK) may vote, provided they are aged 18 or over, are registered, and are not disqualified by insanity, membership of the House of Lords or by being sentenced prisoners. Voting is not compulsory, and a general election normally attracts about 75 per cent of the electorate, a decline in participation of about 8 per cent since 1945. The candidate in a constituency who gains most votes is returned as Member to the Commons. In this 'first-past-the-post' (FPTP) system, other candidates, even if they come close to the winner, will not get a seat in Parliament.

If a Member of Parliament resigns, dies or is made a peer during the lifetime of a Parliament, a by-election must be held in his or her old constituency to elect a new member. No candidate requires the backing of a political party in order to stand for election, but it is very rare for an independent candidate to be elected. MPs are normally chosen by the constituency branch of the party, from a list of suitable candidates issued by the party headquarters. Where the winning party in an election only just gains the greatest proportion of the national vote, this can lead to a substantial distortion of democratic will in actual representation in the Commons. The 1987 and 1997 election results clearly reveal the problem:

General election results		
Party	% of vote	% of MPs
1987		
Conservative	42.0	57.7
Labour	31.0	35.2
Liberal Democrats (as Alliance)	23.0	3.4
1997		
Conservative	31.0	25.0
Labour	44.0	63.6
Liberal Democrats	17.0	7.0

Election night 1997: Stephen Twigg, the successful Labour candidate applauds as the Conservative Defence Minister, Michael Portillo, learns that he has lost his seat. Portillo's dignity in defeat did much to restore his popularity.

The party system

The political party system has evolved since the eighteenth century, and since the first half of the nineteenth century has been essentially a two-party system. Today, this two-party contest is between the Conservative Party (still known by their previous nickname, the 'Tories') and the Labour Party, which emerged at the end of the nineteenth century as a result of the introduction of universal male suffrage and the decline of the Liberal Party.

The Conservative Party is the party of the Right, identified with the idea of economic freedom and until 1979 with the idea of resistance to change. It has successfully portrayed itself as the party of patriotism. As in the nineteenth century, it appeals to a 'property-owning democracy', and as a result its support tends to lie with the wealthier classes, receiving much money from major business and financial institutions. It gives emphasis to the importance of law and order, and the maintenance of strong armed forces to protect British interests.

Prime Minister Tony Blair with his deputy, John Prescott. Representing the centre and the left of the party respectively, they seemed an ideal 'winning ticket' for the 1997 general election.

The Liberal Party, which traces its origins to the eighteenth century 'Whigs', merged with the new Social Democratic Party in 1988 to become the Liberal Democrats, after fighting the 1987 election unsuccessfully as an alliance of both parties. It seeks to attract the votes of the middle ground between Labour and the Conservatives, but has also tended to attract opponents of the Conservatives, dominant in the south of England, and opponents of the Labour Party, dominant in the north. It is the party keenest on constitutional and electoral reform. It also prides itself on being less tied to either capitalist or union interests, and being free to offer more radical policies.

Flag-waving Conservatives at their annual conference. Following their defeat in 1997, the new leader William Hague discouraged such demonstrations of right-wing patriotism.

Labour is preeminently the party of social justice, though its emphasis is less on equality than on the achievement of well-being and opportunity for all members of society. It tends to give the collective well-being of society slightly more importance than individual freedom. It was once committed to public ownership of major industries, and to economic planning. It now favours an entrepreneurial but socially aware economy. The trade union movement, which founded the Labour Party, has lost the influence it once had over the party.

Paddy Ashdown, who became leader of the Liberal Democrats in 1988.

Since 1945 the Conservatives have formed eight governments and Labour seven, although in practice during the period 1945–97 the Conservatives have governed for 36 years and Labour for only 17. Domination of the Commons by the Conservatives, 1979–97, revealed the weakness of the first-past-the-post electoral system. They have enjoyed a large majority in successive parliaments although at the elections of 1979, 1983, 1987 and 1992 more people voted against the Conservative Party than voted for it.

The House of Commons

The dynamic power of Parliament lies in the House of Commons. Its 659 members represent 529 constituencies in England, 40 in Wales, 72 in Scotland and 18 in Northern Ireland. There are only seats in the Commons debating chamber for 370 members, but except on matters of great interest, it is unusual for all members to be present at any one time. Many MPs find themselves in other rooms of the Commons, participating in a variety of committees and meetings necessary for an effective parliamentary process.

The shape of the Commons debating chamber makes an important comment on the political process in Britain. Unlike many European chambers which are semicircular, thus reflecting the spectrum of political opinion in their seating plan, the Commons is rectangular, with the Speaker's (the presiding MP) chair at one end, and either side of it five rows of benches running the length of the chamber. On one side, to the Speaker's right, sits Her Majesty's Government and its supporters, and on the other Her Majesty's Opposition, composed of all Members who oppose the government. The front benches on either side are reserved for members of the Cabinet and other Ministers, and Opposition spokesmen, known as the 'Shadow Cabinet', respectively.

Behind them and further down the chamber sit MPs from their own party, known as 'back-benchers'. The layout hints at two features of British political life: that it has traditionally been a two-party system and that the process is essentially adversarial (indeed, a red line on the floor in front of each front bench still marks the limit – a little more than two swords' lengths – beyond which a Member may not approach the opposite benches). The Speaker is chosen by a vote of the entire House, although in practice the party leaders consult their supporters in order to achieve informal agreement beforehand. The Speaker is

Betty Boothroyd, Speaker of the House, standing in front of her official portrait wearing her robes of office.

responsible for the orderly conduct of business, and is required to act with scrupulous impartiality between Members in the House. In the words of one past Speaker, 'It's not my duty as Speaker to bend arguments in any way, but to ensure that everything that happens here is seen clearly by those who put us here. We are, after all, the servants of those who put us here: the electorate.' The Speaker is assisted by three Deputy Speakers. Unlike peers, who can only claim expenses, MPs are paid salaries, approximately twice the average national wage, but substantially less than most MPs could earn outside the Commons.

The House of Lords

The upper chamber of Parliament, the House of Lords, is not democratic in any sense at all. It consists of four categories of peer, totalling 1,197 members in 1996. The majority are hereditary peers, currently about 750, of whom only about half take an active interest in the affairs of state. A smaller number, about 400, are 'life' peers – an idea introduced in 1958 to elevate to the peerage certain people who have rendered political or public service to the nation. The purpose was not merely to honour but also to enhance the quality of business done in the Lords. Only one-quarter of these life peers are women. All life peers are created on the recommendation of the Prime Minister of the day, with nominations also sought from opposition parties. Nine of the most senior judges, the Lords of Appeal in Ordinary (commonly known as the 'Law Lords'), are also entitled to sit in the Lords. Finally, alongside these secular peers, the Lords Temporal, are the 26 most senior bishops and archbishops of the Church of England, the Lords Spiritual. The Law Lords and the Lords Spiritual are the ancient non-hereditary component of the Lords.

Until 1911 the Lords were able to reject draft laws, known as bills, passed in the Commons, and thus frustrate not only the government of the day, but also the will of the Commons. Since then the Lords have been unable to challenge financial legislation, and have only been able to delay other legislation (since 1949 for no more than one session) but not prevent it. Their only other surviving discretionary power is to veto an attempt by the Commons to prolong its own life beyond its five-year term. The role of the Lords, therefore, is now more to warn than to frustrate over-zealous governments, and they have done this more by the proposition of amendments to legislation which causes them unease, than by direct opposition.

The House of Lords in session. Peers with no party affiliation sit on the 'cross-benches' at the back of the Chamber. The Lords Spiritual, all Anglican bishops, may be seen on the right of the picture.

Although there are over 1,000 peers entitled to sit in the House of Lords, average daily attendance is only about 300 and most of these are life peers who retain a strong interest in the affairs of state. The Lords conduct their business in a far more orderly fashion than the Commons. The House is presided over by the Lord Chancellor, the senior law officer of the state. The position is not like that of the Speaker, for the Lord Chancellor is not impartial, but a government officer. He or she is responsible for the administration of justice and is also an automatic member of the Cabinet.

A larger number of peers support the Conservative Party than the other parties. Those active peers who support Labour or the Liberal Democrats, plus the independent peers (who have 'cross-benches' across the back of the chamber to sit upon), are together almost the same in number as the Conservatives. This preponderance in favour of the Conservatives arises partly because the majority of hereditary peers sympathise more with the Conservative Party than its opponents. Also Labour declined to nominate candidates for life peerages for a period during the 1980s since its party policy included abolition of the Lords, on the grounds that it was an undemocratic anachronism. Despite this preponderance, however, no Conservative government can be absolutely sure of a majority, if its proposals are controversial. Peers, of whatever party loyalty, are far freer to vote according to their own convictions, rather than party policy, than are members of the Commons.

Parliamentary procedure

Each parliamentary session begins with the 'State Opening of Parliament', a ceremonial occasion in which the Queen proceeds from Buckingham Palace to the Palace of Westminster where she delivers the Queen's Speech from her throne in the House of Lords. Her speech is drafted by her government, and describes what the government intends to implement during the forthcoming session. Leading members of the Commons may hear the speech from the far end of the chamber, but are not allowed to enter the House of Lords. During the next five or so days, the government and Opposition debate aspects of the Queen's Speech in the Commons and vote on the amendments which the Opposition proposes. Since the speech is a statement of policy, defeat on any such vote would oblige the government to resign.

The Queen and Prince Philip attending the State Opening of Parliament, a ceremony largely invented a century ago to add prestige to the role of the monarch.

For most of the year the Commons adopts a routine of meeting each weekday afternoon, and 'sitting' until about 10.30 p.m. although it sometimes sits beyond midnight. On Fridays the Commons sits from 9.30 a.m. through to 3.00 p.m., rising early in order to allow MPs to return to their constituencies for the weekend, where they must make themselves available and accessible for local matters, complaints and attendance at formal functions. The proceedings of Parliament are public, and space is available for a small number of people, especially the press, to listen. Since 1803 the proceedings of Parliament have been published the following day as *Hansard*, named after the man who first began to publish the record. Proceedings of both Houses are also now televised, the Lords since 1984 and the Commons since 1989. The manner in which business is conducted is the result of custom and precedent, from which have emerged 'standing orders' which govern the details of practice in each House.

Tony Blair speaking at the Despatch Box in the Commons during Prime Minister's Question Time. On his right is his Chancellor, Gordon Brown.

Each day begins, after brief opening formalities, with Question Time, lasting approximately an hour. MPs are able to ask ministers or other MPs questions on any point they may choose. Questions must be handed in 48 hours ahead, to allow ministers and their departmental staff time to prepare an answer. Naturally, both the Opposition and the party of government seek to use this period in order to reveal the weakness of their opponents. Once a minister's formal answer has been given, supplementary questions may be asked which the minister is expected to answer. Ministers and their civil servants are expected to have anticipated what further questions may be asked. Supplementary questions are used by the Opposition to outmanoeuvre a minister and reveal a weakness in government policy, or by an MP anxious to persuade the government to modify its course of action. On two afternoons each week the Prime Minister will answer questions on general policy matters. These occasions are usually the most lively.

After Question Time, the main debate of the day takes place. Time is given on 24 days during a session for individual MPs representing neither government nor Opposition to introduce debates or 'private Members' bills'. But most of the time available in any parliamentary session is devoted to scrutiny of government spending, and debating new bills the government wishes to introduce. The system of debate is much the same in both chambers. It originates in a 'motion' (a proposal) 'moved' (proposed) by a minister or Member of the House. The Speaker then proposes the question as a subject of debate.

This is not as spontaneous as it may seem. The Leader of the House (appointed by the government) agrees with the Prime Minister the general business, including debates, which they want. The Leader of the House has cabinet rank, and is responsible for planning the transaction of government business in the Commons (a Leader is appointed in the Lords also), and for enabling proper debate of those matters of concern to the House. Twenty opposition days each session allow the Opposition to choose the subjects for debate. At the end of a debate the Speaker asks MPs if they accept the motion. If there is disagreement, there is a division as MPs enter either the 'Aye' (yes) or 'No' lobbies, corridors running either side of the Commons chamber. A bell rings throughout the House six minutes before the lobby doors close to enable MPs, wherever they may be in the House, to vote. Party 'whips' (or managers) stand outside the door of the lobby into which they expect their party's members to pass. Unless it is a free vote, members who ignore party policy risk the strong displeasure of the party leadership. Indeed, the leadership may 'withdraw the whip' from a disobedient member, in other words suspend him or her from party membership either temporarily or in a few cases, expel that member from the party. Without membership of the party, an MP's political career is only likely to last until the next general election.

Parliament's most important function is to create law. A draft law takes the form of a parliamentary bill. Most of these are public bills, implementing government policy. A bill is normally only drafted after exhaustive consultation with concerned professional, voluntary and other agencies. Proposals sometimes take the form of 'white papers', stating government policy, which can be debated before a bill is introduced. 'Green papers' are published when the government wants a full public discussion before it formulates its own proposals.

The process of passing a public (or government) bill is similar in both Houses. Its publication in printed form is announced in the chamber, and this announcement is called its 'first reading'. Its 'second reading', usually a few weeks later, is the occasion for a full debate in the House, unless there is general assent that a debate is unnecessary. If necessary the bill is passed to a committee which considers whether amendments would be desirable in the light of MPs' criticisms or concerns. At the 'third reading' the revised bill is considered in its final form, and a vote taken if necessary. The bill then passes through the Lords in a similar fashion. Once a bill has completed its parliamentary procedures, it is sent to the Queen for royal assent (the third formal element of Parliament), by which it passes into law as an Act of Parliament. Royal assent has not been refused since 1707.

Parliamentary committees

It is natural that in both the Commons and the Lords committees should be formed to consider specific matters or bills passing through Parliament. The Commons have a number of 'standing committees' which examine bills during the procedural stages until they become law. Scotland, Wales and Northern Ireland are all represented by permanent standing committees. In addition, standing committees are appointed to consider specific bills. Between 16 and 50 MPs are normally appointed to a standing committee, usually reflecting the balance of party representation in Parliament.

In 1979 a new and important 'select committee' system was created to examine and monitor government departments and policies, and the manner in which ministers discharge their responsibilities. One reason for doing this was the difficulty individual MPs had in scrutinising government activity adequately. Another was the increase in party discipline which made it difficult for MPs to act independently of party policy. Members of the governing party tended to support government policy and action; those of the opposing party tended to criticise it. There had already been one or two select committees for

particular matters, but this was the first time a comprehensive scrutinising of government departments had been attempted.

The select committee system consists of 17 individual committees 'shadowing' the expenditure, administration and policy of the main government departments. Each committee has a more or less permanent cross-party membership, all of whom have acquired considerable expertise in their respective fields. They give an opportunity for MPs to act more independently of their party than they are able to do in the debating chamber. During the period of Conservative government in the 1980s, for example, a number of select committees, including their Conservative members, were strongly critical of the government.

This, briefly, is the constitutional and political system of Britain. As will be seen in the following chapter, the system as currently operated gives rise to considerable controversy. Some people are dissatisfied with its fundamental principles, and others with what they believe are the dangers of the way the system actually operates.

Further information

WEBSITES

The Monarchy (official) www.royal.gov.uk
Parliament www.parliament.uk
Government www.open.gov.uk (select any government department as lis

PRINTED MATERIAL

Coxall, Bill and Robins, Lynton 1994 *Contemporar British Politics* Chapters 6–10, 12–15 Macmillan
Hennessey, Peter 1989 *Whitehall* Secker and Warbu
Hennessey, Peter 1996 *Muddling Through: Power, Politics and the Quality of Government in Post-War Britain* Indigo
Pimlott, Ben 1997 *The Queen: A Biography of Elizabeth II* HarperCollins
Silk, Paul 1987 *How Parliament Works* Longman

QUESTIONS

Section analysis

1 **The Crown** What are the powers of the monarch?

2 **Whitehall** What does 'Cabinet government' mean? What are its strengths and weaknesses?

3 **Westminster** What made the Commons strong enough to defeat the Crown and to become more important than the Lords during the seventeenth century?

4 **The electoral system** Which party suffers most from the first-past-the-post system?

5 **The party system** Explain the main differences between the Conservative and Labour Parties.

6 **The House of Commons** Draw a simple diagram showing the shape and layout of the House of Commons debating chamber. Give reasons why you think this arrangement is better or worse than the more common semi-circular debating chamber.

7 **The House of Lords** What value does the House of Lords have, if any, in a democracy? Give reasons for your opinion.

8 **Parliamentary procedure** Do you think the 'parliamentary day' is the most useful way to deal with matters of public policy and the enactment of law? Compare it with the practice of the parliamentary chamber in your own country.

9 **Parliamentary committees** Why are parliamentary select committees valuable?

Chapter analysis and discussion

1 Find evidence in the text to support or contradict these statements:
   a Britain is a completely democratic country.
   b There is a balance in government between partisan politicians and an impartial civil service.

c The House of Lords is of little constitutional or political value.
d The first-past-the-post electoral system does not necessarily serve the electorate well.

2 Britain is a democracy, yet its people are not, as one might expect in a democracy, constitutionally in control of the state. Does this surprise you? If so, why?

3 Who rules Britain: the Crown, the Commons, the Lords, the Prime Minister, the Cabinet or the Civil Service? Where does the greatest power lie in your country?

4 If you were British, which political party would you support, and why?

Visual interpretation

Here is a diagrammatic representation of the theoretical political hierarchy. Do you think it reflects reality? (Refer to *Westminster – the seat of Parliament – see page 29*.) If not, draw your own diagram.

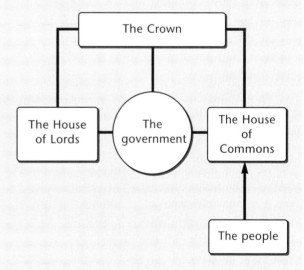

3 Government and politics: debate and change

The previous chapter gives a brief outline of the way in which Britain's constitution and government work. The practice, however, is a good deal more complex in many respects, since the system has evolved gradually and been shaped by tradition and precedent rather than through a coherent and logical constitutional framework.

The monarchy

The apparent solidity and permanence of British custom and tradition are highly deceptive, for the institutions which appear to embody the permanence of these traditions are not static. The monarchy is a good example. Although already limited by the Constitutional Revolution of 1688, its function changed radically from the mid-nineteenth century onwards. In the 1860s and 1870s there was open talk of republicanism. However, Queen Victoria, ably advised by her Prime Minister, remodelled the monarchy to make it appear as the public symbol of national unity and as the paragon of family life in Britain. The rapidly growing middle and working classes of Britain's cities loved it. Most of the formalised ritual, for example the State Opening of Parliament and Trooping the Colour, were invented at this time to generate a feeling of timeless tradition as a counterweight to the social shock waves of the Industrial Revolution. The monarchy offered the public a romantic link with a largely imaginary past. Because Britain was victorious in both world wars, the monarchy survived to become the focal point of the nation. George V attended the first football Cup Final at Wembley and made use of the radio to become a popular monarch. George VI and his consort, Elizabeth (now known as the Queen Mother), made the monarchy yet more popular in the Second World War. By their refusal to leave Buckingham Palace after it had been bombed, and by their tours of badly bombed parts of London and other cities, they became the two most loved people in Britain.

When she came to the throne in 1952, Queen Elizabeth II sought to continue in the same tradition, and to give the various elements of society a sense of belonging, unity and purpose beyond material well-being. So immensely popular was she that, if anything, people were even more deferential to her than to her father. She personified something precious and vulnerable. No newspaper dared question the reputation of the Royal Family. Self-censorship was exercised for fear the public would shun a 'disloyal' newspaper.

The Queen receives a bouquet from an admirer in the crowd. The British still remain deferential towards the Royal Family.

It was not until the late 1960s that the Palace felt a change of style was required to 'sell' the Royal Family to the public. Television was the chosen medium. The result, a programme entitled *Royal Family*, revealed the Queen as a conventional middle-class woman in her private family life. It inevitably changed the public perception of a family which had previously maintained its privacy, and stimulated public interest to know more of its secret life. In particular the press sought to discover and reveal what was intended to remain secret, above all the love lives of the Queen's children, particularly that of the future king.

Charles's problem was to find a suitable bride, who by law had to be a Protestant and by the hypocritical demands of public propriety had to be 'pure'.

At the age of 32, Prince Charles became engaged to a shy girl of 19, Lady Diana Spencer who was, in the words of one commentator, a 'virginal, Protestant aristocrat'. It seemed like a fairytale outcome, and their wedding in July 1981 was watched by a larger television audience than virtually any previous event.

Thus the monarchy seemed to go from strength to strength. It was possible for one leading biographer to remark with complete confidence: 'Today in 1986 (the monarchy) stands for essentially the same values as it stood for sixty years ago and as it will do sixty years ahead.' Never before had the Royal Family been the subject of such national and international fascination. Despite the obvious contradiction between democracy and monarchy, the public was able to hold two opposing views at the same time: that the monarchy embodied national identity and was therefore important but that it was also a harmless but colourful part of our heritage.

In reality the monarchy had, since Queen Victoria's time, acquired quasi-religious importance for many people in Britain.

Most nations require some intangible element of mystery in their sense of identity. For the British the monarchy effectively separates this element from executive power. The credibility of this 'mystery' demands that the monarchy retains its dignity. Walter Bagehot, whose book *The English Constitution*, published in 1862, quickly became a classic analysis of the way in which Britain is governed, wrote of the Crown: 'Its mystery is its life. We must not let in daylight upon magic. We must not bring the Queen into the combat of politics, or she will cease to be reverenced by all combatants; she will become one combatant among many.'

Since 1987 or so, partly as a result of press intrusion, but to a large degree because of the activities of members of the Royal Family, the daylight was let in and that mystery and magic have been lost. In 1987 some of the Queen's children took part in an inane slapstick television show, *It's a Royal Knockout*. The intention had been to present a more modern light-hearted image, but it involved a complete loss of dignity. Diana, too, soon proved a liability as well as an asset to the monarchy. She quickly became the most

glamorous woman on the world stage. She stole attention from Prince Charles, and in her charitable work began to outshine the other Royals. She also found herself in an ambivalent relationship with the press, both detesting their intrusive pursuit of her and yet needing their attention. She did not behave in the restrained way expected of the House of Windsor, but allowed her feelings free expression. The public loved her for it, but the Windsors were not pleased.

In the meantime the monarchy began to face other problems. From the time of the Falklands War in 1982, Margaret Thatcher seemed consciously to model herself on the sixteenth-century Queen Elizabeth I, one of England's most charismatic monarchs. It was no secret that the Queen disliked Thatcher's regal pretensions, which seemed to challenge the status of the Queen herself. Prince Charles began to express views in areas of public life that proved controversial, and was also suspected of disliking the Prime Minister. There was also growing criticism of the cost of maintaining the Royal Family. Quite apart from its substantial private wealth, the taxpayer funded the activities of the Royal Family through a system known as 'the Civil List', which had operated since 1689. It was tax free, and allowed the sovereign on the one hand to retain unused money but on the other, to be free to ask for more should it be needed. Demands for greater accountability grew, as did questions about the Royal Family's expensive lifestyle. Its most conspicuously lavish spending was on two little used forms of transport, the Royal Train and the Royal Yacht *Britannia* (now decommissioned), which by 1991 cost £2.3 million and £9.2 million respectively in annual maintenance. In November 1992 a major fire at Windsor Castle occurred. Initial sympathy gave way to anger when the government announced it would pay for the repairs, especially once it became known that the Castle had not been insured. Within the month the Queen decided that she and Prince Charles must pay tax in future on their private assets and income and that the Civil List payments to all members of the Royal Family except herself, her husband and her mother would be ended. Less well known was the fact that she now paid for other members of her family out of 'the Duchy of Lancaster', a large land and investment holding administered by the government, and therefore hardly her private property, but enjoyed by the sovereign. She managed to reduce the cost of the monarchy to the taxpayer from £53 million in 1991 to £42 million in 1998, a reduction of 38 per cent.

However, the fire at Windsor Castle was hardly the worst of the Queen's troubles in 1992. Almost every month brought some calamitous development in the lives of her children. In January the Duchess of York, Prince Andrew's wife popularly known as 'Fergie', was reliably reported to be having an affair. In February Princess Diana, on tour with her husband in India, posed alone in front of the Taj Mahal, conveying the unmistakable message that her marriage was also in trouble. In March the Duke and Duchess of York announced their separation. In April Princess Anne and her husband were divorced. In June a young journalist, Andrew Morton, published a book entitled *Diana: Her True Story*. It contained information which Diana herself clearly wanted made known about her unhappy marriage. Among other things, it made public Charles's long-standing relationship with Camilla Parker Bowles. It was, in the words of Ben Pimlott, the Queen's biographer, 'a moral classic about a young woman who had entered the legendary world which millions dreamt about, and who found that the "model family" was, indeed, a myth'. Further revelations came in quick succession as the newspapers competed to buy the most lurid stories, photographs and tapes of eavesdropped telephone calls involving various members of the Royal Family. When it was clear that they could no longer remain together, it was announced at the end of the year that Charles and Diana were to separate. It was little wonder that the Queen publicly referred to 1992 as her '*annus horribilis*'.

At first it seemed politically desirable that Charles and Diana should not divorce, but just live separate lives. But in November 1995 Diana gave a long television interview for the BBC in which she frankly admitted to her own adultery as well as revealing the destructive effect of Charles's affair with Camilla Parker Bowles. She also talked about her own problems of depression and her charitable work. What she said also made public the dysfunctional nature of the Royal Family. The Palace had been neither consulted nor informed concerning the broadcast. Dramatically, Diana's appearance was faultless, as someone said at the time: 'restrained, unfaltering and unforgettable.' Within days the Queen wrote to both Charles and Diana strongly advising them to divorce at the earliest moment. Apart from her fury at the interview, she was anxious to remove Diana from the Royal Family before she did further damage to the monarchy. They were divorced in 1996. One

The unforgettable face of Princess Diana during her BBC Panorama interview when she spoke of her anguish as her marriage to Prince Charles disintegrated.

year later Diana was killed in a car crash and Britain was overwhelmed with emotion. Diana had qualities which the Royal Family seemed to lack: warmth, elegance and spontaneous compassion born of the tragedies in her own life. Amid mounting public criticism, the Royal Family seemed to have little idea how to respond, and it apparently required Tony Blair, who referred to Diana as 'the people's princess', to advise the Royal Family to abandon protocol and show greater public feeling. Where can the monarchy go from here? Its popularity has suffered enormously, apparently as the result of one calamitous marriage. In fact, the loss of respect reveals a much more complex process, to do with the hypocritical expectations of the public. In 1996 an opinion poll revealed that while one-quarter of 18-24 year-olds thought Britain would be better off without a monarchy, only one-fifth thought it would be worse off. Furthermore, while 73 per cent were satisfied with the Queen, people were satisfied or dissatisfied with Prince Charles in equal numbers. In 1991 over 80 per cent had thought he would make a good king. An opinion poll among the mourners at Princess Diana's funeral showed that 72 per cent thought Prince William rather than Prince Charles should inherit the throne. However worrying this may be for the Royal Family, it also suggests that the British people do not yet want a republic, even though approximately half the population no longer expect the monarchy to survive another 50 years, a fourfold increase since 1988. The majority seem to want a change from the present formality and protocol to something more accessible. Yet because the hereditary principle is in such contradiction with democratic values it is difficult to see how this can logically lead anywhere but eventually to a republic.

Doubtless the Royal Family will continue with possibly its most important function, the support of charitable work. Each year its members carry out approximately 2,000 charitable engagements. In the words of the historian, David Cannadine, 'Charitable activity [has] become the place where the royal culture of hierarchical condescension and the popular culture of social aspiration, have successfully merged.' Yet the number of people who welcome 'hierarchical condescension' is diminishing.

After Diana's death the Royal Family began to modify its image in order to survive. But can it

Diana, the dead princess, is carried past her close male relatives into Westminster Abbey.

Prince William, the eldest son of Charles and Diana, has the winning shy look of his mother. Will the monarchy still be in existence when his time comes?

reverse the growing feeling that the monarchy is irrelevant, especially to the younger generation, or answer the fundamental question of whether Britain at the beginning of the twenty-first century really needs a monarchy? No political party for the foreseeable future will open a debate, regardless of its private views, since to do so can only lose votes.

The constitution

In the eighteenth century, as a result of the 1689 political settlement (see p.26-27), Britain was more democratic than any other European state and maintained its reputation as a democratic model well into the twentieth century. But is it a leader of European democracy today?

Increasing doubts have been voiced concerning the state of Britain's democracy. The Conservative governments of the 1980s were all voted to power by a minority of the electorate, yet reshaped the country. They centralised power in Whitehall to an unprecedented degree, seriously weakening the strength of local democracy. Underlying such concerns was a more fundamental one, that the haphazard development of Britain's unwritten constitution was no longer a sufficient safeguard of

democratic rights. To critics, the idea of the Crown in Parliament no longer works since neither the Queen nor the Lords can effectively oppose a government which commands a majority in the Commons. In fact there is no constitutional protection at all either for the nation as a whole or for individuals against a political party commanding a majority in the Commons. By law even the courts cannot challenge the legislation of Parliament. In the words of one of Britain's most able lawyers, 'An elected government untrammelled by constitutional limits or constraints, is a menace to our liberties whether it be a dictatorship of Right or Left, of a majority or a minority.'

In 1988 a group of distinguished politicians, lawyers, academics, writers and journalists began to campaign under the title Charter88 (harking back to the charter of 1688) for wide-ranging reforms. They called for a Bill of Rights, to protect individual liberties, and for a written constitution to define and limit the powers of Parliament. Undoubtedly this call was partly explained by a belief that government during the 1980s had curtailed personal liberties more than any previous post-war government. During the 1980s Britain had been found guilty of infringing the European

The myth of tradition: the Queen at the ceremony of Trooping the Colour. Behind her ride Prince Charles and Prince Philip. The ceremony was only invented at the end of the nineteenth century.

Convention on Human Rights more often than any other member of the European Community. In 1990 the European Court of Justice made an historic decision: that British courts must suspend any Act of Parliament which imperils the rights of citizens guaranteed by European Community law. Parliamentary sovereignty is, therefore, already limited by European Union membership. Shortly after coming to power, the Labour government also took steps to incorporate the European Convention on Human Rights into domestic law. Britain had been one of the first to sign the Convention in 1950. It was one of the last to incorporate it into domestic law.

Reform of the House of Lords

Charter88 also called for the reform of the House of Lords, to make it a democratic and non-hereditary chamber. There had been various demands to abolish the House of Lords since the nineteenth century. The Conservatives liked the Lords with its built-in Conservative majority of hereditary peers. Labour had backed away from reform because of perceived difficulties in creating an effective upper chamber that would not weaken the authority of the Commons. If both chambers

were elected but were also in disagreement, how could the Commons insist its will must prevail?

However, when Labour came to power in 1997 it promised to reform the Lords. 'As an initial, self-contained reform, not dependent on further reform in the future,' its election manifesto proclaimed, 'the right of hereditary peers to sit and vote in the House of Lords will be ended by statute.' It also promised to review the appointment of life peers to ensure a sufficient number of cross-bench peers to prevent any one party enjoying an overall majority, but also to reflect more clearly the proportion of votes cast at the previous election. Yet will this be enough? Life peers have never fulfilled their purpose of representing experience outside politics. Besides, if people are only made Lords as a reward for a successful career, or to remove a troublesome politician from government, it will remain 'an old folks' home'. Labour says it wishes to turn the Lords into an organ of democracy. Can this be done, and can it be truly representative? It will only reflect the pluralism of British society if it is elected, in which case it will cease to be the Lords in any meaningful sense, except it might continue to meet in the same gilded chamber.

The honours system

If Labour goes this far, should it also reform the honours system? Twice a year the Queen approves a long list of people for a wide variety of different kinds and grades of honour. The present honours system is so arcane that few understand it. The honours themselves largely belong to two obsolete institutions: feudal chivalry which is 500 years out of date, and the British Empire, which is 50 years out of date. They are awarded partly for achievement, but the grade of award is determined by social status. A senior diplomat might be appointed KCMG (Knight Commander of the Order of St Michael and St George), known irreverently as 'Kindly Call Me God'. There is only one higher rank for a diplomat, GCMG (Grand Commander), so senior indeed that 'God Calls Me God'. A middle-ranking civil servant's efforts may be recognised with an OBE (Order of the British Empire). A primary school principal can only hope for an MBE (Member of the British Empire). Prime Minister Blair indicated he may change this hierarchical structure. 'Why should a school principal not receive a knighthood?' he asked shortly after becoming Prime Minister. But the system will still encourage a sense of hierarchy and the deference that goes with it. Currently, many honours go to people already well rewarded both financially and in career terms. Traditionalists wish to keep the present system, but modernists would like it reformed to be open, explicable and appropriate to a modern society.

The honours system: Paul McCartney, the former Beatle, showing the medal he received with his knighthood.

Government: the difficulties of reform

From 1945 up to the 1960s, the two-party system seemed to ensure good government. The combination of Cabinet government and party discipline in the Commons seemed to provide a balance between efficient government and public accountability. This was partly the result of broad inter-party consensus on a welfare state, a mixed economy (with certain industries nationalised) and full employment. By the mid-1960s growing economic difficulty raised questions about the effectiveness of this kind of government. Many felt that greater long-term economic planning was required to ensure growth and stable prices. One attempt to achieve this was through tripartite consultation and coordination between government and two traditional adversaries, the Trades Union Congress (TUC) and the Confederation of British Industry (CBI). It was not a success, since neither adversary was able to guarantee the cooperation of its membership. Furthermore, governments seemed either unable or unwilling to implement realistic long-term planning and investment, and the experiment failed to modernise industry in the way the rest of Europe was doing.

In 1979 the consensus on broad objectives was broken by Margaret Thatcher. She promised to 'roll back the frontiers of the state', reduce public expenditure and encourage a free-market economy. Her premiership marked the beginning of a far sharper ideological conflict between the two major parties at a time when the demands of government needed more cooperation and less conflict. The privatisation of nationally-owned industries certainly liberated much of the economy from the deadening hand of government control. But she only partially 'rolled back the frontiers' of the state, as she had promised to do. Essentially she changed their configuration. Although the Civil Service shrank, political power became more centralised and more concentrated in Whitehall, and those constituencies of interest beyond the small circle of power became weaker. The Labour government of 1997 promised to reverse this centralising process and possibly to break the mould of the two-party system, the long-cherished desire of the Liberal Democrat Party, by inviting other parties to participate in constitutional reform, and restructuring the way Britain is governed.

The problems, however, are formidable. The system of decision-making at the top has grown more complex, diffuse and extensive. That leads to a loss of government unity as, in the words of one senior civil servant, 'Ministers in Cabinet rarely look at the totality of their responsibilities, at the balance of policy, at the progress of government towards its objectives as a whole.' Improved policy-making coordination and more long-term strategic planning will be vital.

Are government ministers capable of this? One frequently repeated criticism is that Westminster provides too small a pool from which to draw sufficiently talented ministers. There is an increasing need for a wider range of thinkers who can view the distant future more readily than ministers who are harassed by short-term political demands. It is likely therefore that policy research groups will increasingly be brought into the governing process.

Another fear, certainly for senior civil servants, is that a new minister may either fail to grasp the complexities of forging coherent policies, or be so headstrong that he or she will press ahead with ideas which the permanent departmental staff are convinced are fundamentally wrong. The duty of civil servants, having argued their case is to support their minister, unless they believe he or she is contravening an agreed policy, in which case it is their duty to record their protest. This also raises a difficult question regarding ministerial responsibility. It used to be the case that a minister would resign as a point of honour following a serious failure within his or her department. In recent years ministers have been much less willing 'to act honourably'. They have some justification. With the growing complexity of each government department, they must remain accountable for policy failure, but can hardly still be held responsible for serious mistakes by the 'machinery' of the department, unless these stem from faulty policy. Labour promised to establish a special select committee to redefine ministerial responsibility.

There has also been a serious problem of overload, with ministers and civil servants trying to cope with an increasing workload. This problem is not new, and the first attempt to remedy it was made in the mid-1950s. Today, the problem is worse than ever. One recommendation made then, but ignored, was to create regional bodies which could relieve central government of some of its burden. Although this has not yet happened, regional devolution in England is possible, following the creation of Scottish and Welsh assemblies (see p.133-135).

Another problem is the traditional British obsession with secrecy. Much of the governing of Britain has always gone on in secret. The Cabinet's tradition of secrecy conceals a much wider network hidden from public view. In theory power should reside in the Commons, yet there are probably about 200 formal committees working on different aspects of government policy under Cabinet direction. Yet with the exception of four – defence and overseas, economic strategy, home and social affairs, and legislation – which in 1979 the Prime Minister admitted existed, the remainder are secret. Officially they do not exist, and those who participate in them may not even admit to their existence. Yet these committees are the 'engine room' of government. According to constitutional theory, power should rest where the public can see it, but in practice Britain is governed by a largely hidden system. Prime Minister Blair has promised more open government and a Freedom of Information Act, to make government more transparent.

In the past governments deliberately gave information to journalists without allowing them to name the source, sometimes to test public reactions and sometimes to undermine the Opposition or even the position of an uncooperative minister, as happened on several occasions during the 1980s. Such action invited similar behaviour from upset government servants, as also happened during the 1980s. In 1997 Labour announced it would abandon these 'off the record' briefings to journalists, and would appoint an official spokesman.

The Civil Service

Britain prides itself on a politically impartial Civil Service. This, in theory, is because the Civil Service Commissioners responsible for selecting civil servants are answerable to the Queen, and not to the Prime Minister. The system was established as a result of the Northcote–Trevelyan report of 1854. It has produced a service of great excellence, in the words of one elder statesman, 'surely one of the most talented bodies of men ever to be engaged in the art and science of civil government'.

Indeed, the ethical quality of the Civil Service has been generally outstanding, higher than that expected in business or industry. For Peter Hennessy, the leading commentator on Britain's bureaucracy, its qualities are:
(1) probity – there is no 'hand in the till'; (2) care with evidence and respect for reason; (3) a willingness to speak the truth to those in power (i.e. ministers) but a readiness to carry out ministerial instructions to the contrary, if overruled; (4) an appreciation of the wider public

Civil servants are famous for the subtlety and sometimes ambiguity of the statements they make to the public.

interest when there is danger that the policy of central government is made without due care; (5) equity and fairness in treatment of the public; (6) a careful concern for the law; (7) a constant concern for Parliament, its needs and procedures – i.e. no lying and no misleading; (8) a constant concern for democracy.

As another commentator has written, 'It is difficult for politicians to conceive that civil servants can be driven by a desire to do public good in a way that is detached from party preference.' These are high standards – achieved mainly through the maintenance of a tradition of exacting standards over the past century. It cannot be said that the Civil Service does not from time to time fall short of these standards. The highly popular television series, *Yes, Minister*, demonstrated how such high standards need not necessarily prevent devious cunning. One Cabinet Secretary in the 1980s became notorious for his admission that he had been 'economical with the truth', a phrase which entered the English language. Nevertheless, the

standards remain, and are the qualities of which any civil service would rightly be proud.

However valuable such qualities might be, they do not guarantee an effective civil service. Thatcher saw the Civil Service she inherited as an obstruction to her will, and an inefficient corporate body that badly needed to be driven by the kind of values that drove the free market. She was determined to compel the Civil Service to be a dutiful servant of government more than an aloof source of disinterested policy advice, to reduce its size and to be more efficient at delivering services to the public. From 1979 to 1996 Conservative governments reduced the size of the Civil Service by one-third, from 732,000 to 500,000 staff, the smallest bureaucracy since 1939. From the early 1980s there was also a drive to increase efficiency and eliminate wastage, achieving a saving of about £325 million yearly. For example, no fewer than 27,000 different printed forms were scrapped as unnecessary. Three guiding principles were more clearly established for civil servants: that they should have (1) a clear view of objectives; (2) well-defined responsibilities and (3) the information, training and access to expert advice in order to exercise responsibility effectively.

Still, the government, including some civil servants, were dissatisfied. The Civil Service, they felt, was too monolithic, with too many people involved both with the execution of policy or services and also with the formulation of policy. It was decided to separate the two functions, and from 1988 a major reorganisation entitled 'The Next Steps' was commenced. It was the most radical shake-up of the Civil Service for a century, separating policy-making from operational matters. Government ministries were reduced to a small core of advisers and policy analysts to support ministers in the formulation of policy. The bulk of the Civil Service, however, was hived off into many different 'executive agencies', each designated to carry out specific tasks and headed by a chief executive. While answerable to the departmental minister, each executive agency is entirely responsible for its own operation, thus leaving more senior civil servants free to plan policy. By the end of 1995 109 such agencies had been created, with over 70 per cent of all civil servants now employed by one of these agencies. A further 57 candidates were earmarked for executive agency status. In all, something in the order of 85 per cent of all civil servants were destined to belong to an executive agency.

Some senior civil servants were unhappy with the process, partly through their own loss of power and authority, but also because the reorganisation led to blurred accountability and the removal of direct accountability to Parliament. They also felt the Civil Service was in danger of losing its public service ethos.

There is a continuing debate concerning the ability of the Civil Service to respond to the demands of contemporary government. Peter Hennessy has suggested that the demands on central government in the twenty-first century might well be: short-term crisis management; medium-term planning for programmes proposed by a political party and adopted in Parliament; strategic thinking on central issues of the state (defence, energy, foreign policy, the welfare state and so forth); the management of tax-gathering and social security; and managing major services such as national health and education.

He is also concerned, however, by the question of who enters the Civil Service. The Northcote–Trevelyan report found that 'the superior docility of young men renders it much easier to make valuable public servants of them, than of those more advanced in life'. As a result, the present system largely excludes entry into Whitehall's higher ranks from outside the Civil Service. In addition, recruitment to the junior ranks is from a relatively small section of society. This is most strongly seen in the diplomatic service. Over two-thirds of the top cadre of diplomats studied either at Oxford or Cambridge University. Few are female, and virtually none are from an ethnic minority. Even in the rest of the Civil Service one need only look at the background of its top people to recognise there is strong uniformity of background. Barely any permanent secretaries have entered the Civil Service in mid-life from outside the system, the overwhelming proportion having entered direct from university. It had been widely assumed that the pattern was becoming more varied.

Hennessy and others argue strongly in favour of bringing in experience and maturity at a senior level from outside the Civil Service, people who can advance fresh ideas and who are unencumbered with 'the departmental view'. This 'departmental view' is the collective but unwritten state of mind on a wide range of subjects which slowly becomes the accepted wisdom within a ministry. One of those eager to employ more outsiders was Sir Peter Kemp, the senior civil servant who implemented 'The Next Steps' until his retirement in 1992. He still thinks there is much to be done, particularly at the interface between ministries and the executive agencies:

It is the people who stand between ministerial decisions and the autonomous agencies which have to execute them which the Civil Service lacks. This is the administrative equivalent of the familiar British trait of having good ideas but not being able to turn them into practice. We need more of these 'production engineers', individuals to whom broad policy decisions can be remitted, whose job it would be, with the help of a team, to make them fly, and who would be responsible if they did not.

Sir Peter Kemp, *Beyond Next Steps: A Civil Service for the 21st Century*

Quangos

One of Thatcher's targets for removal were the so-called 'quangos' which she had inherited from previous administration. The term 'quango' referred to a variety of institutions and organisations lying on the fringes of government. There were just over 2,000 such bodies in 1980, of which three-quarters were advisory. One-quarter, however, were a good deal more substantial, for example the Arts Council, the British Council, the Countryside Commission and the Commission for Racial Equality, all areas in which the government of the day felt that a 'quasi-autonomous non-governmental organisation' would be able to act more effectively than one within the direct constraints of government. Thatcher halved the number of those she inherited. But she also created a great many more as part of her programme of 'rolling back the frontiers of the state'. The new ones, however, were more integral to government services to large segments of the population, for example the National Health Service trusts (see p.195-196) or 'opted-out schools' (see p.150), urban development corporations, housing action trusts, and regulatory 'watchdogs' created to monitor recently privatised but hitherto public services, like gas, water, electricity and the railways. All these new quangos were arguably discharging rather more fundamental duties of government. Those who favoured such quangos pointed to the increased efficiency or standards which they had achieved or promised to achieve in the future. The critics had two main objections. First, the government freely appointed whom it pleased in order to run these various bodies. By 1996 there were 7,700 such bodies disbursing £54,000 million of public money. Forty per cent of such appointees were directly identified as either members of, or strong supporters of the Conservative Party. The Parliamentary Public Accounts Committee warned of a regression into 'a system of patronage and privatised carelessness'. The other closely related objection was the loss of democratic control. In the words of one administrator in 1997: 'The growth of fringe bodies is a retreat from the simple democratic principle evolved in the nineteenth century that those who perform a public duty should be fully responsible to an electorate ... . '

As with the Civil Service itself, the debate concerning the balance between efficiency and accountability is set to continue.

Parliament: in need of reform?

Is Parliament really sovereign, or is it merely a 'rubber stamp' for government, as many critics say? Because any government, by definition, enjoys a majority in the Commons, in practice Parliament's main function is hardly to pass legislation. That is done by the government and its supporters. As one parliamentary report in 1978 noted, 'The balance of advantage between Parliament and Government in the day-to-day working of the Constitution is now weighted in favour of the Government to a degree which arouses widespread anxiety ... . '

It was for this reason that over 50 Commons select committees were established soon after. Although these were not given the power to compel

evidence from ministers, both ministers and officials have increasingly, and voluntarily, testified to them. Since 1980 these committees have had the power to act not only as policy investigators but as legislative committees as well. Commons select committees have undoubtedly strengthened Parliament's power against deaf government.

The real function of the Commons is as a forum in which to examine and criticise government administration. Government must defend its conduct convincingly. Its other important function is to prepare young politicians for holding office in government. Yet there is wide unease concerning the functioning of Parliament as a check on government. Margaret Thatcher, for example, participated in parliamentary debate very much less often than her predecessors, and was harder for the Opposition to attack, since she was less frequently exposed to the dangers of debate. Labour has promised to restructure Prime Minister's Question Time to make it more effective. This is not only a matter of reducing the amount of sterile 'tit-for-tat' debate. It also means that the governing party must stop using the occasion for its backbenchers (those MPs not holding ministerial office) from 'planting' questions at the direction of the party whip, or asking questions simply to flatter the Prime Minister. Both main parties are guilty of this practice. One newspaper started naming the MP it thought most

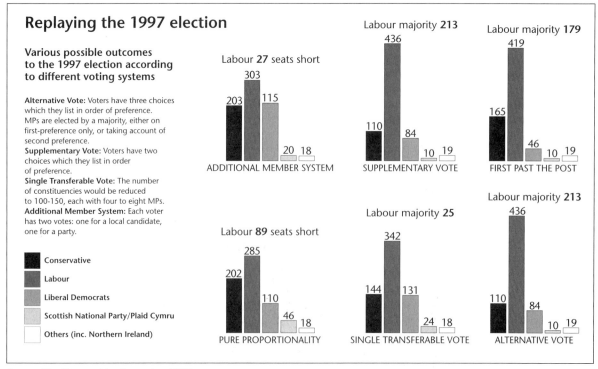

Replaying the 1997 election

Various possible outcomes to the 1997 election according to different voting systems

Alternative Vote: Voters have three choices which they list in order of preference. MPs are elected by a majority, either on first-preference only, or taking account of second preference.
Supplementary Vote: Voters have two choices which they list in order of preference.
Single Transferable Vote: The number of constituencies would be reduced to 100-150, each with four to eight MPs.
Additional Member System: Each voter has two votes: one for a local candidate, one for a party.

■ Conservative
■ Labour
■ Liberal Democrats
■ Scottish National Party/Plaid Cymru
□ Others (inc. Northern Ireland)

Labour 27 seats short
303
203 115
20 18
ADDITIONAL MEMBER SYSTEM

Labour 89 seats short
285
202
110
46 18
PURE PROPORTIONALITY

Labour majority 213
436
110
84
10 19
SUPPLEMENTARY VOTE

Labour majority 25
342
144 131
24 18
SINGLE TRANSFERABLE VOTE

Labour majority 179
419
165
46
10 19
FIRST PAST THE POST

Labour majority 213
436
110
84
10 19
ALTERNATIVE VOTE

Source: *The Observer* 21st September 1997

sycophantic as 'Creep of the Day'. There has been a general decline of independence among MPs as a result of the increase in party discipline and the knowledge among many backbench MPs that if they hope for government office one day, they must avoid any public challenge of party policy.

The quality of Parliament also depends upon the importance given it. British MPs have been among the worst-paid and worst-equipped legislators. As a result of this low level of pay, some MPs have had some kind of outside employment. In the early 1990s a series of scandals, almost exclusively affecting Conservative MPs, compelled Prime Minister Major to establish two judicial inquiries. One was into the secret approval by ministers and civil servants of the sale of arms to Iraq (the Scott Inquiry, see p.49, 139), and the other, the Nolan Inquiry, was into venality among MPs, in particular undertaking to ask particular questions in Parliament in return for payment by outsiders. The findings of both reports seriously damaged the reputation of the Conservative Party, and led partly to its 1997 defeat. Labour promised to implement the Nolan recommendations to ensure probity in public life, and also widen their application.

Not only are MPs among the worst paid in the European Union, but the Commons also sits for twice as many hours as most Western legislatures. An average backbencher spends 67 hours per week on parliamentary business while Parliament is sitting, and 48 hours while it is in recess. How should the burden be lightened? Labour indicated it would look at the anti-social hours of parliamentary sessions, which frequently go on late into the evening.

Electoral reform

It is, perhaps, inevitable that with a growing debate about the kind of government Britain should have, and about its unwritten constitution, there has also been increasing discussion of the need for electoral reform.

This was accelerated by the acute distortions of the present first-past-the-post (FPTP) system during the 1980s, whereby the Conservatives, although a majority of the electorate voted against them, enjoyed an overwhelming majority in the Commons. The virtue of FPTP, its champions claimed, was that it usually ensured strong government. Those who spoke of reform invariably advocated proportional representation (PR). In 1997 Labour established an independent commission to consider what system to put to a national referendum, and invited the Liberal

Democrats to participate. The Conservatives were not invited since they formally opposed any change to the electoral system. The Liberal Democrats were the strongest and oldest advocates of PR, having suffered disproportionately under FPTP.

The arguments in favour of PR seemed clear until its different forms were theoretically applied to the 1997 general election. Each system was then shown to have considerable disadvantages. At some stage, however, the electoral commission will have to invite the electorate to decide what it wants: to keep the present FPTP system or to choose one out of several imperfect PR options. A fundamental problem with PR is that it never serves the interests of the governing party, since it will always reduce its margin of majority. For the Liberal Democrats, on the other hand, PR is the only realistic road whereby they can achieve sufficient 'critical mass' in elections to have real impact in national politics.

Labour promised that regardless of whether PR was eventually adopted for Westminster, it would be the basis for the election for the European Parliament in 1999. The perceived success, or failure, of PR in this election, and in the Scottish Parliament (see p.136) is likely to influence public attitudes to PR for the UK.

Yet if the electorate opts to retain the present system, calls for constitutional reform will continue. No government once elected will wish to restrict its own powers. The idea of introducing constitutional restrictions on Parliament's sovereignty is strongly opposed by several leading politicians. As one veteran politician remarked, 'British democracy is – for better or worse – based on absolute sovereignty of Parliament ... What Parliament has given away, Parliament can take back.' This is precisely the point that reformers fear. A Bill of Rights without a written constitution which limited Parliament's sovereignty might prove worthless. It may be that only a constitutional crisis will persuade the electorate whether or not a written constitution is necessary.

One danger with greater proportionality is of a 'hung' parliament, in which no party is able to form a government on its own nor conclude a coalition agreement with another party. In this situation the Queen would be in the difficult position of deciding how to resolve a constitutional deadlock. It would force her to exercise powers which have long lain dormant. Even without a hung Parliament, the monarch, through the phrase 'the Crown in Parliament' masks the effective sovereignty of the Prime Minister of the time. Without a written constitution what would happen if either the monarch or the Prime Minister decided the other was acting unconstitutionally? Such possibilities raise the whole question of the function and standing of the monarchy in Britain at the end of the twentieth century.

Changes in the electorate and political parties

Electoral results in the period 1979–87 showed a growing north–south divide, with the preponderance of Conservative control of the 'core', and intensified Labour dominance in the 'periphery'. Despite traditional Conservative dominance in the south, until 1979 Labour had won many seats in the south and east of Britain, particularly in London. Yet by 1987 it could win only 23 seats in Greater London and two in the rest of the south. Conservative constituencies became more Conservative, Labour ones became more strongly Labour, with fewer 'marginal' parliamentary seats and more predictably 'safe' ones, hardly helping a lively democratic system. Along with the growing disparity between the richest and poorest fifths of the population, this growing electoral divide threatened the sense of national unity.

By the late 1980s electoral commentators were seriously questioning whether Labour would be able to win another election since its constituency of support was dwindling. Labour's declining constituency had been foreseen. A leading party member had forecast in 1959: 'The Labour Party will probably decline ... by about 2 per cent at each successive general election.' It was a prophecy that proved reasonably accurate. Labour could expect to go on winning on the periphery of political power: in Wales, Scotland and the north of England. Moreover, the continuing drift of population to the south loaded the electoral scene further in the Conservatives' favour. So also did the rapid decline of the working class. This had been estimated at 47 per cent of the electorate in 1964, but was only 34 per cent by 1983, while the middle class – managers, professionals, supervisors and white-collar workers – increased from 36 to 51 per cent in the same period. Furthermore, in 1970 class identity had been a main determinant in the way people voted. Twenty years later this could no longer be assumed. The Conservatives experienced a slight but progressive loss of middle-class votes. But this did not compare with the large loss of blue-collar and clerical votes lost by Labour. A more important determinant had become tenure, home ownership or company share ownership, but the pattern was uneven across the country. In 1987, for example, barely half London's electorate voted according to class identity, while more than

Slick presentation at the Labour Party Conference: some Labour supporters fear that traditional Labour ideas have been sacrificed in favour of clever but empty presentation.

three-quarters of Glasgow's did. There was also anxiety, particularly for Labour, since it kept on losing, at the decline in the overall voter loyalty to the two main parties. In 1951 97 per cent of the vote had gone to one or other main party, but by 1987 this had fallen to 73 per cent. Moreover, much voting had become negative: voting to keep a disliked party out of power, rather than enthusiasm for the party that was supported.

Thus Labour faced severe problems at the beginning of the 1990s. In the 1960s and 1970s it had needed no more than a 3 or 4 per cent swing to get into power. By 1990 Labour could expect only 35 per cent of the national vote, and it needed more than a 10 per cent swing in its favour overall to win. Since the 'blue-collar' manual worker class was rapidly shrinking, Labour also needed to build support in those areas in which it was not represented, the inner and outer 'core' areas, by reinventing itself and by throwing off its less electorally attractive characteristics. It began to distance itself from the trade union movement, openly accepting that the unions had wielded too much power in the past and had been too undemocratic. Each union had been able to cast a 'block vote' at the annual Labour Party conference, in other words the entire vote of the union's membership. At one time virtually all trade union members supported Labour, though they might not agree with their own union's use of their vote. In the 1964 election 73 per cent of trade unionists voted Labour. By 1987 this had fallen to 43 per cent, and yet the unions were still able to cast 5.7 million votes at the conference. Many party decisions at the conference were merely the outcome of a trial of strength between the unions. From 1993 Labour no longer allowed trade unions to cast the 'block vote' on behalf of its membership at the annual party conferences. This was a controversial decision since Labour largely depended on union funding, particularly for election campaigns. Labour was able to persuade the unions to continue to support Labour financially, but it also made a major effort to build up the party membership among those who did not belong to a union.

Although it had never been truly socialist, Labour also formally abandoned its philosophy of nationalisation for major industries in 1995, and also quietly abandoned central economic planning. It accepted, in a way it had not up to the mid-1980s, more use of market forces and less central control. But, in the words of one senior Labour politician, it continued to believe that 'a socialist willingness to intervene in the national interest in order to make good the deficiencies of the market

is a necessary ticket to our industrial future'. In practice this means encouraging diversity, individual enterprise, decentralised economic organisation and more consumer choice. In addition, although traditionally suspicious of Britain's membership of the European Community, from 1987 Labour openly supported full participation as essential to the country's political and economic future.

It also began a strategic campaign in favour of a less class-based ideological stance, and working 'for the many, not the few', as its slogan stated. It began to call itself 'New Labour', to make a crucial distinction from traditional Labour. It projected a classless image, wooing the class of junior white-collar workers whose abandonment of Labour had proved crucial to the Conservative victory in 1979. It also sought to attract women voters, who had traditionally tended to favour the Conservatives, by putting great emphasis on qualities it believed would appeal to them. It also concentrated its efforts on young people, particularly those voting for the first time. After the disappointment of the 1992 election it also identified 91 'critical' parliamentary constituencies which were realistically winnable at the next election, and put specific effort into them.

All these efforts were amply rewarded in 1997 with a landslide victory. Labour's biggest gains were in the south east of Britain, with precisely those groups it had aimed at. Overall 45 per cent of women and 56 per cent of the under 30-year-olds voted for Labour. Although the Conservatives had undoubtedly lost credibility and so were almost certain to lose the 1997 election, the size of Labour's victory indicated how a party could pick itself up after a period of great weakness by good strategic planning and a careful change of image.

One further point should be noted. Although it probably did not change the way people voted significantly, Labour was determined to increase the number of women MPs. Until it was declared illegal by a law court, Labour enforced 'women only' lists of candidates for local constituency parties to choose from. Partly as a result of this 'positive' discrimination, a total of 120 women were elected to Parliament in 1997, almost twice the number elected in 1992. Yet this was still only one-third of the total needed to achieve parity between men and women representatives in the Commons. Even if Labour did not attract many voters by this policy, it made the almost all-male Conservative Party look old-fashioned. For women, of course, the issue is critically important.

Now it is the Conservatives' turn to try to reinvent themselves. After their slightly surprising victory in 1992, the Conservatives found themselves severely weakened in the Commons, and more severely weakened ideologically. The central issue of ideological dissent was the question of participation in the European Union. A few Conservatives favoured Britain's withdrawal. The largest group, however, wished to remain in an economic community but feared both monetary union and closer political integration. Another group favoured monetary union but recognised that Britain was not yet ready for this. This group was fundamentally favourable to progressively closer ties with the rest of Europe. However, the 'Euro-sceptics' were able to appeal to the xenophobic part of the Conservative Party's character. The inability to resolve the schism on this vital issue, even within the Cabinet, made an electoral defeat in 1997 virtually inevitable.

William Hague became leader of the Conservative Party in 1997, aged only 36. His future as leader is likely to depend on his ability to defeat Labour.

Suddenly the Conservative Party seemed not only bitterly divided, but also deeply disorganised, old-fashioned, anti-democratic and highly resistant to change. Straight after the 1997 election it was said mistakenly that the Conservatives had lost because so many of their supporters had stayed at home. The truth was more worrying. The party's local associations, their views, and the recruitment of new party members were all ignored throughout the 1980s. In 1979 party membership had been 1.5 million, but had dwindled to 300,000 by 1997.

The youth branch, the Young Conservatives, once had half a million members, but by 1997 numbered only 7,000. Most devastating of all, by 1997 half the Conservative Party's membership was 65 years of age or older. By the election in 2002 one-third of these might well be dead. Only 16 per cent of the membership was under 45, and only 5 per cent under 35 years of age, almost the exact reverse of Labour membership. Following the 1997 defeat the Conservative MPs elected William Hague as John Major's successor. Hague was only 36, and many felt sceptical about his competence to carry out the reforms necessary to make the party electable.

The changing character of the electorate obviously has long-term implications for Britain's political parties. It was the political centre which first recognised the basic changes that had been taking place. By the end of the 1980s, an analysis of surveys carried out over more than ten years showed class loyalties slowly giving way to a new system of values. According to this analysis, there are three broad categories of voter. First, there are those concerned with survival and security, who value the virtues of loyalty and solidarity. They are generally people on lower incomes who vote Labour. They are about 30 per cent of the population and are in decline. Second, there are those ambitious for success, wealth or power, for whom outward appearances are important. They are 'self-made', natural Conservative voters. By 1990 these were reckoned to be 34 per cent of the population, but also in decline. Third, there are those concerned with personal development and individual freedom, with a tendency towards strong moral motivation, for example concern about world ecology, nuclear power or weapons, or civil liberties. Such people constitute 36 per cent of the population and are increasing.

The Liberal Democrats were the first to make political use of this survey, to demonstrate that their own political views most closely reflected the growing third category. Although this close identity is undeniable, it is less clear whether the party will be able to attract them because, until PR is introduced, it can hope for electoral progress based upon little more than negative voting – the hostility of some voters to the dominant party – in the south, the Conservatives and in the north, Labour. From their viewpoint it is a frustrating position. The 1997 general election was good for the Liberal Democrats. They obtained 46 seats with only 17 per cent of the overall vote, the result of shrewd targeting of winnable seats. However, they face serious problems. Much of their 1997 support came in constituencies in the form of negative voting, in other words, where a voter's preferred party was considered too weak to have a chance. It is highly unpredictable whether the Liberal Democrats will continue to benefit from the 'protest' vote. They are also endangered by Labour's move to the centre of British politics, leaving them as arguably the real representative of the 'radical left'. Everything for the Liberal Democrats hangs on the introduction of PR, when they could hope to attract about 100 seats and thus possibly transform the political scene from a two-party to a three-party contest.

It is difficult to tell whether the decline in support for the two main parties will continue. What, however, has become clearer is that there are a growing number of 'single-issue' activists. These belong to that third category of people concerned with personal development and individual freedom, and who have a strong moral motivation. They come from a broad range of social class, from the unemployed and the so-called underclass at one end of the spectrum to highly educated professional people at the other. In the 1980s women from these different classes combined to protest against nuclear weapons. In the 1990s other powerful coalitions have formed around issues such as the inhumane transport of live animals, the use of animals in medical or cosmetic research, to environmental issues. From 1993 new major roads plans that cut through open countryside, ancient woodlands or other ecologically valued areas were opposed not merely by formal protest but also by direct action. Protesters climbed into those trees scheduled for felling. Others dug complex and almost impenetrable tunnels in the path of the new road, in which they hid. These acts of protest attracted enormous publicity and affected government policy. By 1996 government had become a good deal more apprehensive of 'single-issue' coalitions than it had been a decade earlier. It remains to be seen whether single-issue politics will have a lasting effect on British politics.

Further information

WEBSITES

The Monarchy (unofficial)	www.royalnetwork.com
Political parties	www.conservative-party.org.uk
	www.labour.org.uk
	www.libdems.org.uk
Government economic policy	www.hm-treasury.gov.uk
Political issues	www.bbc.co.uk (search facility)
Charter88	www.charter88.org.uk

PRINTED MATERIAL

Adonis, Andrew, and Pollard, Stephen 1997 *A Class Act: The Myth of Britain's Classless Society* Chapter 5 Hamish Hamilton

Barnett, Anthony 1997 *This Time: Our Constitutional Revolution* Vintage

Haseler, Stephen 1993 *The End of the House of Windsor: Birth of a British Republic* I B Tauris

Kemp, Peter 1993 *Beyond Next Steps: A Civil Service for the 21st Century* Social Market Foundation

Marr, Andrew 1995 *Ruling Britannia: The Failure and Future of British Democracy* Michael Joseph

Morton, Andrew 1997 *Diana: Her True Story* Michael O'Mara Books

Nairn, Tom 1988 *The Enchanted Glass: Britain and Its Monarchy* Hutchinson Radius

Sampson, Anthony 1992 *The Essential Anatomy of Britain: Democracy in Crisis* Hodder and Stoughton

McKay, George (ed.) 1998 *DIY Culture: Party and Protest in the Nineties* Verso

QUESTIONS

Section analysis

1 **The monarchy** Do you think the Royal Family has a future? Give reasons for your answer.

2 **The constitution** If Britain has managed perfectly well since 1688 without a written constitution, does it need one now? Give your own opinion.

3 **The honours system** Is there any defence to be made of the present honours system?

4 **Government: the difficulties of reform** Questions are being raised about the effectiveness of the British system of government. What are they? What changes would you propose?

5 **The Civil Service** What do you think are the chief strength and main weakness of Britain's Civil Service? How should the weakness be tackled?

6 **Quangos** What are the two principal objections to the quangos created by the Conservatives, 1979–97? In your view, do these offset the virtue of greater efficiency?

7 **Parliament: in need of reform?** In what ways can Parliament act as a check on the power of the government? (Refer back to Chapter 2 if necessary.) Do you think Parliament's powers should be greater, and if so, how?

8 **Electoral reform** Argue the case for and against a change in Britain's electoral system.

9 **Changes in the electorate and political parties** How are former political loyalties among the electorate changing? How do you think this will affect the three main parties?

Chapter analysis and discussion

1 How did Labour reinvent itself? And what factors led to the Conservatives' collapse in 1997?

2 Having considered this chapter, what kind of reformed system of parliamentary democracy (i.e. kind of state; type of legislature and executive bodies; electoral system) do you think would prove most acceptable to the British electorate? Give reasons for your thinking.

Visual interpretation

1 Consider the opinions expressed in the graphs and table below.

a What implications do these opinions contain for the Royal Family?

b How do you think the opinions expressed here might subsequently have been affected by Princess Diana's death?

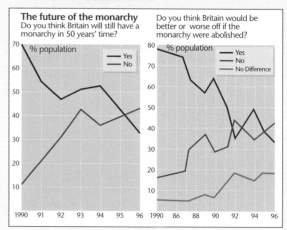

Source: MORI 1996

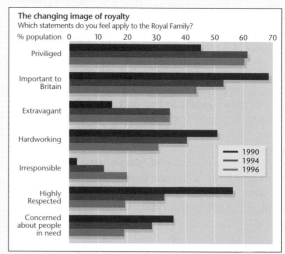

Source: MORI

2 In the 1997 general election Labour won 43 per cent of the total UK vote. Compare the theoretical results for the same general election as shown in the graphs on page 48. Do these results strengthen or weaken the case for PR? Which system of PR would you favour, and why?

4 *The forces of law and order*

There was a time, between 30 and 40 years ago, when the broad mass of British people felt confident and proud about their system of justice, and in particular the quality of the police force. There has been a loss of innocence since then, most strikingly the result of some spectacular miscarriages of justice. In 1989 four Irishmen, 'the Guildford Four', were released after 15 years' imprisonment, when it was revealed that the police interrogation on which they had been convicted in 1974 had not been properly conducted. They had been found guilty of causing a bomb explosion in a Guildford pub. The following year, the conviction of seven other people, 'the Maguire Seven', found guilty of running a bomb factory in the 1970s, was quashed. And the year after that, 1991, another six Irishmen, 'the Birmingham Six', convicted for a bomb explosion in Birmingham in the 1970s, were also released because their convictions were unsound.

Through the 1990s there has been a steady trickle of other revelations leading to the release of people convicted for murder. In 1996 the police admitted that James Hanratty, one of the last men to be hanged in Britain for murder over 30 years earlier, was in fact innocent. The same year it was agreed to review two other suspected cases of miscarried justice. All these cases revealed disturbing aspects of police methods: obtaining confessions by improper means; withholding vital pieces of evidence because they weakened or undermined the case for prosecution; faking evidence; failing to check within the police force when doubts arose about a particular officer's methods. Concern for such miscarriages, however, has been offset by the public's anxiety over rising crime rates and its desire that criminals be caught and punished.

The legal system of England and Wales

The law is one of the most traditional areas of national life and the legal profession has jealously protected its position against outside attack. Its main virtue is its independence from the system of government and as such, a safeguard of civil liberties. Its main vice lies in its resistance to reform, and the maintenance of its own privileges which may be contrary to public interest.

The legal system for England and Wales (there are separate ones for Scotland and Northern Ireland) does not have a criminal or civil code, but is founded upon two basic elements: Acts of Parliament or statute law, and common law which is the outcome of past decisions and practices based upon custom and reason. Common law has slowly built up since Anglo-Saxon times 1,000 years ago, while Parliament has been enacting statutes since the thirteenth century. Almost all criminal law is now set out in Acts of Parliament, while the greater part of civil law still depends upon common law, the weight and guidance of previous similar decisions.

European Community law also applies to Britain by virtue of its membership of the European Union and it takes precedence over domestic law. In 1997 Britain finally took steps to incorporate the European Convention on Human Rights into domestic law.

Dealing with crime

The initial decision to bring a criminal charge normally lies with the police, but since 1986 a Crown Prosecution Service (CPS) has examined the evidence on which the police have charged a suspect to decide whether the case should go to court. Generally it brings to court only those cases which it believes will be successful, a measure to avoid the expense and waste of time in bringing unsound cases to court. However, the collapse of several major cases and the failure to prosecute in other cases have both led to strong criticism of the CPS.

There are two main types of court for criminal cases: Magistrates' Courts (or 'courts of first instance'), which deal with about 95 per cent of

A Crown Court in session. These proceedings may not be photographed.

criminal cases, and Crown Courts for more serious offences. All criminal cases above the level of Magistrates' Courts are held before a jury. Civil law covers matters related to family, property, contracts and torts (wrongful acts suffered by one person at the hands of another). These are usually dealt with in County Courts, but specialised work is concentrated in certain designated courts. The High Court deals with more complicated cases and is divided into three: the Family Division, which deals with family law, divorce and adoption; Chancery, which deals with corporate and personal insolvency, interpretation of trusts and wills; and the Queen's Bench, which deals with contract and tort cases, maritime and commercial law.

Types of court	
Civil	*Criminal*
House of Lords	House of Lords
Court of Appeal (Civil Division)	Court of Appeal (Criminal Division)
High Court: Chancery Family Queen's Bench	
County Court	Crown Court
	Magistrates' Court (Juvenile Court)

There are about 400 Magistrates' Courts in England and Wales, served by approximately 30,000 unpaid or 'lay' magistrates or Justices of the Peace (JPs), who have been dealing with minor crimes for over 600 years. JPs are ordinary citizens chosen from the community. They are appointed by the Lord Chancellor, but on the recommendation of advisory committees of local people. These committees sometimes advertise for applicants. They are required not only to interview, but to make their selection not only on suitability but also ensuring that composition of 'the Bench' broadly reflects the community it serves. In recent years women and members of ethnic minority communities have been recruited to moderate the once overwhelmingly white, male, character of the JP cadre.

A court normally consists of three lay magistrates who are advised on points of law by a legally qualified clerk. They may not impose a sentence of more than six months imprisonment or a fine of more than £5,000, and may refer cases requiring a heavier penalty to the Crown Court.

A Crown Court is presided over by a judge, but the verdict is reached by a jury of 12 citizens, randomly selected from the local electoral rolls. The judge must make sure that the trial is properly conducted, that the 'counsels' (barristers) for the prosecution and defence comply with the rules regarding the evidence that they produce and the examination of witnesses, and that the jury are helped to reach their decision by the judge's summary of the evidence in a way which indicates the relevant points of law and the critical issues on which they must decide in order to reach a verdict. Underlying the whole process lies the assumption that the person charged with an offence is presumed to be innocent unless the prosecution can prove guilt 'beyond all reasonable doubt'. Recent complex cases involving financial fraud have opened a debate as to whether certain kinds of case should be tried by a panel of experts capable of understanding fully what a case involves.

Like Parliament, Crown Courts are adversarial, contests between two opposing parties. Neither the prosecution nor defence counsel is concerned to establish the 'whole' truth about the accused person. Both may well wish to avoid aspects which weaken their case that the accused person is either guilty beyond reasonable doubt, or that sufficient reasonable doubt exists for that person to be declared 'not guilty'. It will be recalled, however, that the withholding of vital evidence by the police has led to serious miscarriages.

A person convicted in a Magistrates' Court may appeal against its decision to the Crown Court. If unsuccessful, the appeal may be taken to the Court of Appeal (Criminal Division), but seldom obtains a reversal. The Court of Appeal dislikes overturning a Crown Court decision unless the evidence is overwhelming or there has been some error of legal procedure. The highest court in the land is the House of Lords, which will consider a case referred from the Court of Appeal where a point of general public importance seems to be at stake. In practice the Lords are represented by five or more of the nine Law Lords.

The treatment of offenders

The sentence passed on an offender is decided by the judge or magistrate, within the limits for the offence set down by Act of Parliament. Punishment may take the form of a fine, imprisonment, or probation under the supervision of a professional probation officer. The death penalty was suspended in 1965 and abolished in 1969 except for treason, although application of the death penalty even in this circumstance would be highly controversial. Had it remained in force the Guildford Four would probably have been hanged. It is this awareness that probably spells an end to efforts by some MPs, supported by over half of the

electorate, to reintroduce hanging. The wrongful conviction of innocent people discredits the finality of hanging.

Imprisonment is used significantly more in Britain than elsewhere in Europe. In 1995 the detention rate in England and Wales was 99 per 100,000 of the population, in Scotland 110, and in Northern Ireland 106 per 100,000. Only Spain and Portugal in Europe have higher rates, while most members of the European Union have a rate of about 55 per 100,000. The debate over imprisonment has always had a political edge. The Conservative Party has always prided itself on being 'the party of law

The grim interior of a prison may offer suitable punishment, but it is questionable whether it helps inmates to become fulfilled and productive members of society.

and order'. In practice this has meant it has encouraged greater use of custodial rather than non-custodial sentences. The belief in stiff punishment as deterrence, retribution and the protection of society, derives from the moral view that criminality stems primarily from envy, greed and malice. The weakness of this argument lies in the fact that barely one in 50 crimes committed leads to a conviction.

Labour and the Liberal Democrats tend to view criminality as the consequence of social conditions rather than intrinsic individual moral wickedness. They blame it on social failure: poverty, poor housing, unemployment and educational failure leading to greatly diminished prospects in life. The weakness of this argument lies largely in the inability of any government within its five-year term of office to sufficiently transform the social context in which crime occurs, and the argument therefore lies largely unproven.

Both points of view eagerly select the academic data of criminologists to vindicate their viewpoint. Within these two collective viewpoints there is, of course, a spectrum of opinion. This is especially true of the Conservative Party, which has a hard-line right-wing element, that would like a return to capital and corporal punishment, the 'hanging and flogging' lobby as they are colloquially known to those who disapprove of such methods. The Conservative left wing tends to deplore such methods and believes, like Labour that the causes of crime are largely social. It is not surprising that the rate of imprisonment increased under Conservative government from 47,000 in England and Wales in 1979 to 62,000 by 1997, a 30 per cent increase. Fluctuations in prison population figures over the period partly reflect which wing of the Conservative Party the Home Secretary of the day belonged to. The prison population fell from 50,000 in 1988 to about 44,000 by 1993, thanks to Home Secretaries of the centre and left of the party. In 1993, however, a particularly hard-line right-wing politician was appointed. As a result of his stringent policy, based on the slogan 'Prison works', prison numbers increased at such a rate that by 1997 six prisons held up to 50 per cent more inmates than they had been designed for, and it was reckoned that in order to keep pace with the increase one new jail would be needed every month.

Prison conditions became a cause of major concern during the different Conservative administrations. During the 1980s there were repeated disorders in prisons. Prisoners rioted over the serious level of overcrowding and the decaying and primitive conditions of many prisons. In 1991 it was finally decided to provide proper toilet facilities instead of the 'slopping out', or buckets, that had been in operation since Victorian times, and were finally acknowledged to be degrading. The installation of a toilet in each cell was completed in 1996.

An unhappy aspect of the system is the imprisonment of those 'on remand', that is, awaiting trial. In 1978 there were 5,800 held on remand, itself arguably too high a number. By 1997 there were no less than 10,000 people held, many for months and sometimes over a year, awaiting either trial or sentencing. The fact that during the 1980s 5 per cent of people held on remand were acquitted and 35 per cent given non-custodial sentences suggests that the remand policy requires careful reassessment. The suicide rate among those on remand, especially among young people, is higher than among convicted prisoners, let alone among the population at large.

The Conservative government decided in 1991 to contract private sector security companies to perform custodial tasks. By 1996 four prisons were privately operated, with more scheduled for privatisation. From 1997 all escort services were contracted out. The advantage lay in saving valuable police and prison officer time on escort duties. It raised the question, however, of the public accountability of such methods.

Labour came to power with the slogan 'Tough on crime and tough on the causes of crime', an attempt to refute Conservative accusations that it was soft on crime. So it insisted on individual responsibility for crime while still arguing that it would tackle the causes, which lay in social deprivation. Following the mass shooting of schoolchildren by a deranged gunman in the Scottish town of Dunblane in 1996, Labour legislated to ban the private possession of all handguns. It also promised to introduce a crime of 'racially motivated violence' to protect ethnic minorities from intimidation.

Young offenders

The age of criminal responsibility is 10 (except in Scotland where it is eight). Children between the ages of 10 and 17 usually appear before a Juvenile Court, where it is decided whether the child should continue to live within the family, subject to supervision, or whether he or she should be taken into local authority care (with foster parents or in a community home). Such offenders normally attend special schools. Some are required to attend special centres on Saturdays, for leisure activities and skills training. Some are required to do community service, for example, a set number of hours decorating the houses of elderly or disabled people, or building an adventure playground. All arrangements must be reviewed every six months. Such arrangements may seem responsible, but are they adequate? Britain has a serious problem with young offenders, who commit seven million crimes a year. Very few young offenders are caught. The peak age for committing crime is 15. One in four criminal offences is committed by teenagers under 16. By that age crime is already a lifestyle for many.

Hardly surprisingly, concern has grown in recent years at the high number of re-offenders among those under the age of 17 taken into care or put into detention centres. One alternative, the 'supervision-in-the-community' scheme started in 1987, was able to show that the re-offence rate among those it had helped was half that of similar offenders who had been sent to prison. The Conservatives also experimented with methods used in the United States. They tried 'boot camps', prisons run on stringent military lines, in the hope that they would transform young offenders. They were not a success. Labour promised to target youth crime in a variety of ways. It promised to halve the time from arrest to trial and thus reduce the period on remand. It promised to change the system whereby people who offended repeatedly could be given a number of 'cautions' but not necessarily a sentence. Instead, for a first offence a person could be given a warning, and for a further offence they could be given a sentence (but not necessarily a custodial one). It also promised to make parents responsible in law for their children's behaviour. It decided to make youth offenders meet and apologise to their victims, in the belief that when confronted with the pain and suffering they had inflicted many would not offend again.

The legal profession and the courts

Traditionally the legal profession has been divided into two distinct practices, each with entrenched rights: only solicitors may deal directly with the public, and only barristers (professional advocates) may fight a case in the higher courts (Crown Courts and the High Court). Both have maintained their own self-regulating bodies, the Law Society for solicitors and the Bar for barristers. A member of the public dissatisfied with the services of a solicitor may complain to the Law Society, but this does not often take action against its own members except in the case of some gross offence or negligence. The Law Society has often infuriated members of the public by advising them to take their complaint to another solicitor.

A black barrister. There is a need for many more barristers from ethnic minorities to achieve proportionate representation in law practice.

There are only about 5,000 barristers, and they are the senior branch of the legal profession. Traditionally, only they have been able to reach the top of the profession, a High Court judgeship. In order to become a barrister, a candidate must obtain entrance to one of the four Inns of Court (law colleges which date from the Middle Ages), complete the legal training and pass the Bar examination. The Inns of Court have maintained their autonomy and privileges, and been more resistant to attempts at reform than almost any other British institution. A newly qualified barrister enters the 'chambers' of an established one, and slowly builds up experience and a reputation as an effective advocate in the higher courts. In due course, a successful barrister may be appointed a Queen's Counsel, or QC, known within the profession as 'taking silk'.

There is no judicial profession in England. All judges are appointed by the Lord Chancellor from among experienced barristers. Some become circuit judges, of whom there are about 300, assigned to the County Courts throughout the country. Above these are about 50 High Court judges, who deal with more important or difficult cases around the country, and about 30 other judges, all of whom belong to one of the divisions of the High Court of Justice (see p.61).

The Central Criminal Court, the Old Bailey, the scene of many famous criminal trials. The Old Bailey has existed since 1539, but the present building dates only from 1907.

The Lord Chancellor combines three distinct functions. As head of the legal hierarchy, he selects judges, QCs and magistrates and may preside over the Law Lords if he so wishes. He is Speaker (presiding officer) of the House of Lords, theoretically responsible for discipline there. Finally, as a political appointee, he is a member of the Cabinet and the government's chief legal adviser. In theory, therefore, the authority of the legislature and executive of Britain are not separated. However, it is a firmly understood tradition, that while judges may not declare an Act of Parliament void, their independence from government is a fundamental duty.

England has fewer professional judges than most countries, eight per million compared with 34 per million in the United States and even more in some countries. Ralf Dahrendorf, one of Britain's foremost academics, who grew up as a German, puts it another way: 'Britain is neither a litigious society in which individuals and groups fight out their battles by calling on the courts, nor is it a state society in which the courts are used as instruments of explicit domination. ... Where there is liberty, the law is always the second best instrument for defending it.' However, Britain became progressively more litigious during the 1980s, with the explosive growth of court cases to settle disputes in the workplace, health service and schools. This is an ominous indication of the absence or failure of intermediary bodies capable of resolving disputes without recourse to the courts.

The way in which judges are selected remains a matter of controversy. The Lord Chancellor's freedom to appoint judges allows successive products of the Bar to reinforce what Anthony Sampson, a leading analyst of British institutions, calls 'the most extreme British example of a closed and self-regulating community'. They tend to be detached from the broad sweep of society, almost entirely white, male, privately educated and belonging to the professional middle class. Take for example, the composition of the four most senior echelons of the judiciary in 1997:

Composition of the judiciary			
Category	Men	Women	Ethnic minorities
Law Lords	12	0	0
Appeal Court judges	31	1	0
High Court judges	97	7	0
Circuit judges	512	30	5

The Conservative government's Lord Chancellor from 1987 to 1997, Lord Mackay, was remarkable for two reasons. He was the son of a railwayman, educated within the state system. As a Scottish advocate, his whole professional career had been outside the English Bar. His appointment caused a considerable stir. Disturbed by the narrowness of intake into the judiciary, he introduced advertising and modern selection methods in 1994 in order to encourage a wider range of barristers into applying for the judiciary. However, he probably recognised it would take a long time to transform the elitist character of the judiciary.

In 1988, Labour advertised for the very first time for the job of High Court judge, with the words 'the Lord Chancellor will recommend those who appear to him to be best qualified regardless of ethnic origin, gender, marital status, sexual orientation, political affiliation, religion or (subject to the physical requirements of the office) disability'. But an applicant was required to have been a circuit judge for at least two years and a barrister for 10 years. It is therefore bound to mean that women and ethnic minority groups will remain severely underrepresented in the senior ranks of the judiciary for many years to come.

The legal system of Scotland

The Scottish legal system is similar to the English one, but is more influenced by Roman law, like other systems in Europe. Its main courts are the Sheriffs' Courts (like Crown Courts) for civil and criminal cases and the Court of Session for civil cases. The Court of Session is divided into an Outer House (a court of first instance) and the Inner House (a court of appeal). The Inner House has two divisions of four judges respectively, one under the direction of the Lord President, and the other under the Lord Justice Clerk. Less serious criminal cases are tried in the Sheriff's Courts (like Crown Courts) and District Courts, but more serious ones go to the High Court of Justiciary. Juries in Scotland are made up of 15 rather than 12 citizens. Minor offences are dealt with in District Courts (the equivalent of Magistrates' Courts). The senior law officer in the High Court of Justiciary and in all Scotland is the Lord Justice General, and the Lord Justice Clerk is second in rank.

In Scotland, the Lord Advocate is responsible for all prosecutions, a much older arrangement than England's Crown Prosecution Service. The work is carried out on his behalf by his deputy, the Solicitor General for Scotland, and by local officials, known as 'procurators fiscal'. The Secretary of State for Scotland, always a Scottish MP, but usually also one who is a lawyer by profession, is responsible for the appointment of most judges.

The police

In early 1990 a major feature article in one of Britain's leading papers was entitled, 'What's gone wrong with the police?' It referred to the frequency of scandals during the 1980s involving the police. These scandals concerned the excessive use of violence to maintain public order (urban riots in 1981, the miners' strike in 1984–85, the anti-poll tax riots in 1990); violence in the questioning of suspects (particularly, but not exclusively, in connection with Northern Ireland); the fabrication of evidence and the extortion of forced confessions (the 'Guildford Four' and the

Police arrest an anti-motorway protester in east London. Not all arrests are this gentle.

'Birmingham Six' (see p.55); and corrupt practices, for example the falsification of records concerning the successful solution to crimes. It also commented on the severe loss of morale among the police, and the high number of police who resign from the force on account of stress.

Certainly until the 1960s, the British police force was a source of pride. Unlike police in almost every other country, the British police officer enjoyed a trusted, respected and friendly relationship with the public. The 'bobbies on the beat' made it their business to learn about their neighbourhood. In return, the public placed a high level of trust in their integrity. This was probably a rosy, idealised view of the police, but it was a genuine source of pride that almost alone in the police world, the British bobby was unarmed. As Ralf Dahrendorf says, 'It is hard to exaggerate the significance of the fact that the British police did not, and very largely do not, carry weapons.' The British police are probably still among the finest in the world, but clearly there are serious and growing problems. A survey commissioned by three

authoritative police associations at the end of the 1980s reported that one in five people believed the police used unnecessary force on arrest, falsified statements, planted evidence and used violence in police stations. It also reported that only 43 per cent of white people interviewed and only 29 per cent of blacks believed the police treated all people fairly. In such circumstances there is clearly a critical need to rebuild public confidence. But what should be done? The problem is partly structural. In 1997 there were 52 separate police forces operating in different parts of the country. There is a debate here between the demands of efficiency and of local democratic control. In practice there is a high degree of coordination between police forces, particularly with the increasing use of the Police National Computer which can rapidly provide every police officer in communication with his own police station details on anyone with a previous criminal record or, for example, the details of the owner of any vehicle he or she might see in the street. Coordination also occurs at the highest level through the Association of Chief Police Officers.

A police woman at work. There is still a temptation to assign women police officers to community rather than criminal work.

Each force is answerable to a local police authority, whose composition is traditionally one-third magistrates and two-thirds local councillors. Police authorities have limited powers. They can appoint the chief officer (the Chief Constable), subject to Home Office approval, and they may ask questions and advise concerning police work. In 1995 the Home Secretary reduced the largely elected character of these authorities by appointing people to serve in them. Labour indicated it might legislate to ensure that every member was elected rather than selected, and to increase the powers of the police authority. It is not difficult to sense growing politicisation around who controls the police. In the case of London's Metropolitan Police (the 'Met'), the authority is the Home Secretary himself. In practice the Home Office has greater direct influence on each police force than the local police authority has.

Each Chief Constable is responsible for all operational and administrative decisions. The police authority cannot give direct instructions on such matters, nor can the Home Secretary (except in the cases of London and Northern Ireland). In 1966 a judge ruled that a Chief Constable, like any police officer, cannot be told which particular laws to enforce or refrain from enforcing. Traditionally Chief Constables have disliked local attempts to control even more than those of central government. The result is that except in the case of police violation of the law, or a case of gross negligence, it is extremely difficult for elected representatives at the local level to exercise direct control. In the 1984–85 miners' strike, for example, the local police authorities were powerless to moderate the aggressive tactics adopted by the police to defeat the miners.

Until 1987 the police investigated alleged police malpractice themselves. Although a Police Complaints Authority now exists, it does not command great confidence. In 1992, for example, it received 19,289 complaints of which it considered 9,200. However, only 904 cases, less than 10 per cent of those considered actually resulted in disciplinary proceedings, and only 97 in criminal charges. Many people believe that police malfeasance is much more widespread than these statistics would suggest.

Until 1984 no British citizen had any formal protection against police intimidation except customary ones, the right to silence and the right to see a solicitor. The right to silence was removed in Northern Ireland in 1988, and in Britain in 1993. Since 1984 there have been statutory codes of practice to be followed in the arrest and questioning of suspects, including the requirement to tape-record (for court use) all interrogations. This should improve things but it should be remembered, in the words of one ex-policeman, that 'Cells and detention rooms are known as places where officers can free themselves from legal and formal organisational rules.'

In an age of increasing popular violence and disrespect for law and order, the great challenge for the police is to recapture the respect of the public. Frustrating as this may be for the police, the challenge is to show greater restraint rather than aggression under provocation. It is also to shift the emphasis back from the more exciting image of armed or armoured law enforcement to a softer image of policing in the form of the friendly but firm neighbourhood bobby. In the longer run, the way the public feel about the police is of fundamental importance to police ability to control crime and maintain public order. Unfortunately, neighbourhood policing has far lower status than crime control.

As the challenges of modern society became more complex, the response of the Conservative government was to give the police more manpower and more money. Between 1979 and 1992 expenditure on the criminal justice system (police, courts and prisons) doubled in real terms to £9,000 million, of which the police spent £5,400 million. However, there is no indication these extra resources had any effect at all on recorded offences which rose from 1.6 million in 1971 to 2.5 million in 1980 to 5 million in 1995 in England and Wales. In other words, the steepest increase in crime coincided with the greatest increase in crime prevention expenditure. Even these statistics, however, are probably only a fraction of the real crime figure. Furthermore, the failure of increased spending on crime prevention to affect crime figures suggests the answer to crime must lie elsewhere.

Further information

WEBSITES

Police	www.police.co.uk
New Scotland Yard	www.open.gov.uk/police/mps/home.htm
Lord Chancellor's Department	www.open.gov.uk (select Lord Chancellor's Dept)
Amnesty International	www.amnesty.org.uk (select UK country report)

PRINTED MATERIAL

Coxall, Bill and Robins, Lynton 1994 *Contemporar British Politics*, Chapters 17 and 31 Macmillan
Griffith, J. A. G. 1991 *The Politics of the Judiciary* Fo

QUESTIONS

Section analysis

1 The legal system in England and Wales
What are the two basic sources of English law?

2 Dealing with crime There are two main types of criminal court in England and Wales, Crown Courts and Magistrates' Courts. What are the differences between them?

3 The treatment of offenders How does the British way of treating offenders differ from treatment in your country?

4 Young offenders Which of the various treatments of young offenders mentioned in the chapter will be the most effective, in your opinion? Or do you think a combination of treatments would be preferable?

5 The legal profession Do you think that a relatively small legal profession, as in Britain, is desirable? Give your reasons.

6 The police What has gone wrong with the police? Based upon the information given, list the basic concerns the average citizen might have.

Chapter analysis and discussion

Which of the following statements are correct, and which are incorrect? Find textual evidence for your decision.

1 Partly as a result of the wrongful imprisonment of the Guildford Four and the Birmingham Six
a the legal system of England and Wales was questioned by Lord Mackay.
b the Crown Prosecution Service was established.
c the public have less confidence in the police.

2 The legal system of England and Wales
a is based on a written legal code.
b assumes that a person is innocent unless he or she has been proved guilty.
c has more professional judges than most other countries.

3 In England and Wales
a the highest court is the House of Lords.
b Magistrates' Courts are presided over by Justices of the Peace who have a legal training and receive a salary.

c a jury of 12 citizens decides on the defendant's guilt or innocence in a Crown Court.

4 The police in Britain
a make the initial decision to bring a criminal charge against someone.
b do not generally carry guns.
c are controlled chiefly by local police authorities.

Textual interpretation

1 *We expect him [the average police officer] to be human and yet at the same time para-human. We welcome official protection, yet resent official interference. We employ him to administer the law, and yet will ask him to waive it. We resent him when he enforces a law in our own case, yet demand his dismissal when he does not elsewhere … We expect him to be a member of society, yet not share its prejudices and values.*
(The Commissioner of the Metropolitan Police 1987)

Do you consider this an adequate defence for police conduct as described by the author? Give reasons and evidence for your point of view.

Visual interpretation

1 Consider this graph. Does it satisfactorily explain Britain's high prison population?

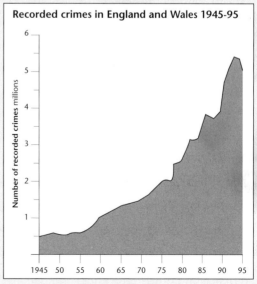

Recorded crimes in England and Wales 1945-95

Number of recorded crimes millions

1945 50 55 60 65 70 75 80 85 90 95

Source: *Protecting the Public*, White Paper

5 Local government

A changing system

Regrettably for the student, local government in Britain is complex, inconsistent and in a long phase of restructuring. Two basic issues lie behind recent changes: the search for improved efficiency, and the ideological conflict between those, usually belonging to the political Left, who believe local government is a vital component of democracy and those, mainly of the Right, who argue that people are more interested in efficient service than local democracy. Thus the Conservative period of office, 1979–97 was characterised by the drive for efficient and low-cost services, while Labour since 1997 has sought to recover a degree of local democracy.

It may be helpful to provide a short history before looking more closely at the system. Although the county system of local administration dates back 1,000 years to Saxon times, the first systematic framework of local councils was established in the late nineteenth century. Broadly speaking, a three-tier system was introduced, consisting of county, borough or district and parish councils. These councils and their achievements were a source of great civic pride, wittily described by Sidney Webb, an early socialist:

> The town councillor will walk along the municipal pavement, lit by municipal gas and cleansed by municipal brooms with municipal water and, seeing by the municipal clock in the municipal market, that he is too early to meet his children coming from the municipal school ... will use the national telegraph system to tell them not to walk through the municipal park, but ... to meet him in the municipal reading room.

It was only in the 1960s and 1970s that major restructuring of the system took place, the result of major changes in population size and distribution and of the growth of conurbations (the growth of one town to reach a neighbouring one). In the 1970s six 'metropolitan' counties (Greater Manchester, Merseyside, Tyne and Wear, West Midlands, West Yorkshire and South Yorkshire) were created in an attempt to rationalise and reduce costs. A two-tier system of administration was introduced in England, Wales, and most of Scotland, whereas in Northern Ireland a single-tier system was adopted. London is a special case. It was the first city to have its own elected authority, established in 1215. London, also, was the first city anywhere to establish a complex civic administration to coordinate modern urban services: transport, housing, clean water and sewage systems, and education. Local government in London was reorganised in 1965 with the establishment of the Greater London Council (GLC), and 32 subsidiary borough councils and the Corporation of the City of London (see p.70), a much smaller number of administrative bodies than hitherto. In 1986, however, the Conservative government abolished the GLC (discussed below) and the other six metropolitan county councils, transferring most functions to the lower tier of borough or metropolitan district councils. A handful of unelected coordinating bodies was left in place.

Local government services: rubbish collection.

By the early 1990s England (with the exception of Greater London) and Wales were divided into 53 counties, within which there were approximately 370 districts. In mainland Scotland there were nine regions, divided into 53 districts, and the three authorities for the groups of islands (Shetland, Orkney and the Western Isles). In Northern Ireland a two-tier system had been reintroduced.

In 1992, however, a Local Government Commission was established to review the existing structures, boundaries, and electoral arrangements. In particular it was asked to review the two-tier system. Although it recommended that most remain undisturbed, it proposed the introduction of single-tier, or unitary, councils in certain cities. By the beginning of 1997 14 unitary councils had been established in England, with the possibility of more. In Scotland 29 unitary councils replaced the previous system of nine regions and 53 district councils. As for Wales, 22 unitary authorities replaced the previous eight county councils and 37 district councils. In Northern Ireland a single-tier system was tried once again, but with certain bodies directly responsible to central government.

A mayor carrying out his official duties at a celebration in an old people's home.

England			Scotland	
county councils	(34)		unitary councils	(32)
joint authorities	(6)	(conurbations)		
unitary authorities	(45)	(mainly cities but some counties)	**Wales**	
London borough councils	(33)	(including the City of London)	unitary authorities	(22)
district councils	(238)			
metropolitan district councils	(36)		**Northern Ireland**	
			district councils	(26)

As a result of this confusing history virtually no one, apart from the government officers concerned and a handful of academics, has much idea how local government is organised across the United Kingdom. Frankly, most people have only a vague idea of how their own local authority works.

County (or unitary), district and borough councils provide the range of services necessary for everyday life. The county councils usually look after the wider and larger responsibilities like planning, transport, highways, traffic regulation, health, education, and fire services. In principle, the local authorities have control over the local police, but in practice their control is extremely limited since the police may argue that they are directly answerable to the Crown (see p.62). District councils are usually responsible for local taxation, leisure and recreation, environmental health, housing, and refuse collection. The

borough councils in London are responsible for most of the services provided by county and district councils. The Metropolitan Police is responsible for all London (except for the City of London) and there is a single fire service for London. London Regional Transport, which is outside local authority control, provides transport in London.

Each county or borough department negotiates with the appropriate central government ministry concerning its affairs, for example, education, or highways and transport. The introduction of local regulations, 'bylaws', may only be done with government approval. Scotland, Wales and Northern Ireland each have a minister who is responsible not only for that country, but also for adapting the function of government to the conditions of each particular country, thus coming between other government ministries and the local authorities of these three countries. The establishment of parliamentary assemblies in Scotland and Wales (see p.133-135) will variously affect these arrangements.

It is a basic principle of local government that local people can devise a better system for the local context than can central government. As a result there is no standard system, since in each county the local authorities have the freedom to organise and administer services as they think will best suit the area. Closely related to this efficiency principle is the democratic one – the right of people to organise community affairs as they think best.

Each authority is composed of elected councillors, who form the governing body, and permanent local government officers, the local equivalent of the civil service. Elected councillors, unlike MPs, remain unpaid, although they can receive an allowance for performing council business and also allowances for necessary expenses. Most of those who stand for election, predominantly men, are local business or professional people, but a growing number of women seek a political career in local rather than national politics. Some work for purely idealistic reasons, while others may be politically ambitious or believe that their position as councillor will help advance their own business or professional standing. On average, councillors spend at least 30 hours weekly on council business, but it is perhaps noteworthy that women councillors tend to spend 22 per cent more time on council business than men, while Labour councillors spend 30 per cent and Liberal councillors 20 per cent more time than Conservative ones.

Each council elects a chairman, or in boroughs a 'mayor', and in Scotland a 'provost', almost invariably from the majority party represented on the council. Councillors are elected for four years in England and Wales and three years in Scotland. All councils, except at parish level, delegate committees, usually composed of certain councillors and some appropriate officers employed by the council, to consider policy, problems and expenditure in particular areas of council activity, for example education. Generally, the public may attend any council or committee meetings. Local government employs 1.4 million salaried officers. All senior local government officers are appointed only with approval from the appropriate government ministry.

Expenditure by local authorities is about one-quarter of total public expenditure, and one-third of this local government expenditure is on education (see p.149). Almost 80 per cent of local government expenditure is financed from central government. The balance is raised locally, by local taxation and by the collection of rents, fees and payments on property or services provided by the council. The system of both central and local finance for local government is complicated and controversial, and is discussed more fully below. Central government is expected to ensure the funds necessary to provide adequate services, and to offset the differences in wealth and service requirements between different areas. These differences are particularly great between, for example, a densely populated but wealthy area in the south east of England, and a remote, thinly populated part of highland Scotland.

The tension between central government and local democracy

There has always been a tension between local and central government, between civic freedoms expressed locally and intervention by central government. This tension, which has been growing since 1945, raises important questions about local freedoms and the power of central government. The political party in power tends to insist on the importance of central government intervention, while the opposition party strongly defends the right to local democracy. In 1976, for example, a Labour government told all local authorities to arrange secondary education on non-selective lines, forcing them to combine the traditionally separate schools for children deemed to be of higher and lower ability at the early age of 11. A few local authorities successfully defied the government.

The long-cherished independence of local government, however, has been slowly eroded over the years by a variety of processes. In the nineteenth century the majority of candidates were independent citizens, concerned solely with the well-being of their town or county. From the late nineteenth century onwards, however, national political parties began to sponsor candidates in local elections. In this way political loyalties at a national level began to displace local considerations and determine how people voted. Today there are virtually no independent candidates left, except in one or two remote rural areas.

Consequently, today people usually dismiss the qualities of each individual candidate in favour of party loyalty, an unfortunate fact since local issues are often quite different from national ones. It

Public consultation is an important task in local government. Here local children examine the model for a proposed housing scheme.

makes local government unnecessarily adversarial. Sometimes a conflict of loyalty arises for councillors who wish, in spite of their party loyalties and the contradictory directions received from party headquarters, to pursue a policy in the local interest. Some councillors risk expulsion from their party for disobedience.

National parties all use local government as a 'nursery' for those ambitious to enter Parliament. Between 1945 and 1979 45 per cent of Labour and 25 per cent of Conservative MPs entered Parliament after service as a councillor in local government. As with the constituency system, the tendency to vote for a party rather than an individual undermines the chief advantage of a localised political process, and it is hardly surprising that most local council elections usually attract barely 40 per cent of the electorate, roughly half that of national elections, and substantially lower than those in other Western European countries. People either feel local government is unimportant or that it is too remote and party-based to respond effectively to their needs.

People also often use local elections as a way of protesting against the government of the day. Many local authorities are often 'captured' by the party of opposition, and this characteristic is interpreted as a register of the government's unpopularity. This was most dramatically demonstrated during the period 1979–97, when Conservative-controlled councils were virtually eliminated. They were not particularly strong in 1979 and although they were much stronger in the county councils outside the cities, they did control 188 borough, city and district councils, out of a total then of roughly 400 such bodies in England. By 1996 they still controlled only 12, and had also lost control of 35 out of 36 county councils.

How large should local authority areas be? There is a natural tension between the demands of democracy and efficiency. Compared with other European countries Britain has chosen decisively in favour of administrative efficiency. In other parts of Europe there is one council member for every 250–450 people. In Britain there is a councillor for every 1,800 people. For this reason also local government in Britain is far less effective as a democratic forum than it could be. It seriously reduces the chances of effective consultation and participation, not to mention well-informed voting, and that raises questions about how far efficiency can be achieved if the local population are not fully consulted.

Since 1979 local government has been severely weakened by conflict with central government. Technically Parliament is sovereign and may grant or limit the powers of the local authorities which administer Britain at the local level. However, there has always been a bargaining relationship between central government and local authorities. Throughout the 1970s both Labour and Conservative governments accepted a consensual approach through consultation, and this process allowed central government to incorporate local government more closely into its policies.

This relationship changed dramatically after 1979. The new Thatcher government was driven by two considerations. One was the ideological belief that government by definition was inefficient, wasteful and sapped individual initiative, and should therefore be minimised. It also believed that the public was not interested in local democracy but in the delivery of efficient and low-cost services. This was undeniable, until things went wrong, and then those affected became very interested indeed in their democratic rights. The other consideration was a political one. A majority of local authorities were Labour-controlled and they were seen, along with trade unions, as bastions of resistance to the revolution Margaret Thatcher was determined to achieve. The government was therefore determined that the local authorities should submit to central authority. So it ceased to consult them and issued directives instead. Of these the most significant was the imposition of spending limits. It did this in two ways. It scrutinised local authority budgets and limited, or 'capped', the funds they were allowed to raise through 'rates', the old local property tax. From 1983 those authorities which tried to defy the government soon experienced its second means of securing obedience. They simply received reduced central government funding until they agreed to comply. By 1985 there was an atmosphere of open defiance by many local authorities, led by the Greater London Council and some of the metropolitan counties, all of which were Labour controlled. Thatcher took the simple expedient of passing an act through Parliament to abolish them, transferring their functions to the local boroughs, and establishing a handful of residual bodies to oversee such matters as transport, fire services, etc. Greater London was left as the only capital in the Western world without its own elected body.

A local council meeting in progress.

Indeed, the GLC was replaced by services provided by five government departments, 32 boroughs and 27 quangos. The message to other local authorities was simple: if they would not do as they were told, they would be replaced or ignored. In taking these steps, Margaret Thatcher directly contradicted the verdict of her great nineteenth-century Conservative predecessor, Benjamin Disraeli: 'Centralisation is the death-blow of public freedom.'

Having successfully brought the local authorities to heel, the Thatcher government decided to bring market forces further into local government. It decided to convert local authorities from 'providers' into 'enablers', by requiring them to contract out council services to the most competitive bidder. For example, councils were encouraged to contract private care companies to take care of the elderly, and to use housing associations for the provision of homes. The council remained the 'gatekeeper' but paid others to be the 'provider'. It was possible to reduce costs substantially, but in the process it was felt that democratic accountability was lost. One area in which this was felt very strongly was housing. In

1980 local authorities still owned about 30 per cent of the nation's housing stock. They controlled this housing, making it available to those in need of housing. Most tenants became permanent but some moved out to buy property of their own, thus making a small amount of housing available each year for homeless people. The government ruled that local authorities had to sell their housing stock to the tenants if the latter wished to buy. This was particularly offensive to Labour councils, which had always viewed the provision of proper housing for all residents, regardless of wealth, to be the first responsibility of local government. In order to curb spending, councils were forbidden to sell land or property in order to benefit financially. Most of the proceeds of all such sales had to be handed to central government. This prevented local authorities from using the funds received by the sale of council housing to build more publicly-owned homes.

The Thatcher government's next move was to scrap the old 'rates' property tax, and replace it with what it called a Community Charge, in effect a poll, or capitation, tax. It wanted every single person within a local authority area to pay an

Typical local authority housing constructed on the edge of town.

equal sum for the services to which everyone had access. Rates had been based upon the size of each dwelling, and therefore tended to apply a graded charge according to wealth. The poll tax, as virtually everyone called it, was considered extremely unfair even by many Conservative supporters. It was also highly inefficient. Rates had to be collected from 17 million people. The new charge had to be collected from 35 million people, a much harder task. It was introduced into Scotland in 1989 and into England and Wales in 1990. It provoked riots and a widespread refusal to pay. It was also a factor in Margaret Thatcher's downfall later that year. John Major's administration quietly dropped the poll tax and replaced it with a Council Tax, essentially a graded property tax, with rebates for the poorest and for people living alone.

By the early 1990s local authorities felt battered by the constant stream of measures enforced by central government. No fewer than 124 Acts of Parliament which affected them had been passed during the 1980s. There was also resentment and a widespread suspicion in many local authorities that they were penalised for not being Conservative-controlled. In 1990 for example, 21 local authorities were capped because they planned to spend on average 12.5 per cent more than the Standard Spending Assessment allowed. Not a single Conservative-controlled council was capped. Conservative Berkshire increased its spending by 20.6 per cent but remained untouched, while Brent, a Labour-controlled London Borough, was capped when its spending rose by only 1.4 per cent.

Yet of all the local authorities it was Westminster which attracted most adverse attention. As one of only two Conservative-controlled councils left in London, it received so many different kinds of grant and relief in 1995–6, that a local authority in the Midlands reckoned that had it enjoyed a similar level of government help it would not have needed to ask anyone to pay the Council Tax and would have been rich enough to meet its budget commitments and also pay £1,000 to each household! In 1996 also, as a result of seven years' research into Westminster Council's housing sales, the District Auditor found six senior councillors guilty of gerrymandering.

On coming to power, Labour announced that local authorities should be less constrained by central government and more accountable to local people. Labour proposes abandoning capping, but retaining powers to curb what it calls 'excessive' rises. It will also allow councils to choose whether

or not to put services out to tender. Each council will be required to produce a performance plan. London will again have an elected authority, and an elected mayor. Labour also promised to introduce regional assemblies for England if there is a clear desire and also popular consent.

There is, however, no guarantee that Labour councils will not display corrupt practices as Conservative ones have done. Corruption flourishes where one party enjoys absolute control. One or two Labour councils in the Glasgow area have a reputation for corruption. Rooting out corrupt practices remains a constant task. Nor is there any guarantee that the Labour government will not be tempted to limit real local democracy if it finds local authorities unwilling to comply with its policies. It was possibly with these issues in mind that Tony Blair promised a tough code and independent investigations into alleged corruption, and promised to revitalise local elections, arrange the direct election of mayors and overhaul local government committee structures. With a Labour administration in control of the state, the public will punish it when it is unpopular by voting Conservative councillors back into the town hall.

Further information

WEBSITES

Local Government Information Unit	www.lgiu.gov.uk
Local Government Association	www.lga.gov.uk
Local government	www.open.gov.uk (select 'local government' from the functional inde

PRINTED MATERIAL

Byrne, T. 1994 *Local Government in Britain* Penguin
Coxall, Bill and Robins, Lynton 1994 *Contemporary British Politics* Chapter 11 Macmillan
Leach, Steve, Stewart, John and Walsh, Kieron 1994 *The Changing Organisation and Management of Local Government* Macmillan

QUESTIONS

Section analysis

1 A changing system What are the two driving forces behind changes in local government?

2 A changing system Which of the following people are elected and which are appointed? Which are paid and which give their services free: a councillor, a local government officer, a chairman, a mayor, a provost?

3 A changing system Decide which of the following are the responsibility of the county councils, and which are the responsibility of the district councils: transport, housing, fire services, waste disposal, environmental health, highways.

4 Central government and local democracy Why did the Conservative government abolish the planning body for London? Do you think it was a desirable step to take? Give reasons for your opinion.

5 Central government and local democracy Should councillors be independent or members of national political parties? What advantages or disadvantages do you see in each?

Chapter analysis and discussion

1 Which of the following is the best explanation of the conflict between local and central government in Britain? Give reasons for your answer.
a There is a permanent, inevitable and natural conflict between locally expressed civic freedoms and the national interest.
b Central government wishes to increase its control, particularly in areas where its political opponents are strongest, while local government seeks to retain its own powers.
c From 1979 central government under the Conservatives abandoned consensual arrangements arising from consultation.

2 Opinions in Britain differ on the following points. What is your opinion?
a Local government should no longer be the nursery for those ambitious to enter Parliament.
b Local government should not be monopolised by the national political parties.
c There should be central planning bodies for the major cities, especially London.

3 Find textual evidence to support these statements:
a Central government pays for more than half the expenditure of local government.
b The Conservatives compelled local councils to surrender most of the money gained from the sale of housing or land to central government.

Textual interpretation

Consider the following statement:
On the one hand, large units of government are necessary in urban-industrial society in order to achieve efficiency, economies of scale, functional effectiveness and an adequate capacity to plan and organise; on the other hand, small units of government are necessary to preserve the attributes of grassroots democracy …

1 Where do you think the balance should lie in terms of local government's size and powers?

2 Has local government in your country found this balance?

6 *Working Britain*

The economic problems

Britain was the first country both to industrialise and to develop a capitalist economy. By 1800 its share of world trade stood at approximately 40 per cent. In 1850 it had as many merchant ships as the rest of the world put together and it led the world in most manufacturing industries. Its lead, however, did not prove durable. Early in the twentieth century it was overtaken by the United States and Germany. After two world wars and the rapid loss of its empire, Britain was unable even to maintain its position in Europe. For a once great political and economic empire it has been a humbling process.

After 1945 Britain tried to find a balance between government intervention in the economy and an almost completely free-market economy such as existed in the United States. Neither system seemed to fit Britain's needs. The former seemed compromised between two different objectives: planned economic prosperity and the means of ensuring full employment, while the latter promised greater economic prosperity at the cost of poverty and unemployment for the less able in society. Both Labour and the Conservatives were reluctant to break from the consensus based on Keynesian economics (see p.7-8).

People seemed complacent about Britain's decline, reluctant to make the painful adjustments that might be necessary to reverse it. Prosperity increased during the late 1950s and in the 1960s, diverting attention from Britain's decline relative to its main competitors. In 1973 the Conservative Prime Minister Edward Heath warned: 'The alternative to expansion is not, as some occasionally seem to suppose, an England of quiet market towns linked only by steam trains puffing slowly and peacefully through green meadows. The alternative is slums, dangerous roads, old factories, cramped schools, stunted lives.'

By the mid-1970s both Labour and Conservative economists were thinking of moving away from Keynesian economics which were based upon stimulating demand by injecting money into the economy. As described in the Introduction (see p.8), it was the Conservatives who decided to break with the old economic formula completely. Returning to power in 1979, they were determined to dismantle the corporatist state, and to remove the regulations and controls from finance and industry. They decided to lower taxes as an incentive to individuals and businesses to increase productivity; to leave the labour force to regulate itself either by pricing itself out of employment or by working within the amount of money employers could afford; to abolish exchange controls and, finally, to limit government spending levels and use money supply (the amount of money in circulation at any one time) as a way of controlling inflation. On this last point Prime Minister Margaret Thatcher told the Commons, 'If our objective is to have a prosperous and expanding economy, we must recognise that high public spending, as a proportion of GNP (gross national product), very quickly kills growth ... We have to remember that governments have no money at all. Every penny they take is from the productive sector of the economy in order to transfer it to the unproductive part of it.' She had a point: between 1961 and 1975 employment outside the wealth creating sector of the economy increased by over 40 per cent relative to employment within it.

From 1979 to 1997 the Conservatives put their new ideas into practice. Income tax was reduced from 33 per cent to 24 per cent. For higher-income groups the reduction was greater but this did not lead to any loss in revenue, partly because fewer people tried to avoid lower-rate tax, but also because a larger number of people progressively fell into the upper, 40 per cent, band. However, the government also increased Value Added Tax (VAT) on goods and services to 17.5 per cent from the rates of 8 and 12.5 per cent which were both in use in 1979. In the meantime it gave every encouragement to a free-market economy. Measured purely in financial terms the results were dramatic. By 1987 the FT-SE (pronounced 'footsie' but standing for Financial Times–Stock Exchange) index of share values was five times higher than it had been four years earlier, in 1983. But the belief that it would force industry to become 'fit and lean' led only partly to greater efficiency. It also led to the collapse of much of Britain's manufacturing industry.

Thatcher's belief that 'monetarism' alone, based on the supply of money, could produce the revolution she sought proved ill-founded. The resulting surge in unemployment dramatically increased public expenditure. By 1995 every unemployed person cost £9,000 yearly in income support and lost tax. In the decade 1985–95 1.64 million workers aged 55–64 lost their jobs prematurely. Social welfare spending rocketed to deal with the rise in unemployed and prematurely retired people. But even without this result from their own policies, the Conservatives would have found the task of reducing public expenditure insuperable. Whatever savings could be made did not offset increased costs from less avoidable factors. One was the burden of an ageing population. In 1979 there were 2.9 million people over the age of 75, but this figure rose to reach 4.2 million by 1997. Another was education. Enrolment in higher education doubled in the same period.

By 1985 it was clear that monetarism was not a panacea for Britain's economic ills, and it was quietly abandoned. Its damage had been considerable. By 1983, as a result of the new policy and for the first time in more than 200 years, Britain imported more manufactured goods than it exported. As a House of Lords select committee in 1985 stated, continued deindustrialisation posed 'a grave threat to the standard of living and to the economic and political stability of the nation.' Britain's share of world trade fell by 15 per cent and its manufacturing sector shrank by 10 per cent in the years 1979 to 1986, while at the same time the import of manufactured goods rose by 40 per cent.

There were some successes, but at a price. In the early 1980s British Steel was an industry in decline. By the late 1980s it was the most efficient in Europe. In 1980 the production of one ton of steel had taken 12 man hours. By 1988 this figure had been reduced to 3.7, achieved not only by increasing efficiency but by shedding most of the workforce, from 130,000 in 1980 to 50,000 in 1987.

Overall, unemployment in Britain rose from 1.5 million in 1979 to over 3 million by 1983 and fell to 2.5 million by the end of the 1980s, partly due to a reduction in the workforce and also to the narrowing of the official definition of unemployment. The only real bonus Britain enjoyed was the oil resources discovered mainly in the North Sea in the 1960s, whereby it became the world's sixth largest oil producer. Oil revenue softened the impact of the recession from 1979 to 1985, reaching an annual peak of £12 billion by 1985. Much of the oil revenue was spent on social security for those unemployed. After a brief boom in the mid-1980s, the country moved into recession again in 1988, with rising interest rates, inflation and a balance of payments crisis. By 1990 it was in the deepest recession since 1930, and it proved longer and deeper than the recession that hit other members of the European Union. Inflation, temporarily controlled, rose to over 10 per cent and was only checked from rising further by high interest rates which also had the side effect of discouraging economic growth. By 1990 the manufacturing industry had barely recovered from the major shrinkage in the early 1980s. What had survived was more efficient, but in the meantime Britain's share of world trade in manufactured goods had shrunk from 8 per cent in 1979 to 6.5 per cent. Britain's balance of payments was unhealthy too. In 1985 it had enjoyed a small surplus of £3.5 billion, but in 1990 this had changed to a deficit of £20.4 billion.

Property prices reflect the state of the economy. Many homes were repossessed and sold by money-lending institutions in the early 1990s.

The difficulties led to widespread 'downsizing', as companies shed staff in order to survive. The Conservative heartlands, notably the south east, were particularly hard hit this time. The recession affected the property market, leading to a collapse of prices. The banks, which had fuelled the property boom, had to write off £20,000 million in bad debts. Many people who had borrowed large amounts of money in the form of mortgages for the houses they had purchased could no longer keep up their monthly repayments and lost their homes as the banks seized them (see p.191).

The level of commercial interpenetration by multinational companies greatly increased during the 1980s. A survey in 1987 showed Britain to be the major recipient of foreign investment in Europe. For example, 30 per cent of Japan's total West European investment, and 36 per cent of US investment in the European Community came to Britain. By 1989 10 per cent of Britain's workforce, were employed in the top 1,000 foreign-owned companies in the country.

Partly as a result of reduced employment possibilities, small businesses increased rapidly, from 2.4 million in 1980 to 3.7 million by 1997. However, many failed to survive, some as a result of poor management, but many because financial conditions are harsher in Britain than in most of the European Union. Small businesses remain important, not only because large businesses grow from small ones, but also because over half the new jobs in Britain are created by firms employing fewer than 100 staff. Currently 7 million people work in companies with fewer than 50 employees.

The Conservatives' greatest transformation was the privatisation of wholly or partly government-owned enterprises. They reduced the size of the state-owned sector by over two-thirds, privatising approximately 50 major businesses by 1996. The greatest two benefits of privatisation were that it forced prices down and forced standards of service up to the benefit of customers and shareholders. By 1990 20 per cent of the adult population were share owners, a higher proportion than in any other Western industrialised country. There was no question of taking these enterprises back into public ownership, even by a Labour government.

After the departure of Thatcher, the Conservatives quietly returned to a form of Keynesian economics. Taxes increased again so that by 1996 the average personal burden of taxation had increased by 18 per cent since 1979, from 31.1 per cent to 37.2 per cent of earnings. However, the recession was followed by a loss of confidence in the value of

sterling and its massive sale on the money markets, which led to Britain's humiliating exit from the European Exchange Rate Mechanism (ERM) in 1992. Following this disaster Britain adopted the tightest fiscal policy for many years, with a strong commitment to keeping below an inflation ceiling of 4 per cent. Unemployment and interest rates fell steadily, and growth picked up. However the Conservative record still looked bad: in the years 1959–79 annual average growth had been 2.75 per cent. In the years 1974–94 the figure was only 2 per cent. Britain's international trade position seriously deteriorated too. By 1997 it ranked only eleventh out of 15 European Union members, with its share of world trade reduced to 6 per cent.

The Schlumberger building in the Cambridge Science Park, a symbol of innovative technical enterprise.

There are some bright spots amid the gloom. Britain became a world leader in the production of microprocessors. 'High-tech' industries have developed in three main areas, west of London along the M4 motorway or 'Golden Corridor', the lowlands between Edinburgh and Dundee, nicknamed 'Silicon Glen', and the area between London and Cambridge. The Cambridge Science Park, symbolised by its modernist Schlumberger Building, is the flagship of high-tech Britain. Beginning in 1969, by 1998 the Park contained 76 high-tech companies. In all, there are 50 science parks in the United Kingdom, hosting over 1,200 companies, mainly in computing, biotechnology, chemistry, electrical engineering and robotics. Apart from the City (discussed below), recorded music is a strong export sector. Britain publishes 100,000 new books yearly, and boasts the largest

Dundee Technology Park. These parks often offer financial inducements in order to persuade companies to relocate.

export publishing industry in the world. Eight out of the 10 most profitable retailers in Europe are British. Two of the 25 top global retailers are British, and four of the top 10 food retailers in Europe are British. The Body Shop, a great success story of the 1980s, had 1,200 outlets in 45 countries by 1997, 80 per cent of these outlets being outside the United Kingdom. As Napoleon once scornfully remarked, the British are, indeed, a nation of shopkeepers.

Owners and managers

The most important actors in the economy are, obviously, those who own and manage it, those who finance it, and those who provide the workforce.

The most important lobby organisation for owners and managers is the Confederation of British Industry (CBI), which seeks to support industrial growth and planning, and, through its lobbying of government, to create a climate conducive to efficiency and profitability. It is Britain's major industrial institution with a membership of 250,000 companies. Although traditionally more favourable to Conservative than Labour governments, a reassessment has taken place. It did not like being edged out of consultation with government during the 1980s, nor did it like the Conservatives' policy of maintaining high interest rates as a means of controlling inflation, since this also made it expensive to borrow money for expansion and so reduced industrial growth. The CBI was also critical of the Conservatives' failure to encourage investment rather than consumption. It wanted massive investment in new technology,

and greatly improved road and rail networks. It is inclined to believe that Britain has no choice economically but to accept European Monetary Union (EMU) (see below). The CBI is therefore likely to work with a Labour government more enthusiastically than hitherto, and to distance itself from the Conservatives while they remain hostile to the single currency.

There has been a process of concentration in terms of capital and power. In 1915 the top 100 manufacturing firms controlled only 15 per cent of manufacturing output, but after 1970 they controlled over half. Consequently there are fewer interest groups controlling the CBI, and their individual influence is greater.

During the period of Conservative government a range of lobby groups representing finance and commerce increased their influence, while bodies representing manufacturing, professional and public sector interests were weakened. Under Labour the balance is likely to change, with manufacturing and the public sector being given a greater hearing.

The financial sector

There has been a long tradition of directing the economy through the financial institutions which together are known as 'the City', and which until 1986 were all located in the 'Square Mile' of the City of London. The Bank of England, the retail and wholesale banks, insurance companies (most notably Lloyds) and the Stock Exchange of the City have for a very long time played an important role in Britain's economy, not only because they are the nerve centre of national finance but because such a large proportion of Britain's wealth has been invested by the City overseas. Indeed, apart from income from tourism, the City has been mainly responsible for Britain's large annual invisible exports which have done so much for the national economy.

The Bank of England, which serves as Britain's central bank has three main traditional roles: to maintain the stability and value of the currency; to maintain the stability of the financial system in Britain and help maintain it internationally; and to ensure the effectiveness of the financial services sector. It also advises government and provides banking services to government, the banking system and other central banks. The Bank is implicitly responsible to a considerable extent for the proper working of the City.

Traders in the London Financial Futures Market. The stress involved is evident on the faces of those bidding.

There are two principal kinds of bank: retail banks for personal and small business accounts, normally known as 'the high street banks'; and wholesale banks which handle large deposits at higher interest rates. Many of these are known as 'merchant banks'. In the mid-1980s the building societies (mutual societies owned by both savers and borrowers which traditionally lent money to house purchasers) were allowed to become publicly-owned enterprises, in practice banks. As a consequence of general financial deregulation during the 1980s, most financial institutions found themselves offering a wide range of financial services, blurring the previous distinctions between one kind of finance house and another. By 1996 there were no fewer than 375 banking institutions licensed to operate in Britain, and over 100 foreign banks licensed to take deposits.

In order to increase the City's role as an international financial centre, the old exclusions which limited who could operate in the City were removed in 1986. This deregulation, popularly known as the 'Big Bang', allowed any foreign financial institution to participate in the London money market. London became the undisputed leading financial centre in Europe, and the third in the world (alongside New York and Tokyo). Before 1986 all City stockbroking firms were British. By 1990 154 out of 408 were foreign owned. The main investors in British stockbroking are the United States, Japan and France. Many foreign banks and finance houses also have offices in the City. London, incidentally, is also the favourite location of the European Union business community. Edinburgh, specialising in fund management, is Europe's fourth largest financial centre.

Since the Big Bang, the City has seen frenzied financial activity. For example the brokers of the London International Financial Futures Market are responsible for about 25,000 contracts daily. Most of these brokers trading in 'futures' (the future relative values of different currencies) are under 25 years old. Very few of these highly paid traders survive the stress beyond the age of 30, and most move to quieter jobs.

A major problem for the City has been the question of regulation. The Conservatives favoured 'self-regulation', based upon the City's long-standing reputation for probity. But this probity had depended upon a very particular ethic within a highly restricted pre-computer world in which it was far harder for dishonesty to escape detection. Government watchdogs since the Big Bang have proved inadequate. Fraud, 'insider trading' (the use of inside financial knowledge for personal profit) and other malpractices were already a cause for concern by 1990. In the first half of the 1990s, however, there were a spectacular string of scandals: the collapse of one foreign bank that had already been refused a licence to operate in both New York and Jeddah and should have been refused one for London; the destruction of one of London's leading merchant banks, Barings, by the uncontrolled speculation of a 'rogue' trader in Singapore; the massive theft of pension funds from his own employees by the magnate Robert Maxwell; and the mis-selling of individual pension schemes by major finance companies to an estimated 400,000 employees following the government's encouragement for the public to opt out of the State Earnings Related Pension Scheme. Perhaps the most spectacular scandal of all, however, was at Lloyds, the 300-year-old insurance brokers.

Lloyds is essentially a market, not a company, where about 167 different syndicates compete with each other and other insurance companies for business. It embodied the idea of personal trust that once characterised the City. In the mid-1980s, when it seemed highly profitable, there were 33,000 wealthy individual investors, known as 'names', who were willing to trade with unlimited liability. At the end of the 1980s a series of massive claims almost overwhelmed Lloyds. Huge losses were reported, for which the names were liable. But a widespread lack of probity in the way the syndicates conducted their business also became evident. A conflict ensued between the 'names', most of whom faced financial ruin, and Lloyds. A special deal was struck in 1996 whereby the losses to these 'names' were limited and outstanding liabilities were reinsured. By 1996 there were only 13,000 'names' still registered with Lloyds.

The British emphasis on guiding the economy through the City's financial institutions gives rise to major problems. Those who invest in the City are often concerned with making maximum profit in the minimum amount of time. This conflicts with the national economic interest. Many industrial ventures require long-term investment,

and show slow profits at first. So great is the drive for increasing share values that finance houses or rival companies frequently become 'predators', seeking to buy enough shares to take over other companies. Target companies are frequently competitors, so there is the added danger of a tendency towards monopoly. In each case the process is concerned not with developing the potential productivity of an enterprise but with quick profit. It is profoundly damaging to industry.

Most industrialised countries enjoy a significantly higher level of industrial investment than Britain where banks, insurance companies, pension funds and building societies frequently prefer to invest in other areas. While the political Right sees the City as a successful network of institutions earning large sums of money by its trade abroad, the Left fears that the City is a drain on national resources, by tempting British capital away from domestic industrial investment, and by exerting political influence through its control of funding and the external value of sterling.

When Labour returned to power it immediately made its mark on the City. It gave the Bank of England statutory power to set interest rates, independently of government. Since the setting of interest rates had been a favourite instrument of government for both political and economic ends this move, as one financial journalist remarked, 'transformed 300 years of political economy and manipulation of the Bank of England'. In effect, Labour abandoned a key lever for short-term considerations, in favour of allowing the Bank to set interest rates purely as part of long-term economic strategy. In increasing the Bank's independence Labour also took steps to ensure that its decisions were more open and also more accountable to the House of Commons, and to change the composition of the Bank's governing Court from exclusively white male middle-class bankers living mainly in the Home Counties to include a range of industrial and business experience representing the whole of the United Kingdom.

Labour also promised new regulatory structures to enhance the international reputation of the financial market in London and to provide fresh protection for small savers, pensioners and investors, to encourage greater investment. It also indicated it would apply regulations regarding share profits to deter short-term buying and selling and to encourage longer-term investment. It also promised to legislate to stop anti-competitive practices, but to encourage competition between the privatised utilities. On taking office, Labour raised a 'windfall' tax on the privatised utilities, which had made enormous profits thanks partly to the Conservative government having sold these utilities, notably gas, electricity and water, substantially below their market worth. It used this windfall tax to fund its 'welfare to work' programme, designed to help unemployed young people into employment.

The trade unions

From 1945 until 1979 the trade union movement, representing organised labour, was a central actor in the British economy. Workers had first been allowed to form unions in 1824. The Trades Union Congress (TUC) was established in 1868 as a coordinating body. The TUC's concern that the workers' interests be represented in Parliament led to the establishment of the Labour Party in 1900. The unions dominated Labour until the 1990s. With membership reaching eight million by 1918, the unions became major players in the economy. The close working relationship achieved with government during the Second World War left the unions well placed in 1945 to play a central role in state planning in the post-war years, a role accepted as legitimate by both the Conservatives and Labour.

Union power grew after 1945, with the number of members increasing, but with fewer and more powerful unions as a result of amalgamation. In 1960 there were 650 unions with 9.8 million members; in 1980 there were 438 unions with over 12 million members. Union centralisation was a response to the growing concentration of capital power. By the mid-1970s over 25 per cent of the workforce were employed in firms of over 10,000 employees in the private sector alone. By 1979 the largest union had two million members.

During the 1960s and 1970s the unions became so powerful that no government could operate without consulting them. 'Beer and sandwich lunches at Number Ten' became a well-known feature of political life. A major reason for poor industrial relations was that in most manufacturing enterprises several different unions were represented, and these had difficulty agreeing equitable rates of pay. In 1974 a miners' strike brought down the Conservative government and five years later widespread strike action, during the so-called 'Winter of Discontent', brought down the Labour government.

The Conservative government elected in 1979 saw the unions as the prime enemy of a market economy and determined to reduce their power

by law. It introduced union laws in 1980, 1984, 1988 and 1993 which had two main aims. The first was to restrict and regulate the power of unions in industry, and the second was to shift the balance of power within each union, in the belief that ordinary members of unions would moderate the behaviour of their officials. The laws reduced picketing rights (rights to assemble outside workplace entrances to discourage anyone entering during a strike) and the right to secondary action (sympathy strikes or other action at workplaces not directly involved in the dispute); made union leaders liable to legal prosecution if they organised a strike without a secret ballot of the membership; forbade union-only labour agreements, known as the 'closed shop'; threatened union funds for any violation of the new laws; insisted that all union leaders should be subject to periodic elections by secret ballot; and required that the members of each union should vote on whether they should have a political fund (an apparent attempt to destroy the financing of the Labour Party).

Union power was further weakened by a serious fall in membership, from 12.2 million (53 per cent of the employed workforce) in 1979 to 8.7 million by 1989 and 6.7 million by 1998. Most of the shrinkage was explained by growing unemployment and by a shift in the economy from heavily unionised manufacturing to barely unionised service industries. Furthermore, the TUC was almost completely excluded from consultation with government – there was no more beer and sandwiches at Downing Street.

During the 1980s more unions merged, partly because of falling membership, but also to adapt to the increased power of employers to insist on arrangements with a single union at the workplace rather than several, as had traditionally happened. By 1995 only one union, recently formed out of smaller ones, had a membership of over one million.

Changing circumstances, not only in Britain, but in the industrialised world generally, brought great stress to the labour movement, particularly to those unions most resistant to economic and technological change. The stress placed upon the trade union movement produced major tensions between 'modernists' who wished to break away from old-style trade unionism and provide a fresh type of service to its members, and the Left of the trade union movement, which clung to the old working-class ideologies. By 1997 the modernists had decisively won the contest. Most ordinary union members accepted the wisdom of single-

A striker's picket at a factory gateway following the dismissal of 320 staff. Note the crude but effective placard slogans.

union deals with employers. Meanwhile the nature of union membership had been changing, with a proportionate increase of white-collar and female members, and a dramatically increased proportion (25 per cent) of members who were share owners. Each of these three growing categories under-mines the male-dominated / working-class / leftist ideologies of traditional trade unionism. Partly because of diminished power, and partly because modern union members are much less adversarial than their forebears, by 1996 strike action had reached the lowest level since records began in 1891.

Although union power may be diminished, it is not destroyed. At a policy level unions have shifted the focus of their efforts to broader issues of labour relations, like the establishment of a legal minimum wage, legal workplace rights and industrial democracy. The TUC itself is unlikely to recover its previous powers because the five or six major unions that dominate it also need it less, since they feel they have sufficient influence individually.

There is greater realism about the past, including a recognition that union power in the 1970s has proved a long-term disaster, and that the abuse of

power was anti-democratic. Since the early 1990s British unions have tried to learn from their less adversarial European counterparts. They have also changed their attitude to the European Community from hostility to enthusiasm.

Union relations with Labour have also changed. Labour will not repeal Conservative union legislation. While still relying on union funding, it has progressively reduced union voting power at its annual Conference, which in 1990 still controlled 90 per cent of the conference vote through use of the 'block vote' (whereby union leaders could cast the vote of their total membership). In 1996 it was agreed that the maximum trade union vote at Labour Conference should not exceed 50 per cent of the total. It was accepted that perceived union control over Labour damaged the latter's electoral prospects. In the words of one union leader, John Edmonds, 'We know that we don't want a confusion of roles between unions and government. We know that this makes the electorate very very anxious.' Many union leaders believe that greater detachment from Labour can be good for them too. A survey of potential recruits by one union showed that the single biggest reason for not joining was union influence on the Labour Party. A greater distance

John Monks addressing the TUC annual conference as its General Secretary in 1996. Monks is known as a moderniser, willing to abandon traditional ideology.

will help the unions to campaign more effectively on the issues that concern them, regardless of the party in power. As John Edmonds says, 'The unions' role is to give workers confidence to change, so that it doesn't just depend on the employer's whim.'

The workforce

There are currently approximately 35 million people of working age in Britain, and there will be no substantial change in this level until after the year 2000. However there has been a massive change in employment patterns. In 1970 barely 20 per cent of the workforce was female compared with 46 per cent of the workforce in 1995. In 1955 42 per cent of employees were in manufacturing compared with 18 per cent 40 years later. During the same period employment in the services sector more than doubled to 76 per cent of the workforce.

Other developments indicate job loss, job insecurity or workplace stress. Out of those households in which there was someone of working age in 1996, one-fifth contained no adult in work. Overall, by 1996 full-time male employment had fallen by 20 per cent since 1977. There has been a massive growth in self-

employment, mainly among men, who have either experienced unemployment or decided to escape an employer. By 1996 3.4 million, over 10 per cent of those in work, were self-employed, an increase of 19 per cent since 1986. Part-time work has also greatly increased, accounting for 6.4 million of the workforce by 1995. Eighty per cent of these part-timers are women, an indicator both of the way 'employed' often now means only part-time employment but also that there has been a significant decline in the proportion of men in work. Men are expected to take only 20 per cent of the 1.6 million jobs which will be created mainly in the new service sector by 2006. Temporary employment is another characteristic of changed working circumstances, accounting for 1.6 million members of the workforce. Temporary work grew by 25 per cent in the period from 1992 to 1995. Since the 1980s about two million people are permanently out of work but this masks the fact that each year almost four million are unemployed for part or all of the time.

Those in work are also tending to work longer hours but with falling productivity. It is behaviour symptomatic of people who are frightened that they might lose their jobs. The longer hours are bad for health, standards of work, and family life. British working hours have been increasing over the past decade to an average of 43.4 hours a week by 1995, while the average in the European Union is 40.2 hours and is falling. In his book, *The State We're In*, Will Hutton groups the workforce into three categories: 40 per cent who are either employed or self-employed and who enjoy work security; 30 per cent who are employed but feel insecure because they are without employment protection, benefits like a pension or paid holidays, or because they are either casual workers or on fixed-term contracts; and 30 per cent who are either idle or earning 'poverty' wages. There are one million full-time employees who earn less than half the national average wage. In the mid-1980s it was still possible to claim that, unlike in many other European countries, the majority of British workers might not be very industrious, but at least they were content in their work. That is no longer true. A survey in 1996 revealed that no fewer than 64 per cent of full-time workers would happily give up work if they could afford to do so, and only 20 per cent were sure they would keep on working even if they could afford not to do so.

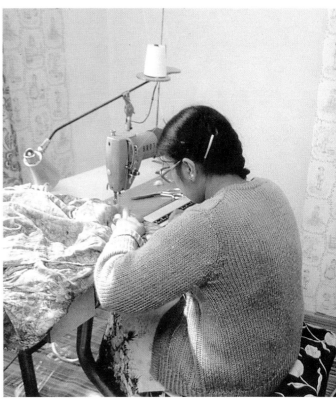

A woman sewing at home. Such 'piece-work', as it is known, is very low paid, but it allows her to work from home.

Britain has one of the least regulated labour markets of any industrialised country. The Conservatives rejected the Social Chapter of the European Community's Maastricht Treaty in order to ensure that British companies could be competitive through low employment costs. Increasing these costs, they said, would put people out of work. On coming to power Labour accepted the Social Chapter, arguing that market efficiency partly depends on people feeling they are being fairly dealt with. Labour also believes Britain cannot compete with low-wage labour elsewhere and should concentrate on activities requiring highly skilled workers. Yet for that training is required. No less than 64 per cent of Britain's workforce has no vocational qualification. In Germany the figure is only 26 per cent. In 1993 Britain had 250,000 people on apprentice training schemes, while in Germany the figure was two million.

There is also a growing gap between the earnings of the rich and poor. The first earnings figures, published in 1889, showed that the highest-paid fifth of the workforce earned 143 per cent more than the national average while the lowest-paid fifth earned 31 per cent less than the average. Exactly a century later official figures showed that

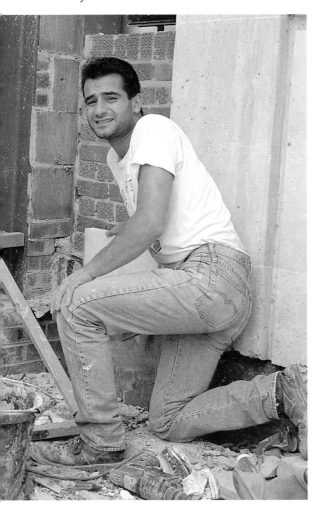

Many builders are self-employed, even if they often work for a larger company on particular jobs.

An unskilled casual worker picking tomatoes will earn very little money.

Under its 'welfare to work' programme Labour first promised to get 250,000 under-25-year-olds off state benefit and into work and then widened the programme to include all unemployed people below the age of 50. It also promised to introduce a legal minimum wage. And it promised to increase vocational training. How far it fulfilled its promises would be judged when it sought re-election in 2002.

The energy industries

It was Britain's development of coal production which determined its economic leadership of the world in the eighteenth and nineteenth centuries. It was only once oil production was itself in decline in 1990, that it displaced coal as Britain's main source of energy. Coal mining was once a powerful and proud industry, but since the defeat of the miners' strike in 1985 economic change has reduced the coal industry to a shadow of its

the top fifth now earned 158 per cent more and the bottom fifth 35 per cent less than the national average. In the years 1945–79 the gap had closed considerably and most of this new inequality occurred in the 1980s. At the bottom of the scale, almost six million full-time workers, 37 per cent of the total full-time workforce, earned less than the 'decency threshold' defined by the Council of Europe as 68 per cent of average full-time earnings. In the 1990s the enormous salaries of directors, sometimes 20 times greater than average earnings in their own company gave rise to public revulsion for these 'fat cats' as they became known. For example, the chairmen of the 10 privatised water companies received pay rises of 571 per cent in the five years following privatisation.

Oil has become Britain's most important energy source. Working on oil rigs is demanding but relatively well-paid.

former self. In 1955 there were 850 working coal mines in Britain. By the end of 1995, after privatisation, only 32 deep mines were still in operation, and three-quarters of their produce was for use in electricity generation. Coal will decline further. It is more polluting and less efficient than natural gas.

Oil and gas were discovered under the British sector of the North Sea at the end of the 1960s. In 1985 Britain was the sixth largest producer of oil in the world but by 1995 had fallen back to rank ninth. It is the fifth largest gas producer. Oil and gas turned Britain from a net importer of energy into a net exporter. In the early 1970s imports accounted for over 50 per cent of Britain's fuel consumption. By 1995 Britain exported 40 million tonnes of oil equivalent (oil, coal and natural gas measured in terms of equivalent oil energy), just under one-fifth of its own energy consumption.

British policy makers have insisted over a number of years that energy should be derived from a balance of different sources. Easily the most controversial of these is the nuclear energy programme. Britain established the world's first large-scale nuclear plant in 1956. It was assumed that nuclear energy would be a clean, safe solution to energy needs. Successive governments promised benefits which its technology was unable to fulfil. Public worries grew over the years, because of the difficulties of dealing with nuclear waste and because nuclear power stations had been built without much idea of how to dismantle them safely once their useful life had come to an end. The question of nuclear energy became a highly emotive subject, particularly after disasters elsewhere. It was only when the government sold the electricity industry into private hands that the costs of nuclear energy became apparent. The real commercial cost by 1990 was twice as high as for a coal-fired power station. Unless a much safer and more efficient system is designed, nuclear power has little future.

In the early 1990s Britain started to take renewable energy sources much more seriously than previously. It is estimated that the combined onshore and offshore wind energy resources could ultimately provide over 60 per cent of the national electricity requirement. Although the technology is still in its infancy, Britain now has one of the major wind generation facilities in Europe. Renewable energy sources are planned to provide 3 per cent of the national energy requirement by the year 2000.

Sellafield, Britain's best known nuclear power plant. It changed its name from Windscale in an attempt to escape some of the unpopularity attached to nuclear energy.

The causes of industrial failure

Why has Britain declined so rapidly from the greatest world power in 1900 to one of the lower-ranking members of the European Union by the century's end? The stress of two world wars and the loss of empire, though not unique to Britain, led to difficult adjustments. Unlike other European powers, Britain failed to rebuild its industries in 1945. Life was sufficiently comfortable that people remained unwilling to make the painful adjustments that might make Britain more competitive economically.

Among the long-standing reasons for Britain's poor performance, perhaps the most complex ones are cultural. One theory is that despite the major economic changes of the Industrial Revolution, the old gentry class (the aristocracy and land-owning families) of Britain did not oppose the rising middle class but made skilful adjustments to allow them to share the ruling culture. This was most evident in Britain's private education system, misleadingly called 'public' schools (see p.152), where a culture of respect for the professions but disdain for industry continued long after the Second World War. Even in the 1980s, while the public school emphasis changed from the

A wind farm. Wind power is an increasingly popular source of power.

Britain also fails to invest in research. In the 1980s the government reduced research budgets at universities and put pressure on universities to direct their research towards practical purposes. Both aspects of this philosophy were opposed in the universities, which claimed that Britain's future depends upon adequate research funding and also the freedom to pursue pure research, not applied to immediate industrial needs, but which advance scientific knowledge more broadly.

Britain's failure to treat these matters properly is most clearly seen in the area of Research and Development (R and D), most of which is directed towards immediate and practical problems. British companies spend less on R and D as a percentage of annual revenue than many European competitors. It partly results from the short-termism of stock market investment.

Another aspect of industrial failure is the absence of 'team spirit'. Little effort is made to interest the workforce in a company's well-being. Joint consultation between management and workers is still a rarity. Too few companies offer a bonus or incentive scheme for increased productivity. In such circumstances it is hardly surprising that many British workers have a leisurely approach to work.

With its vaunted youthful energy, Labour set itself the target of curing these ills.

European Monetary Union

Nothing in the mid-1990s was politically so divisive as the question of whether Britain should enter the European Monetary Union (EMU) scheduled for 1999. The Conservatives were deeply split on the issue and became unelectable. Labour managed to maintain its unity by pledging to join EMU 'when the time was right'. Once elected, Labour indicated this would be after 1999, and probably at least three years later. After the experience of Britain's exit from the Exchange Rate Mechanism (ERM) in 1992, it wanted longer to prepare the economy for monetary integration and also possibly wanted EMU to get over any 'teething' problems. Labour's Chancellor, Gordon Brown told the Commons that 'entering the single currency before we have achieved durable and sustainable convergence (with other EU countries in the economic cycle) would discourage investment'.

Nevertheless, Labour took measures to prepare for entry. Surrendering the power to set interest rates to the Bank of England was a first step. It also

professions to merchant banking, there remained little enthusiasm for industry. For Ralf Dahrendorf, able to observe British society as an intimate member and yet with the eyes of an outsider: 'The upper class is relaxed, the middle class is acquiescent and the working class is passive.'

Britain also failed to give technical and scientific subjects as much importance as its competitors, something noted as long ago as 1868. Technical education has remained weak ever since, when compared with Britain's major competitors. In 1982 a government report stated that 'Britain has one of the least trained workforces in the industrial world.' Britain has a very long way to go in skills acquisition. By the late 1980s only 6 per cent of Britain's labour force had a university degree, compared with 18 per cent in America and 13 per cent in Japan.

A student engineer at a further education college.

allowed business to convert shares into euros, and to pay tax in euros from 1999. Labour was concerned that business should not be disadvantaged by late membership. The advantage of entering EMU included lower interest rates, greater economic stability and possibly higher productivity. The dangers of staying out included the temptation to devalue in order to remain competitive in Europe, with the accompanying penalty of starting another inflationary cycle, and the likelihood that Japanese car and electronic enterprises would move their factories from Britain to other parts of the European Union. There also remained the danger that the financial markets would view sterling as weaker than the euro. Yet there is also a strong case against entry. The loss of control over interest rates as an instrument of fiscal policy amounts to a loss of sovereignty. Britain has always used control of interest rates as a main tool for controlling the economy. Britain is unlike other EU members in the high proportion of mortgage holders (home owners with housing loans) who are very susceptible to interest rates. The limitation on government borrowing also seriously limits government's options. For the Conservatives, however, the whole idea is wrong-headed. As their leader, William Hague, told the CBI in 1997:

> *The danger for Britain is not that we will somehow be left behind in Europe. The real danger for us is that Europe could be left behind in the rest of the world ... the single currency is for all time. British business could find itself trapped in a burning building with no exits.*

Labour has committed itself to a referendum on the issue. By 1997 there were barely 35 per cent of the electorate in favour of EMU, but Labour was confident that, given time, it could persuade a majority of the electorate to support entry.

Further information

WEBSITES

Bank of England	www.bankofengland.co.uk
Lloyds of London	www.lloydsoflondon.co.uk
Confederation of British Industry	www.cbi.org.uk
Trades Union Congress	www.tuc.org.uk
The Industrial Society	www.indsoc.co.uk
Business in the Community	www.bitc.org.uk

PRINTED MATERIAL

Coxall, Bill and Robins, Lynton 1994 *Contemporary British Politics* Chapters 20 and 25 Macmillan

Hutton, Will 1996 *The State We're In* Vintage

Hutton, Will 1997 *The State To Come* Vintage

QUESTIONS

Section analysis

1 **The economic problems** What were the economic successes and failures of the Conservative administrations, 1979–97?

2 **Owners and managers** Why might the CBI's influence now be in decline?

3 **The financial sector** What is the essential danger in the power exerted on the national economy by the City's financial institutions?

4 **The trade unions** Why are Labour and the trade unions happy to be less closely identified with each other?

5 **The workforce** Summarise the changes affecting Britain's workforce since the 1950s.

6 **The energy industries** Does Britain's energy policy differ from that in your country? If so, how?

7 **The causes of industrial failure** Why has Britain fallen behind so many of its European competitors from a position of pre-eminence in 1900?

8 **European Monetary Union** What are the basic advantages and disadvantages to Britain of joining the European Monetary Union?

Chapter analysis and discussion

1 Which of the following statements best summarises Britain's economic position today? Find evidence in the text to support your choice.

a The economic changes introduced by the Conservatives 1979–97 laid the foundations for Britain's economic success.

b The economic changes introduced by the Conservatives did not solve Britain's fundamental economic weakness compared with its competitors.

2 Is Britain's economic decline inevitable? Can its economic position improve? Find arguments to support both points of view.

3 In the mid-1980s almost 90 per cent of the British workforce said they were satisfied with their work situation. Ten years later a survey suggested that over 60 per cent would happily give up their job if they could afford to do so. Can you suggest any possible reasons for these contrasting statistics?

4 Read the following statements about the British economy and compare them with the situation in your country:

a The British economy is partly controlled by the government and partly left to market forces.

b Nuclear energy is very expensive, is not trusted by ordinary people and has no future.

Visual interpretation

Examine the 1997 unemployment map of Britain, and the comparative international table. What do they tell you about Britain's current employment situation?

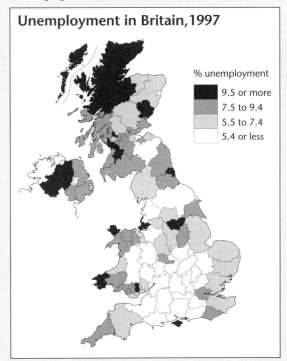

Unemployment in Britain, 1997

% unemployment
- 9.5 or more
- 7.5 to 9.4
- 5.5 to 7.4
- 5.4 or less

Source: *Regional Trends 32* © Crown copyright 1997

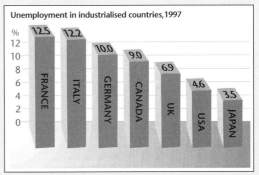

Unemployment in industrialised countries, 1997

Country	%
FRANCE	12.5
ITALY	12.2
GERMANY	10.0
CANADA	9.0
UK	6.9
USA	4.6
JAPAN	3.5

Source: OECD

7 A social profile

It is easy to assume that the population of a country like Britain is stable, but it is a dangerous assumption to make. There is plenty of change going on, even though the population will not reach 60 million from its present 58 million until about 2011, and will start falling again from 2025. As already noted, the population is unevenly distributed across the land, and there has been a persistent drift to the south and south east since the 1980s. But the shape of Britain's population in age and composition has been changing substantially too. Since the middle of the century fertility has fluctuated, rapidly increasing and decreasing (up to 30 per cent variation) in a single decade. This has implications for health and education services, and for employment.

Overall, the 'baby boom' that followed the end of the Second World War, and the subsequent decline in births (to slightly under replenishment level) during the 1970s, are leading to major changes in balance between age groups. The birth rate continues to fall, and the balance between young and old continues to shift. In 1971 24 per cent of the population was under the age of 15. By 1995 this proportion had fallen to about 20 per cent

Old age pensioners on the south coast of England enjoying celebrations to mark the fiftieth anniversary of the end of the Second World War.

while the proportion of over-65-year-olds increased from 13 to 18 per cent.

The British population is already one of the oldest in Europe, and it is currently getting older. In 1990 the median age in Britain was 36 but it will rise to 41 by 2020 before slowly falling again. There will be twice as many people aged 85 or over by 2020 as in 1990. A disproportionate number of the old, incidentally, choose to retire to the south coast and East Anglia, creating regional imbalances.

Britain is also changing ethnically. There used to be an assumption that the British were nearly all Anglo-Saxon, in spite of the substantial immigration of people from continental Europe during the first half of the century. Of course, they were largely invisible. Since black people from the Caribbean were first recruited to fill job vacancies during the 1950s, over two million Afro-Caribbean and Asian people have come to live and work in Britain. With a natural increase they have become 5.7 per cent of Britain's population, but concentrated particularly in London and Leicester (where their density is three times the national average), and in Bradford, Slough and Birmingham (where it is twice the national average).

Despite such changes, broad stereotypical views concerning British society persist. Take, for example, the classic family.

The family

The nuclear family, a married couple with perhaps two children, is still considered the ideal social unit and most young people still aspire to this idea of their own future. Yet as a picture of the way most British people live, it is increasingly unrealistic. If the picture includes the traditional idea of the man going out to work while the wife stays at home, it is now true of less than 10 per cent of households. Even without such a limited definition, only 40 per cent of the population live in nuclear family households, and even within this group a considerable proportion of parents are in their

An east London street market used by members of the local Bangladeshi community.

second marriage with children from a previous marriage.

Social behaviour is rapidly changing. The number of people living alone has risen significantly, from one in 10 in 1951 to more than one in four 40 years later, and it will be one in three early in the twenty-first century. In the same period the proportion of households containing five or more people has halved to fewer than one in 10. The British are clearly becoming a more solitary nation in their living habits. These facts have social implications, for example housing needs in the future (see Chapter 15).

There is an increasing proportion of men and women living together before marriage. For example, in 1961 only 1 per cent of first-time married couples had previously been living together, compared with 25 per cent in 1976, and with over 50 per cent of those aged between 30 and 40 who then got married. By the year 2000 most couples will probably live together before marrying. About one in four of the couples living together, or 'cohabiting', never do get married. In the period 1979–91 the proportion of single, widowed, divorced or separated women aged between 18 and 49 increased from 11 to 23 per cent of women in that age group.

Until 1990 or so it was possible to maintain that marriage was as popular as ever. Recently, however, there has been a rapid drop from the

annual average of 400,000 weddings during the 1980s to only 279,000 by 1996, the lowest ever recorded figure. In 1961 85 per cent of all marriages were for the first time, while today 38 per cent are second marriages for at least one partner. Britain has the highest divorce rate in Europe. Thirty-eight per cent of marriages end in divorce, one quarter of first marriages failing in the first five years. The rate is highest among those on a low income and those who marry very young, say under the age of 24. By 1995 people were also on average three years older when they married, 28 for men and 26 for women, compared with the average ages in 1985.

A traditional wedding group with the bride, groom, parents, bridesmaid, best man and priest.

What happens to those who do not marry? Besides a fall in the total number of marriages each year, there has been an increase in the number of couples choosing to live together but not marry, and also of women who choose to marry later in life. Only one in seven women aged between 25 and 29 was still single in 1979, compared with more than one in three by the mid-1990s. Some women prefer independence, either by cohabiting or by living alone, which they fear they will lose by marriage. Personal development must also partly explain the growing divorce rate. Alongside a social acceptance of divorce greater today than in the 1950s and 1960s, women have been increasingly dissatisfied by the traditional expectations of the woman's role in marriage. They also usually now want the right to pursue a career. Sometimes the husband's difficulty in adapting to the new situation puts a strain on the marriage.

One inevitable consequence of the climbing divorce rate has been the rise of single-parent families. These families often experience isolation and poverty. Single-parent families have been increasing, from 8 per cent of all families in 1972 to 22 per cent by 1995. The great majority of single parents are women. One in three children under the age of five has divorced parents. Forty per cent of children experience the divorce of their parents before the age of 18.

Many single parents face serious hardship. This family occupies very low-cost housing.

There has also been an increase in babies born outside marriage. It is indicative of both the increasing proportion and changing social attitudes that these babies, once described as 'illegitimate', are now described officially as 'non-marital'. In 1961 only 6 per cent of births were non-marital, but the rate has recently risen steeply from 16 to 33 per cent in the years 1983–95. This rapid rise reflects the increase in cohabitation, which accounts for 48 per cent of non-marital births. Unfortunately, cohabitation is no indication of a long-term stable environment for children. Statistics show that cohabiting parents are three times more likely to split up than married parents.

The remaining non-marital births are to single mothers, with the rate being highest in areas of high unemployment and the greatest poverty, suggesting to some analysts that the birth of a child gives a woman in such circumstances someone to love, a purpose in life and also state assistance. There is also an ethnic dimension. On account of traditional patterns of family life, over 40 per cent of Caribbean families are single-parent ones.

What can be made of such evidence? For some, such statistics are evidence of moral decline, and they argue the need to return to traditional values. In the face of the evidence this sounds like wishful thinking.

Is Britain really in moral decline? It would be safer to say that moral values are changing, with less attention to traditional definitions of immorality, and greater emphasis on personal morality being rooted in kindness and respect for others. Many, however, would disagree with this verdict, pointing to the high divorce and non-marital birth rates as evidence of fundamental failure to be kind or to respect others. One retired school teacher and Devon magistrate has this to say: 'You cannot give young people moral tuition in this area (sex) any more. They regard it as an intolerable intrusion into their privacy.' Yet, he continues, 'I must admit that I also find older children more mature, more responsible, more considerate to each other [than the previous generation].' To blame a moral decline on the failure to uphold family values is simplistic. There are other things which must be considered to understand what is going on in society and why. A fundamental one is the matter of social class.

Social class

On becoming Prime Minister in 1990, John Major announced: 'We will ... make the whole of the country a genuinely classless society.' In fact he failed, for the gap between rich and poor grew during his seven years' premiership, but his statement was a clear admission that class is still a real feature in English society, though less so in the Celtic countries. The English are self-conscious about class. Many think it is a thing of the past, because it does not unduly impinge on their daily lives. But it is there, even if it is very different from what it was 50 years ago.

Market researchers in the 1950s applied six classes to Britain, and they have tended to be used ever since. The following figures are for 1992.

Social classes in Britain	
Class	% of households
A Upper middle class (senior civil servants, professional, senior management and finance)	3
B Middle class (middle managerial)	16
C1 Lower middle class (junior managerial/clerical, non-manual workers)	26
C2 Skilled working class	26
D Semi-skilled/Unskilled working class	17
E Residual (dependent on state benefit, unemployed, occasional part-time)	13

(Source: *National Readership Survey*, NRS, 1992/93)

The terms still apply today. The kind of work done not only indicates education and how much is earned, but also the kind of social contact that is usual. Most people generally mix socially with the same kind of people as their work colleagues, and usually live in streets or neighbourhoods which reflect that social grouping. Manual workers tend to mix with each other, as do professionals (doctors, lawyers and senior civil servants) and managers.

This suggests a static situation, but there is major movement between classes. Many people move from one category to another during their working lives. The working class is rapidly declining. In 1911 three out of every four employed or self-employed people were manual workers. By 1950 that proportion had fallen to two out of three, but since then has fallen to 40 per cent or so. Since the 1950s there has been a massive growth of the middle class. But there has also been the emergence of a sizeable 'underclass', as Category E is commonly known.

Class has both crude and subtle components. A combination of wealth and education form the crude indicators. Yet the sense of social class or group is affected by social circle as well as education and wealth. A relatively poor but highly educated family may find itself associating with wealthier but similarly highly educated friends. A traditional landowning but less highly educated 'gentry' family will probably associate with other landowners of similar educational level. There are one or two expensive private schools (part of the 'public school' system, see p.152) which cater for the less intelligent children of the upper élite of the country. But there are also children of those who belong to the upper middle class who go to an ordinary local state-funded school rather than a fee-paying school. The former is likely to remain part of the élite. The latter may function comfortably in a wider range of social classes. There can also be a major class difference between grown-up children and their parents. Marriage outside one's class is much more common than it used to be. Consequently, the 'extended' family, including cousins, will probably include people who in their social life belong to quite different social classes.

The middle class, in particular, has great fluidity and mobility. During the 20 years 1971–91, approximately two million jobs were created in the professional and managerial fields alone, and the whole middle class is constantly expanding. Over half of today's middle class started life in the working class. Their children may well aspire to the upper middle class.

Despite this fluidity, the élite of society, itself a segment of the professional class, takes great care to protect itself. This includes the 'gentry' class made up mainly of landowners, and others who move in the most exclusive English social circles. It sends its children to be educated privately at a public school, where its children obtain a better academic education than normally possible in state-funded schools. More importantly they obtain a sense of social superiority through the public schools' élitist culture. A recent Provost (or president) of Eton College told assembled pupils that they were being educated so as 'to exercise authority'. A boy at John Major's old (state) school had this to say: 'If John Major wants a classless society, then he'll have to abolish the public school sector. We can't have equal opportunities with two different sectors.' Another commented, 'You feel different from them. It's not equal. They start on a different level.'

Unskilled work such as this often indicates low pay and low social status.

Although by no means an exclusively middle class activity, ballet lessons are enormously popular with young middle class girls.

As a skilled worker, a builder can make a good living for himself.

Henley Regatta is a major annual social event for the privately educated upper middle classes.

Young women now normally work on an equal footing with men, while at more senior levels women still face discrimination.

It is also true that the 'top' 1 per cent has enormous influence and control. A handful of outsiders obtain access to this élite. It is sometimes known as 'The Establishment' and sometimes as 'The Great and the Good'. They move easily in the most influential political, cultural or social circles. Anthony Sampson, a leading authority on how Britain is really governed, says: 'The rulers are not at all close-knit or united … (They are) a cluster of interlocking circles, each one largely preoccupied with its own.' The top 1 per cent of wealth holders probably own about one-quarter of the nation's wealth, a large drop from the two-thirds they controlled in 1914 but a larger proportion than one might expect in a modern democracy. The reason that the top 1 per cent has remained so wealthy is inheritance, which is spread around the family to minimise the effects of taxation. The sons all go to public schools, usually the more famous ones. As one sociologist has noted, 'The ruling minority has survived all the transformations from medieval to modern society by a long series of concessions and accommodations in return for retention of privileges and property.'

Traditionally, the young men of this élite went into the professions: the Civil Service, the law, medicine, the armed forces or the Church. That was partly the result of the original public school ethic of 'service'. During the Thatcher years this characteristic changed. Increasingly this élite, but also many members of the upper middle class as a whole, has moved from public service into the private sector: merchant banks, accountancy, management and financial consultancy. The reason is quite simple. Until the late 1970s salaries in the private sector were reasonably comparable to those in public life. But from 1979 private sector salaries soared in the new free market ethos. Today, if you wish to be seriously wealthy there is no point in seeking a career in public service.

There is another factor in the growing importance of wealth within the class system. Generally speaking, people seek marriage partners within their own social group. With more women taking up careers, particularly in the private sector, the wealth differential between a professional-class couple earning £80,000 each and a working-class couple earning £20,000 each is far greater than the differential when it was only the men who were earning. Thus, today, some people describe the new upper middle class as 'the super class'.

Those who think that Britain has a class-ridden society usually think of the contrast between the old moneyed 'upper class', maintained by its great wealth, property and privileged education,

together with the growing economic super class on the one hand, and the underclass of dependent, unemployed or homeless people on the other. But these two extremes are where there is the least social mobility. In between there is huge social mobility.

Nevertheless, the perception of class conflict remains. Since 1964 opinion polls have asked a random sample of people, 'There used to be a lot of talk in politics about the 'class struggle'. Do you think there is a class struggle in this country?' In 1964 48 per cent thought so, a figure which had risen to a remarkable 81 per cent in 1995, reflecting the increasing disparity between rich and poor in Britain.

Gender

Many women would argue that there is a different half of the nation which gets less than its fair share of power, freedom and wealth: the female sex. In spite of the considerable change in social attitudes since 1945, and particularly since the feminist revolution which began in the 1960s, parity has yet to be achieved. Women have entered employment in increasing numbers. In 1971 52 per cent of women between the ages of 25 and 44 were economically active, a figure that by 1995 had risen to approximately 75 per cent. Nevertheless, their position relative to men in employment improves only slowly. In part it is a generational matter. The average pay difference among 35–55 year-olds in 1996 was 22 per cent, among 25–34 year-olds 6 per cent, while there was parity under the age of 25.

Yet the reasons are also more complex, largely to do with the fact that men continue to control the positions of power and of wealth and either consciously or subconsciously usually replace themselves with other men. In spite of having a female monarch and having had a female Prime Minister for over a decade, the difficulties begin at the top. Margaret Thatcher only ever had one other female Cabinet minister, who lasted for less than a year.

In 1989 the Labour Party decided to adopt a system of positive action in favour of women, whereby MPs voting on the composition of the Shadow Cabinet would be compelled to vote for at least three women (out of 18 nominees to Cabinet posts). It also encouraged the selection of women parliamentary candidates. Only 19 women MPs had been elected in the 1979 election, a figure that improved to 41 in 1987 and to 63 in 1992, of whom 39 were Labour. The real breakthrough came in 1997, when 120 women were elected, of whom 101 represented Labour seats. Yet that still left a ratio of five men to every woman in the Commons, a better representation than in southern Europe, but significantly poorer than the Scandinavian countries. There is therefore still plenty of work for the Commons 300 Group, an all-party organisation working towards a minimum of 300 women MPs. On election, Tony Blair appointed five women to his 22-member Cabinet, an indication of the substantial change not only in representation but also in attitudes.

Dame Pauline Neville-Jones is Managing Director at NatWest Markets, a major finance house in the City of London. Her success is exceptional. There are plenty of highly gifted women frustrated by male prejudice.

If one looks at the positions of power in the country, few are held by women, (see p.59), who by 1997 represented over 46 per cent of the workforce. In 1997 only 6 per cent of High Court and Circuit judges were women. In the Civil Service there was no female Permanent Secretary, the senior rank, although there were an increasing number at senior, but lower, levels. In fact, out of 304 Permanent Secretaries between 1900 and 1990, only two have been women. In the words of one high-flier, who ran the Prime Minister's Efficiency Unit until 1996, 'The top of the Civil Service is still dominated by a very traditional male élite which prefers to promote people they feel comfortable with – and that means men with similar backgrounds.' Thus the proportion of women in the top three grades of the Civil Service rose from 5 per cent in 1984 to 11 per cent in

1995. At that rate parity is still at least 20 years away.

This characteristic is widespread. In 1995 the first woman ever was appointed as a police Chief Constable, and it was widely reported as a significant breach of a male dominated preserve. Will she be followed by others? Currently only 1.5 per cent of senior police posts are held by women. In order to succeed in such spheres women must be outstandingly better than men. In 1996 only 7 per cent of university professors were women. While 25 per cent of qualifying doctors are women, only 3 per cent of surgeons are women.

More women succeed in business, but they still attract curiosity. When appointed or sacked, they attract press comment not only on their professional ability but also on their private lives. Men do not receive similar treatment. The retail chain, Marks and Spencer appointed its first female executive board member in 1996. The same year the conglomerate, Pearson appointed its first female chief executive, the first female chief executive for the top 100 publicly quoted (FT-SE 100) companies. Only 3 per cent of company directors are women. Only 11 per cent of all managers are women. Women in career structures often sense that a 'glass ceiling' exists which prevents them reaching the top. Possibly as a consequence, 800,000 women run their own businesses.

Women are also paid less than men. On average, out of the whole labour force, women earn 31 per cent less than men. The average hourly wage for full-time women workers is £7, only 80 per cent of what men earn.

Married women rather than their husbands suffer the career penalties of producing and raising children. A small but growing number of employers ensure that mothers can resume their careers without any damage to their career prospects after having a baby. Few provide crèches for young children in order to encourage women to work for them. The state provides day care for fewer than 1 per cent of under-three-year-olds, thus discouraging women from working. Apart from Ireland, this is the lowest level of provision in the European Community.

For those women who do work, there is an added penalty. Although on average they work shorter hours than men (in 1996, 40 compared with 47), there has been no substantial adjustment of the domestic burden. Women still do about 8 hours more domestic work weekly than men.

Young people

A reversal of previous inequality, however, is taking place among younger people. It starts at school, where girls are now out-performing boys. Fifty per cent of girls now achieve the top three grades of the secondary education examination (Grades A–C at GCSE, see p.147), compared with only 40 per cent of boys. Girls not only work harder at school, but also prepare themselves more carefully at all stages for obtaining employment. They are also increasingly thought to have better skills at teamwork, and the achievement of objectives by consensus.

Teenage parents with baby: Britain has the highest rate of teenage pregnancies in Europe.

This is not solely to do with the fact that boys mature later. Many boys have watched their fathers become unemployed and idle at home. It is a dispiriting role model. Manual work, in which physical prowess was important, notably mining, steel production, heavy engineering, has radically declined. Since 1980 over two million male jobs have been lost. Boys, too, are far more frequently targeted by drug pushers and are twice as likely to be the victims of crime or violence than women. In a society in which an increasing proportion of women have children outside marriage, unmarried fathers have no rights over the children. Such factors add up to a widespread loss of self-esteem, and the loss of an identifiable male role for many boys. A growing number of young women feel they can do without men. Thus, alongside growing gender equality lies the danger of a large number of young men with little purpose in their lives, something which itself may generate major social problems.

All young people tend to worry about employment, to the extent that they are far less rebellious than young people in the 1960s and 1970s. They also have fewer interests outside those spheres relevant to obtaining a job. According to a survey carried out in 1997 by the Industrial Society, only 40 per cent have any interest whatsoever in politics. Most find it irrelevant. But they are more disciplined than they used to be. No fewer than 78 per cent think that discipline both at school and at home is too lax. Sixty-three per cent of them feel school let them down. The Industrial Society drew a picture of an optimistic, 'can-do' generation who want to better themselves through education, while learning practical skills. They aspire to traditional values, for example preferring the idea of marriage and family stability to partnerships, possibly because many know the trauma of parents divorcing. But they are also more isolated than their parents' generation. Only one in five feel they are part of a community, a sad reflection on the atomisation of modern British society.

Ethnic minorities

The ethnic minority communities in Britain comprise 5.7 per cent of the total population but are likely to rise to about 7 per cent in the early years of the twenty-first century, on account of their higher birth rate. In 1950 there were only about 40,000 non-white Britons, mainly in ports like Liverpool, Bristol and Cardiff. People from the West Indies began immigrating to Britain in substantial numbers at that time, in response to labour shortages. During the 1960s and 1970s a large number of people also came from India, Pakistan and Bangladesh.

Britain has a large Chinese ethnic minority. Chinatown near Leicester Square in London is a favourite place for shopping and eating.

These immigrants soon discovered that they were the target of discrimination in class and status. People of Afro-Caribbean and Asian origin have generally had the worst-paid jobs, lived in the worst housing and encountered hostility from white neighbours. The initial view that non-white immigrants would assimilate into the host community was quickly proved wrong. Since the mid-1960s the government has introduced three race relations acts in order to eliminate racial discrimination. But laws were also introduced to restrict immigration, which seemed particularly aimed at thwarting non-white immigrants.

The following table gives the sizes of the main ethnic minority communities in Britain by area of origin, based on the 1991 official population census.

Ethnic minority communities in Britain	
Origin	*Number*
Indian	840,000
Caribbean	500,000
Pakistan	477,000
Black African	212,000
Bangladeshi	163,000
Chinese	157,000

These communities have areas of high concentration. London has the largest concentration of ethnic minority members, particularly Afro-Caribbeans, 60 per cent of whom are Londoners. But people of Indian origin are also highly concentrated in Leicester, those of Pakistani origin have high concentrations in the West Midlands and also in West Yorkshire, while those of Bangladeshi origin are concentrated in east London. In 1997 20 per cent of Londoners belonged to an ethnic minority group, a proportion which will rise to 28 per cent by 2011.

Many British people believe they inhabit an already overcrowded island. Governments have seldom told the electorate that immigrant labour has filled essential areas the British workforce was reluctant to fill. Instead, they have tended to bow to uninformed popular prejudice, that immigration is a problem rather than an asset. Margaret Thatcher, for example, promised that a Conservative government would 'finally see an end to immigration', and spoke of the fears of white Britons that they might be 'swamped by people with a different culture'. Although she failed, her government increased the restrictions on immigration and ended the automatic right of anyone born in Britain to British citizenship. Her remarks reflected widespread but ill-informed prejudice. In fact, immigration has been dropping steadily since its peak year in 1967 and, although this is not widely known, in the 30 years up to 1982 750,000 more people left Britain permanently than entered to settle. Since then immigrants have slightly outnumbered emigrants, by about 70,000 each year. In the early 1990s the government made it much harder for political asylum seekers to find refuge in Britain. For both immigrants and asylum seekers, their applications can take years to be processed because of bureaucratic inefficiency.

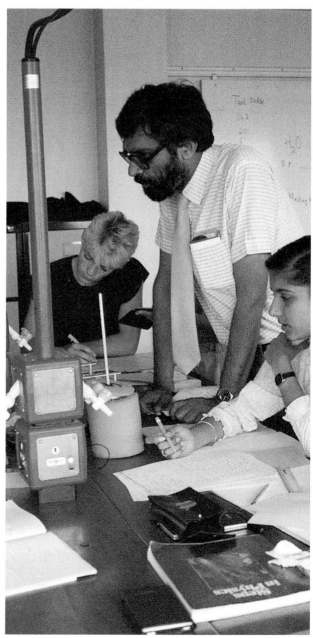

Some schools have a high intake from ethnic minorities, as in this case.

Another complaint frequently levelled against ethnic minority communities is their 'failure to integrate'. At first it was government policy to try to spread immigrants evenly. It did not work for two basic reasons. Most immigrants ended up in the poorest areas, and also they understandably wished to be close to other members of their community. In addition, white families often moved away from areas of high ethnic-minority concentration. The result has been a continuing process of ethnic separation.

Afro-Caribbeans and Asians experience many kinds of disadvantage. They find greater difficulty getting a job. Studies show that a white person is 10 times more likely to obtain a job than a black competitor for it. In 1995 the unemployment rate among black Afro-Caribbeans and Bangladeshis was 24 and 27 per cent respectively. The rate among those of Indian origin was 12 per cent while among whites it was only 8 per cent. A black person is likely to find it harder to obtain credit from a bank or a loan to purchase a house.

Immigrants also tend to receive the worst housing. Thirty-eight per cent of Pakistanis and Bangladeshis report lacking one or more basic housing amenities compared with 11 per cent of whites. It is no surprise therefore that Pakistanis and Bangladeshis are 50 per cent more likely to suffer ill health than whites. Thus, in employment, promotion prospects, housing, health and education, many immigrant communities find themselves significantly disadvantaged.

Difficulties for children from ethnic minorities begin when they go to school. Many members of the ethnic minorities live in deprived inner-city areas where the quality of the schools is worse than elsewhere. Low expectations from their teachers and a sense of alienation from the majority white community are serious disadvantages. Afro-Caribbeans are expected to remain at the bottom of the educational and economic scale. Asians generally do better in formal education than Afro-Caribbeans and many white children. Some parents of Indian origin make major sacrifices for their children to be educated privately. For example, easily the most frequent name on the register of Dulwich College, south-east London's most prestigious private school, is an Indian one, Patel. British Asians of Indian origin are likely to rise to leading positions in the British economy.

The ethnic minority communities feel that they also face hostility from the authorities. In some areas a young black man is 10 times more likely to

A Sikh policeman.

be stopped in the street by police than the average white citizen. Black people feel harassed by such treatment, particularly since a growing number of black youths, the main target of the police, were born in Britain. There is also clear evidence that the police more readily arrest blacks than whites. A study in 1989 showed that although only 6 per cent of the population, blacks made up 20 per cent of those held in custody in England and Wales, and 38 per cent of those held in custody in London, even though ethnic minorities represent only 20 per cent of London's population. Blacks are both twice as likely to be held in custody before trial and twice as likely to be acquitted once their case is heard by a magistrate. Afro-Caribbeans and Asians are frequent targets for verbal abuse, harassment or even attack. In 1996 about 12,000 racially motivated incidents were reported.

Discrimination, or at least a failure to involve the ethnic minority groups adequately, is apparent in many institutions. Only 1 per cent of the army, the police and fire brigade are from ethnic minorities. In all three organisations stories of racial abuse and harassment deter blacks from enrolling. The idea of a black officer commanding a regiment or a police station, let alone becoming a general or chief constable remains difficult to imagine. Discrimination is not confined to such 'macho' organisations. There used to be many black nurses working in hospitals. By 1995 while blacks comprised over 8 per cent of nurses over the age of 55, they were less than 1 per cent of those under the age of 25. Younger black women know that they are unlikely to get promotion, and are looking elsewhere for a career. Yet acceptance and equal treatment are now urgent since the ethnic minorities are expected to double by 2025, when they will constitute 20 per cent of the workforce.

In some places the barriers have begun to be broken down, but it has required determination. Black people have excelled in sport and show business, but these two areas do not confer real power or social authority on them. The idea of blacks in managerial positions over whites is still not widely acceptable. Successive governments have introduced legislation that promises absolute equality for non-white British citizens. But the promise has remained unfulfilled. Government has not done enough to implement functional equality in the areas over which it has direct control, and white Britons have not yet accepted Afro-Caribbeans and Asians who are born and grow up here (now more than 40 per cent of their communities) as being as British as themselves.

Yet, in spite of this bleak picture, the outlook seems positive. A survey in 1997 found that 60 per cent of black respondents felt that racism had lessened during the previous five years. Furthermore, multiracial partnerships are more frequent in Britain than elsewhere, and this is creating a new multiracial identity. By 1991 almost 40 per cent of young black men were married to or living with a white partner, and so were over 20 per cent of young black women. Almost half Afro-Caribbean children come from multiracial homes. Such children tend to embrace a black identity because of the discrimination around them. However, they are thoroughly British. As Trevor Phillips, one of Britain's leading black journalists writes:

It is the young, multiracial crowd who have the flexibility and adaptability that the twenty-first century will demand. For them moving between cultures and using several languages is a way of life that they have imbibed with their mother's milk. Instead of teaching children that the whiter (or blacker) they are, the better, the real advantage may be in being able to count the number of different roots your parents have bequeathed you.

(Trevor Phillips, *The Independent*)

Further information

WEBSITES

Commission for Racial Equality	www.open.gov.uk/cre
Gender and ethnicity issues	www.bitc.org.uk
Black Information Line	www.blink.org.uk

PRINTED MATERIAL

Adonis, Andrew and Pollard, Stephen 1997
A Class Act: The Myth of Britain's Classless Society
Hamish Hamilton

Coxall, Bill and Robins, Lynton 1994
Contemporary British Politics Chapters 24, 26 and 2
Macmillan

Halsey, A. H. 1995 *Change in British Society: from 19 to the Present Day* Oxford University Press

Paxman, Jeremy 1991
Friends in High Places: Who Runs Britain? Penguin

Davies, Nick 1998 *Dark Heart: The Shocking Truth about Hidden Britain* Vintage

QUESTIONS

Section analysis

1 Summarise the main changes to British society in terms of age, ethnic origin and family structure since the middle of the century.

2 **The family** Why is the number of non-marital births in Britain increasing?

3 **Social class** Are class divisions in British society real or imagined? Find evidence in the text to support your argument.

4 **Gender and young people** In what ways are women still disadvantaged in British society? Why might young males, however, feel disadvantaged?

5 **Ethnic minorities** Do you agree with Trevor Phillips's assessment (p.100), or do you think the children of mixed-race partnerships will remain disadvantaged? Find evidence for your point of view.

Chapter analysis and discussion

1 In what ways do you think that class divisions and the gulf between rich and poor are changing in Britain?

2 What predictions can you make about British society? In what ways is it likely to differ by 2010 from today?

3 Both women and ethnic minorities suffer disadvantages in Britain. Do you think those disadvantages are comparable?

Visual interpretation

1 How far does the graph below confirm this chapter's discussion of unemployment rates among different ethnic communities in Britain?

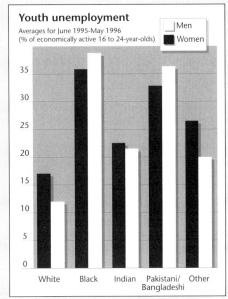

Source: *Labour Force Survey*

2 What does the graph below say about the changing role of women in politics?

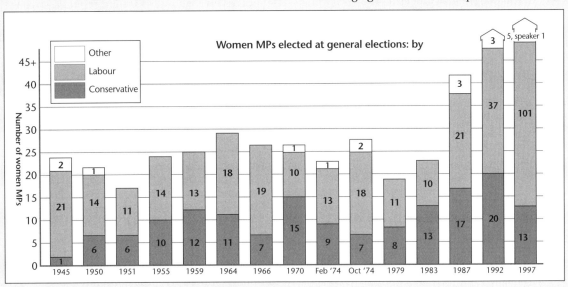

Source: House of Commons (Public Information Office)

8 Culture and style: national self-expression

How do the many aspects of British society discussed in the preceding chapters express themselves? Like any other society, the British like to create an agreeable picture of themselves. The majority like to think the important national values are things like tolerance, decency, moderation, consensus and compromise. They are uncomfortable with terms which polarise, such as: liberation, bourgeois, capitalist, collectivist. They like modesty and understatement, and they prefer practical common sense to pure logic. One writer, contrasting England with neighbouring France, says, 'At times it seems that the French and English national characters could be expressed in a series of antitheses: wit/humour; logic/tradition; gallantry/courage; thrift/expenditure; taste/comfort; town/country; vanity/pride.' Unlike elsewhere in Europe, someone described as an 'intellectual' usually feels embarrassed rather than flattered.

The community and the individual

In spite of having been a centralised state for longer than most European countries, British society is also deeply individualistic in a way which is inseparable from ideas of liberty and localism. This has a long history. According to one sociologist, 'Individualism is built into "custom and practice", and into local work places and community organisations.'

There is a feeling that it is the ordinary people, standing up for their rights in spite of government, who safeguard freedom, in contrast with France where in theory it is the state which upholds liberty. According to Ralf Dahrendorf, 'There is a fundamental liberty in Britain not easily found elsewhere.'

In part this liberty stems from the growth of a variety of institutions in previous centuries, which have strongly resisted the authority of central government. The tradition continues. Unlike in many other countries, local government still clings both to local identity and style. For example, some county names which were centuries old disappeared in the local government reorganisation of 1974. The removal of these names was so unpopular that most of them have since been revived.

This local response illustrates another long-standing characteristic of the British. They have a strong civic sense and participate in public affairs as their birthright. It is at the local level that British democracy is most meaningful. Writing approximately 80 years ago, Elie Halevy, a French writer on Britain, spoke enthusiastically of Britain as 'the country of voluntary obedience, of spontaneous organisation'. It is no less true today. The impulse to organise oneself and one's neighbours in some cause is a strong British tradition. William Beveridge, the 1940s architect of Britain's welfare system, wrote at the time, 'Vigour and abundance of Voluntary Action outside the home, individually and in association with other citizens, for bettering one's own life and that of one's fellows, are the distinguishing marks of a free society.'

About seven million Britons are regularly involved in voluntary activity, ranging from urban community action groups of the political left to local preservation societies, associated with more traditionally-minded people. Choirs, local dramatic groups, shelters for homeless people, the provision of the lifeboat service around Britain's shores, and many other things besides, depend upon the voluntary impulse. There are over 180,000 charities officially registered with the government, and at least 300,000 other voluntary organisations, including sports clubs, trade unions, rambling clubs, protest groups and other unregistered societies. Many charities operate with less than £1,000 yearly. Only a handful operate with more than £1 million. One of the largest of these, the disaster relief and world development agency Oxfam, has a network across Britain of over 800 shops selling second-hand goods and Third-World products, staffed by unpaid volunteers. It raises approximately £100 million yearly. All these

Volunteers taking disabled children fishing.

organisations, great or small, depend upon time, skill and money given voluntarily.

The fine distinctions of speech

A picture of the British as both individualist and yet community-minded is a cosy one, and in many respects the British have a deep sense of cultural cohesion and unity. Yet, in the words of a leading educationist, 'The trouble with the British is that they accept and enjoy the nice distinctions of social class. They love hierarchy and see nothing wrong in the deferential attitude that it breeds.' Nowhere is this clearer than in the question of speech. For the way English is spoken gives away not only regional identity but to some extent class status too. It is, for one sociologist, 'the snobbery which brands the tongue of every British child'. Since the days of Shakespeare, the English of south-east England has been considered the 'standard', for no better reason than that the south east is the region of economic and political power. The emergence of an upper and upper-middle-class mode of speech, 'received pronunciation' (RP), was systematically established through the public school system attended by the boys of wealthier families. It is a recent invention, barely a century old, yet RP persists as the accepted dialect of the national élite.

Broadly speaking, there are two kinds of RP. 'Unmarked' RP suggests no more than that the speaker is well educated (although of course many equally or better educated people speak with a regional accent). This is the dialect of the BBC, and thus it has a kind of authority. Through radio and television, unmarked RP is becoming a more widely spoken accent. As recently as 1981 an internal BBC handbook advocated the pronunciation 'of a person born and brought up in one of the Home Counties, educated at one of the southern Universities'. Then there is 'marked' RP, which indicates high social class and is spoken, for example, by many army officers who come from upper-class families. In both the Falklands and Gulf wars (1982 and 1991), marked RP was fashionable since it suggested leadership and authority at a time of national crisis. Although spoken by less than 5 per cent of the population, those who speak RP enjoy a social authority that contradicts democratic ideals.

Yet RP's social authority is rapidly declining, since it is suggestive of social snobbery and superiority. It no longer elicits such widespread deference. Some regional accents have acquired greater standing. In the early 1990s companies locating telephone-call centres sought the accent that would most suggest trustworthiness, competence and friendliness. While a Yorkshire accent suggested reliability and a West Country accent amiability, it was the Scots accent that scored highly in all three. Prejudice remains against certain accents. One experiment showed that people with a West Midlands accent are trusted less than those with other regional accents. There is prejudice also against some London accents.

Do dialect (a matter of grammar and vocabulary) and accent enrich or impoverish the language? This is a continuing matter for debate among linguists. Some argue that regional accents enhance the sense of local community and that to abandon them is to give way to the accents of the ruling class. Others argue that regional dialects, given their class associations, are socially divisive. Dialect is unlikely to disappear and the debate is likely to continue. At the moment, however, regional accents seem to be prevailing.

The rural ideal

There are many sub-cultures within Britain which reflect age, class, gender, ethnicity and social outlook. Broadly speaking there is a divide between the cultures of the controlling majority and those of the protesting minority, people who feel comparatively weak.

The rural ideal that the majority of the British dream of.

Chatsworth in Derbyshire. Great houses like Chatsworth appeal to the British love of the countryside, but also to nostalgia and deference to the landed class.

One of the most striking aspects of popular mainstream culture in Britain is the love of the countryside. Many people, whether they live in a suburban house or in a flat in a high-rise block, would say their dream home was a country cottage with roses growing over the door. As a nation, the British have made a mental retreat from the urban environment. They have a deep nostalgia for an idealised world of neat hedgerows, cottages and great country houses, surrounded by parkland and eighteenth-century style gardens that looked harmonious and natural. The nostalgia stems partly from a sense of loss which has lingered since the Industrial Revolution two centuries ago, and from a romantic love of nature which has been such a powerful theme in English literature. The National Trust, which owns or manages hundreds of country estates and great country houses, was founded a century ago on the rising nostalgia for a lost rural paradise. Its rapid growth in membership from 315,000 in the late 1970s to 2.4 million in 1997, illustrates its success in encouraging a love of the country and of the past. In 1996 there were well over 11 million visits to National Trust properties. The National Trust can easily become an exercise in national nostalgia, and because so many properties are great houses, it can also pander to a sense of deference to the great landed families.

A basic reason many town dwellers wish to live in the suburbs is to have a garden in which to grow flowers. Indeed, many suburban houses imitate a cottage style. Even in the heart of London, its great parks, such as St James's, Hyde Park and Kensington Gardens, are informal, recreating a rural ideal.

Britain is a country where over 80 per cent of the population live in towns of 50,000 inhabitants or more. Yet most reject the urban industrial culture, viewing life in the city as an 'unnatural' economic necessity. In order to realise their rural dream, on average 300 people every day move to a dwelling in the country. Many upper-middle-class people own a country cottage to which they retreat at weekends. In March 1998 about 250,000 people marched through central London in protest at what they saw as the government's neglect of the countryside. In fact the Countryside March was composed of different lobby groups, some with conflicting agendas, but that was not the point. The significance of the protest lay in the sheer number who attended, many of whom were actually town dwellers. The majority of British may understand little of the real countryside, but it remains sufficiently important to their sense of identity for them to take to the streets if they think it is endangered.

Dress codes

We give ourselves away by how we dress. Nostalgia and traditionalism are also expressed in appearances. The majority of British people dress conservatively rather than fashionably. A small number of the upper and professional upper middle class, for example barristers, diplomats, army officers and Conservative MPs dress in the well-tried styles of the past 50 years or so. Many of the men still have their suits specially tailored, and are thus instantly recognisable as belonging to the upper echelons of society. Yet how they dress is wholly unrepresentative of society in general.

The vast majority of people buy their clothes at the high-street stores, of which Marks and Spencer must be the most famous. They wear the clothes of the British middle classes, perfectly passable but hardly stylish like the dress standards in much of Europe. Indeed, the British still have a reputation for being the worst dressed people in Europe, and they do not really care.

Oxfam charity shops where people can buy a wide range of cheap second-hand clothes.

There is a tolerance, shabbiness and inventiveness in the way some, particularly the young, dress. There can be few countries where people who can afford new clothes deliberately choose to buy the 'cast-offs' of others. Yet in Britain many people, especially students and other young people, happily look for bargains at the thousands of charity shops that exist all over the country. Many who buy their clothes from these shops are genuinely needy. But equally, many are not. They choose to buy their clothes in charity shops because they are cheap and because they sometimes find wonderful bargains: almost new, high-quality items that cost next to nothing. In fact, some of the most dress-conscious young people find astonishing clothes at these shops, and manage to look sensational when they wear them. It is, perhaps, a flair for clothes that is peculiarly British.

Naomi Campbell on the catwalk, wearing a design by the British designer Stella McCartney. British designers are renowned for their sense of style and unconventionality.

Nostalgia and modernity

However, there is an important, and sometimes destructive, tension between nostalgia and individualism. Tradition and creativity are in conflict. The widespread love of the country-cottage look, and the old-fashioned dress style of the upper class, says much about the way the British perceive themselves. Because the past is glorious for the British, they prefer its reassurance to the uncertainty of the future. Speaking of fashion in its wider sense, the journalist Charlotte Du Cann notes the price the British pay for their nostalgia: 'Those who come to Britain want to buy what we sell with utter conviction: our cosy comforting past. The hand-crafted nostalgia that we market so desperately robs contemporary design of its rebellious energy.'

During the 1980s British nostalgia grew more than ever. Forty-one 'heritage' centres were established. More people than ever went to visit England's historic houses. Why? In the words of The National Trust Book of the English House, 'They (English country houses) look back to periods of apparent stability and order that, to some people, seem preferable to the chaos of the present.' By 1996

High-rise housing enjoyed brief popularity when first constructed in the 1960s. Thirty-five years later it is often synonymous with urban deprivation.

there were 2,500 museums in Britain of which half had been established since 1971. But as one museum curator warns, 'If you are not careful you will wallow in nostalgia, in this sort of myth that the past was wonderful. I personally believe the past was awful.'

Anti-modernism has been a prevalent theme in British culture this century. The popular culture of the urban working class, expressed for example, in cinemas, dance halls and football stadiums, has been a poor relation. Britain has a far weaker modernist culture than exists in France or Germany, because the British feel less certain about the relationship between architecture, art, design, craft and manufacture. It is safer to live with the quiet authority of a rural past, than the uncertainties of the urban present.

Nowhere was this tension more fiercely debated at the end of the 1980s, than in the field of architecture. There was a strong revolt against the use of bare concrete, and against the high-rise buildings which had been so popular in the 1960s and early 1970s. But it was also a protest against the unfamiliarity and apparent brutality of modernist architecture. This was popularly associated with cheap public housing and office blocks. In the late 1980s Prince Charles openly championed a return to traditional architecture and building materials, intervening to prevent a modernist addition to the National Gallery, an early nineteenth-century building, and to prevent the construction of what he called a 'glass stump', designed by the great modernist architect, Mies van der Rohe, in the City of London. Prince Charles created a major debate, in which the popular mood was clearly in sympathy with his views. The attack on modern architecture tended to concentrate on the worst examples and to ignore more exciting modern work. Modernist architects had no intention of defending the poor architecture of many cheap modern buildings. As one leading architect, James Stirling, remarked, 'The housing architecture of the 1960s was simply a matter of building more and more houses for less and less money until you ended up with a sort of trash.'

Many architects watched with dismay as important sites were developed in post-modernist, decorative, pastiche styles, as for example in much of the housing in London's redeveloped Docklands; or in the neo-classical style, for example Quinlan Terry's Richmond Riverside Development, which carefully but dishonestly disguised modern offices behind 'tasteful' mock-classical facades. The modernists, of whom Richard

Rogers was a leading champion, insisted that buildings should be, and appear, true to their purpose.

These styles, post-modern and neo-classical, were associated in people's minds with private development in the way that cheap, high-rise, concrete buildings were thought of as the architecture of the welfare state. Thus, post-modern and classical (which are too expensive for low-income families) were associated with the free-market era of Conservative government. At a deeper level, it is difficult to avoid the conclusion that the post-modern and neo-classical challenges to modernism were a popular revolt against the demands and reality of the modern world. The argument goes beyond stylistic conservatism. The retreat from bold modern planning and buildings implies hesitancy, in contrast with, for example, the self-confident modern buildings in Paris. More seriously, it suggests a fear of change, and apprehension rather than enthusiasm about the future.

It may be for this reason that on coming to power, Labour consciously distanced itself from nostalgia and tradition to embrace the young, innovative and exciting. In colloquial terms Labour wanted to promote Britain as 'cool' rather than 'stuffy'. This was expressed most symbolically in the Millennium Dome project designed by the Richard Rogers Partnership, intended as a showpiece of modern design.

In reality, though seldom formally acknowledged or celebrated, foreign modern influences have been immensely important in shaping popular culture since 1945. As a result of the US presence during and after the war, Britain was invaded by American culture – symbolised by chewing gum, jazz, flashy cars and mass production. It spoke of material wealth and social equality and seemed highly subversive to adults, who accepted the existing social order, while being highly attractive to the young. By 1959 almost 90 per cent of all teenage spending was conditioned by a rapidly Americanising working-class taste. It was not destined to last. In the 1960s Britain was more influenced by the apparent sophistication of continental Europe – Italian, French and Spanish cuisine, espresso bars, Scandinavian design, modernist architecture, and even holidays in the

Canary Wharf, currently London's tallest building, is an icon of the Thatcher period. In the foreground luxury housing stands on the river front.

sun. This, too, implied a more egalitarian country than Britain had traditionally been.

In the 1960s this mixture of influences that made up a new popular culture exploded in a distinctly English type of pop music – exemplified by the Beatles, the Rolling Stones and many others – and a revolution in dress and style, expressed most strikingly in the mini-skirt and the exotic range of clothes that expressed social liberation, on sale in London's Carnaby Street. The revolution became permanent as this popular culture seeped into even the upper-class reaches of Britain's youth. It eventually even became acceptable in all classes and for both men and women to wear laundered pressed jeans, the classic working-man's garb, as smart casual dress. Nevertheless, the tension between the popular modernism of rebellious young people and the traditionalism of a staid, silent majority persists.

Urban sub-cultures

Rebellion and dissent belong on city streets. Among those who rejected the English country-cottage culture in favour of a popular urban culture, some remained deeply dissatisfied with their place in society. Virtually all the youth sub-cultures of the politically or economically weaker segments of society had their roots in the poorer parts of towns. In the 1950s it was Teds, in the 1960s Mods and Rockers, in the 1970s Bikers (or Greasers), Skinheads, Punks and Rastafarians, and in the 1980s New Age Travellers (a rural exception), Goths, Pervs and Indie Kids. They reflect a refusal to conform in post-1945 society. Like the rural dream of the majority, some of these sub-cultures are based on nostalgia for a lost world, for example, an imagined traditional working-class culture for the Skinheads, or an idealised Africa for Rastafarians.

The single greatest influence for all these rebel sub-cultures has been Afro-Caribbean. Afro-Caribbean immigrants, and more particularly their children, have felt excluded from mainstream British society. Many feel they have exchanged one colonial situation for another, as a cheap and marginalised labour force. As they were largely confined to depressed urban areas, many whites associated Afro-Caribbean youths with violence and disorder. In 1981 and 1985 riots in London, Bristol, Birmingham and Liverpool were to a considerable extent an expression of Afro-Caribbean frustration with their lot.

At a spiritual level many Afro-Caribbeans, like those still in the Caribbean, dreamed of a golden

The Afro-Caribbean community displays its flair and vibrancy at the annual Notting Hill Carnival.

age in Africa before the slave traders came. These Rastafarians began to wear distinctive clothes, camouflage jackets, large hats in the red, gold and green colours of Ethiopia, and wear their long, uncut hair in 'dreadlocks'. They took to speaking in a special 'patois', or dialect. This was defiance and revolt, until Rastafarians became a recognised and legitimate minority group at the end of the 1980s.

Most important, however, for its cultural impact, has been the black music which came into Britain mainly through the Rastafarian movement. Three particular types, ska, reggae and rap, evolved in the Caribbean and United States but were developed in Britain. 'Break-dance' music came direct from the United States as did 'hip-hop'. 'Nowhere in the world,' according to the style writer Peter York, 'is black American dancing music more cherished than in England.' At first the music spread through informal channels, and homemade tapes. By the mid-1980s there were over 100 different independent reggae 'labels', or companies making tapes and records of reggae music. Afro-Caribbean music and culture finds its most colourful and exuberant public expression in the annual Notting Hill Carnival in London.

Black music, however, became a powerful expression of dissidence and was adopted by other rebel sub-cultures, even those which were openly hostile to the ethnic minorities. Indeed, it is through music that the black and white cultures have fused. The Skinheads, for example, who developed in the 1970s out of an older cult, the Mods, copied black mannerisms and fashions and danced to reggae. According to Ronnie Am, a retired black disc jockey, 'White teenagers loved the music and copied the clothes. This was the biggest adoption of black fashion by white people.' Yet Skinheads were closely identified with extreme right-wing racist views. In general they tolerated Afro-Caribbeans more willingly than the Asian minority. So many Skinheads were violent to blacks and homosexuals, or gays, that they are widely considered to be virtually fascist. They wore heavy boots, jeans and braces, and shaved their hair or cut it very short. They aggressively sought to recover a crude working-class identity which their parents' generation had largely abandoned. By the 1990s the Skinhead movement had virtually disappeared.

The Punks were a reaction to the glamour of the pop-star world of the 1960s and early 1970s. Their appeal to the young was their ability to outrage middle-aged opinion, particularly among the

guardians of social values, like the police and other civil authorities. They did this by using foul language, dressing in torn clothes, wearing Union Jacks, swastikas, mutilating their bodies with safety pins, wearing chains and even articles suggestive of urban waste like black plastic dustbin liner shirts. Punk, too, used black music, particularly reggae, to inspire its own Punk sound. Unlike Skinheads, however, many Punks openly identified with Black Britain. After 20 years, Punks too have virtually disappeared. While the rock-star culture of the 1960s proclaimed a classless society, Punks, Skinheads and Rastafarians, each in their own way, were insisting that they inhabited a world divided, as they saw it, by class and race.

Who is attracted to such cults? Generally it has been young people with low self-esteem, who have done poorly at school. Joining a gang is a means of finding status, and of defying the conventional world in which they have been defined as failures. For example, 'heavy metal' is the music of failure, and the fact that it is widely despised by those who enjoy pop, reggae or soul, is its appeal. Unlike other rebel cults, though, the followers of heavy metal have the manner of victims, and some wear gothic script and grinning skulls, suggestive of morbid interests. The capital of heavy metal is Birmingham, one of Britain's least loved cities.

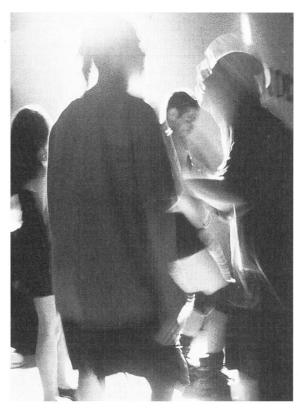

Clubbing, the favourite weekend activity for British youth.

New Age Travellers are more than a romantic movement. They challenge and reject the highly integrated society in which most people now live.

Such cults arise and disappear over periods of a decade or two. Two such youth cults which arose in the 1980s were Ragga and Gothic. Ragga was essentially American-inspired, as their clothing: baseball caps, tracksuit trousers and chunky trainers indicate. Gothic was a home-grown British style – a mixture of 1970s Punk and 1960s Hippie. Typically 'Goths' wore their hair very long and dyed black, and dressed in cheap, loose, black clothes, sometimes embroidered in black and frequently torn. Both boys and girls wore make-up, looking pale with mascara around the eyes. They were non-violent and seemed nostalgic for the youth culture and music of the 1960s. Always a minority movement, it was popular among angst-ridden youth who, in the words of the street style expert, Ted Polhemus, 'are comforted by and attracted to a romanticized, stylish vision of life in the shadow of death'. By the mid-1990s both had virtually disappeared.

Such sub-cultures follow a cycle. They create initial shock and provoke a strong response, particularly from the police. Adherents are frequently portrayed by older people as 'sub-human' or 'just animals'. Their addiction to drugs is sometimes exaggerated as a major threat to society. As the sub-culture gathers momentum it attracts youth in search of a rebel identity (often merely to irritate their parents). Many, perhaps most, adopt it for fun, conforming to the requirements of conventional society during working hours, and playing at rebellion in their leisure time. Meanwhile, the fashion designers commercialise the look and sell it in the clothes shops. The sub-culture rapidly ceases to express serious dissent, let alone being a threat to society. In the end, of course, it is reduced to yet another street style of urban culture.

Each new sub-culture also blends with existing ones in a kaleidoscope of style. According to one black teacher in south London, 'Unlike any other time I can remember, black and white children in working-class areas are wearing identical kits, of the black groups they idolise.' On the other hand, by the late 1980s many blacks were wearing totally different clothes which had no connection at all with reggae or with black America, but which were Italian 'designer label' suits.

One of the most important and significantly different recent sub-cultures, however, are the New Age Travellers who reject urban life to imitate the traditional Roma, forming small communities and moving around the countryside in caravans, to live a natural and idealised simple life. They are the natural descendants of the 1960s Hippies. Like the Roma, their transient lifestyle has made them very unpopular with local authorities, with the police and with the more conservative elements in the population. From 1985 they were engaged in repeated confrontations with the police who were strongly encouraged by the Conservative government to make life hard for them. The trouble they caused, largely accusations of pilfering and leaving litter, were either untrue or greatly exaggerated. Yet while reviled as 'unwashed scroungers', the New Age Travellers have had a profound influence on the whole country. For their supposedly 'cranky' views about an imperilled ecology and environment acquired growing acceptance in the 1990s as the population at large began to appreciate the madness of destroying countryside for the sake of yet more cars. In the mid-1990s the protest movement against the laying of new main roads was led by 'eco-warriors', of whom the most famous was nicknamed Swampy. These eco-warriors were largely from, or drew their inspiration (and appearance) from, the New Age Travellers. They were completely unimpressed by conventional forms of protest, and adopted unconventional but highly effective ways of drawing public attention to the issues (see p.188). As Polhemus states in his book *Street Styles*, the movement 'has become a model for responsible, creative life in the twenty-first century'.

The culture of sport

Britain was the first country to organise sport as a national activity. In the second half of the nineteenth century it organised and exported a number of games, notably football, rugby football, hockey, lawn tennis, golf and cricket. The initial purpose behind organised sport was to provide an outlet for youthful energies at public schools (see p.152-154). It was generally believed to have character-building qualities for future leaders. But it was not long before local businessmen began to organise football and other sports as recreational activity for their workforces. Football clubs quickly sprang up in towns and cities all over Britain, and football was rapidly taken into working-class culture. The Saturday afternoon match was an occasion which working-class men would attend, supporting their local team.

From the 1960s, however, the character of football (and other national sports) began to change. A fundamental reason was financial. As match attendances dropped, clubs sought external help from sponsorship and advertising. Commercial

Skateboarders have adopted their style from American street culture. Skateboarding is now extremely popular in the parks of most British cities.

companies found this profitable. For example, Cornhill Insurance began to sponsor English 'test' cricket in 1980 at a cost of £4.5 million. Beforehand only 2 per cent of the population had heard of Cornhill, while by 1985 20 per cent had done so, and Cornhill had almost doubled its turnover. The decline in spectators forced club managers to make their sporting events less occasions for local support and more displays of spectacular skill. Football clubs started buying and selling players. In the 1950s football heroes, like Stanley Matthews, remained in their local communities. From the 1960s, many football stars moved into expensive suburbs and displayed their newly acquired wealth. Supporters became

Football is more popular than ever but still has a predominately male appeal.

commercial enterprises soon took an interest and several bought control of particular clubs. In 1996, for example, Leeds United was acquired for over £20 million by a leisure company. By the year 2000 15 clubs will be listed on the stock market for public investment.

Thus the game has radically changed. In 1985 ticket sales were the most important source of revenue. By 1995 sponsorship, television coverage and 'merchandising', the sale of goods with the club logo, were collectively set to eclipse ticket sales. In the space of three years, 1992–95, Manchester United increased the annual value of its merchandising from £2 million to £23.5 million. Players are not only bought and sold for huge sums, but receive enormous payment for their performance. There is a price to be paid. Tension now exists between the great magnates who own football clubs and the fans. As a journalist says of one club which is a good business but a mediocre club, 'something crucial has been sacrificed to make the books balance. The club has misplaced its soul.' If football (and other sports) were not run as business enterprises, they might lose television spectators but enjoy greater local participation. However, even though football has become such a spectator sport, at the end of the twentieth century 1.6 million British were playing it as recreation, more than ever before. It remains a truly national game.

primarily consumers, with no involvement in their club. Few members of the teams they supported were genuinely local people who lived in the same community as their supporters. High transfer fees, the glamorous lives of some players, and the lack of participation in the control of clubs, under-mined the traditional involvement and loyalty of supporters. A process of alienation occurred between supporters and clubs. In the 1980s this alienation led some supporters to demonstrate loyalty through their own action, by invading football pitches and controlling the surrounding streets, inevitably leading to violence.
Meanwhile the football clubs have shifted their priority from simply playing the game to becoming profitable businesses. In 1982 only 12 out of 92 football league clubs in Britain made a profit from spectators. Traditionally the clubs were run by committees usually composed of local people who treated the club as a prestigious hobby. All that changed with the creation of the Premier League in 1992, launched with a lucrative five-year television deal with the BBC and BSkyB. Suddenly there was 15 times as much money. Football had become big business, and immediately began to attract private investors. Multimillionaires and

In 1996 the Rugby Football Union abandoned its amateur status and went professional. As in football, the finance has been revolutionised, with the advent of major sponsorship, backers, and the marketing of merchandise. Investors, as one journalist notes, 'see rugby as part of the changing sociological face of the country as we move deeper into a leisure orientated world'. They look forward to handsome returns on their investment. But what will it do for the game?

Over a century ago, the novelist Anthony Trollope listed the sports 'essentially dear to the English nature'. These included hunting, shooting, rowing and horse racing. He was, of course, referring to the 'gentleman class', which through the public school system established football, rugby and cricket as national games. A class dimension to sport persists. Hunting, rowing and horse racing, because of the expense involved, have remained primarily upper-class pastimes. The Henley Regatta, the high point of the rowing season, Royal Ascot, for horse racing, and polo at Windsor remain pinnacles of the upper-class summer season. Golf is still to some extent financially segregated between exclusive private clubs and

Footballers as stars: Alan Shearer, England captain, receiving a rose from an admirer.

municipal facilities. Football remains essentially lower class, but with a growing middle-class following. In 1996 the Professional Footballers Association could not name a single ex-public schoolboy playing in any of the football leagues. On the other hand, while in Wales rugby has always been a mass game, in England it has always been more socially exclusive, with a very high proportion of ex-public school players. Having gone professional, rugby is bound to become more socially mixed.

Despite these areas of exclusivity, sport remains one of the areas in which members of ethnic minorities have demonstrated their ability in a white-dominated society, particularly in athletics, cricket and soccer. The black footballer, Paul Ince, has captained the English football team and the black sprinter, Linford Christie, was the captain of the British men's Olympic team in both 1992 and 1996.

The arts

The British find discussion of their national artistic and intellectual life faintly embarrassing. As the great British art historian, Nikolaus Pevsner, himself a refugee immigrant, remarked over 30 years ago,

'None of the other nations of Europe has so abject an inferiority complex about its own aesthetic capabilities as England.' This inferiority complex owed much to the rise of the Modern Movement which was so strongly rooted in continental Europe, particularly in France and Germany. Britain, in contrast, tended to cling to nostalgic expression in art and architecture.

Yet Britain today has much to be proud of, though its artistic achievements are frequently better appreciated, and known, abroad than at home. In 1976 the American artist Ron Kitaj argued that there were 'artistic personalities in this small island more unique and strong and, I think, more numerous than anywhere in the world outside America's jolting artistic vigour'. Examples easily come to mind. Henry Moore exhibited more widely than any previous artist. Until his death in 1992, Francis Bacon was frequently described as the greatest living artist. Lucien Freud has been described as 'the greatest living realist painter'. David Hockney has been described by one critic as 'one of the most original and versatile artists of his generation anywhere in the world'. Howard Hodgkin and Carel Weight, too, are possibly as well known abroad as at home. Yet in the 1990s Britain experienced a cultural renaissance not seen since the 1960s. One journalist wrote: 'suddenly

Polo, played almost solely by Britain's small upper class.

we are the arts centre of the universe. How on earth did it happen? No one quite knows and no one is as surprised as we are.' Among the younger talent are artists, like Mona Hatoum, Damien Hirst and Rachel Whiteread, and the gifted architect Zaha Hadid.

As in fashion the British seem to enjoy breaking the rules of the current modernist style, and this perhaps is what gives British art such originality. As one art critic wrote recently, 'British artists, who are currently enjoying the highest international standing, have been singularly unaffected by the much vaunted internationalism of the Modern Movement. English art is perhaps beginning to escape from insularity and provincialism through a rediscovery of its Englishness.'

By the mid-1990s the tide had started to turn against post-modernism with its pastiche, nostalgic qualities, in favour of exciting and innovative buildings. Richard Rogers's proposed Millennium Dome has already been mentioned. Norman Foster, who is still better known abroad than at home, is working on the London Millennium Tower, which promises to be the tallest building in Europe. At the Victoria and Albert Museum a new and shocking extension, 'The Spiral', designed by an American, Daniel Libeskind, is also planned. As Jonathan Glancey tells its critics, 'No, it does not "fit in" with the existing streetscape; but then what exactly is there for an architect to "fit in" with in South Kensington's audacious and gloriously eclectic museum land?'

However, there are areas of the arts in which Britain more confidently excels. British theatre is

The Road Across the Wolds, *(1997), a scene from his native Yorkshire by one of Britain's most famous painters, David Hockney.*

among the liveliest and most innovative in the world. Some would argue that the quality of theatre is a good register of a country's democratic values. For it is on the stage that some of the most painful questions can be asked about the way we live, both as individuals and as a community.

Over 300 commercial theatres operate, 100 of these in London, and about 40 of them in London's famous West End. However, the real vitality of British theatre is to be found less in the West End than in the regional, 'fringe' and pub theatres all over the country. West End theatres are essentially commercial. They stage what will fill the house, which means there is an emphasis on musicals, comedy and other forms of light entertainment. They depend on foreign tourists to fill up to 40 per cent of seats.

Much of the liveliest theatre, however, has grown

out of 'rep', the repertory movement which began in Manchester in 1908, and which experienced a major revival from 1958 when the Belgrade Theatre in Coventry was built, the first new regional theatre for over 20 years. While 'rep' as such is no longer really existent, during the 1960s and 1970s 40 theatres were built, rebuilt or extensively renovated. These theatres, however, did not follow the classical tradition of repertoire, a much repeated cycle of well rehearsed plays, nor offer a menu of uncontroversial light entertainment. Instead they presented seasons of plays, each running for about four to six weeks after which they would not be restaged. Certain theatres have become particularly famous for their presentation of new plays and powerful, sometimes controversial productions of classic ones. Among the better known of these energetic centres of dramatic talent are the Glasgow

Citizen's, the Sheffield Crucible, the West Yorkshire Playhouse in Leeds, the Bristol Old Vic, the Manchester Royal Exchange, in London the Royal Court and the Lyric Hammersmith, and others, too, in Leeds, Liverpool, Nottingham and elsewhere. It is these theatres, rather than those in the West End, which stage most of the best innovative British drama today.

Theatre is a powerful instrument of education as well as art and culture. Another significant feature of British theatre is the way in which actors have taken drama to young people, even into primary schools. This has broken down some of the traditional barriers between formal stage drama and the community.

Much of the excellence of these theatres is a result of the intensive preparation and speed with which productions are staged and their short performance lifespan. Their intensity and freshness is not allowed to grow stale. Another important feature, however, is the youthfulness of many of the best productions. Length of experience in Britain is not allowed to stand in the way of talent,

and as a result young people, some recently from drama school, perform many leading roles.

The theatres already discussed almost all receive some government subsidy, but significantly less than most theatres in continental Europe. Some theatres have been unable to continue, and have closed. Most are forced to mix their more adventurous productions with safer, more commercial productions. Nevertheless, even though British theatre laments the lack of support, inadequate financing creates a permanent sense of tension and hardship in which some of Britain's best drama is staged. Fringe and pub theatre doubled in size during the 1980s, becoming a popular form of less conventional theatre. These theatres, like the Almeida and King's Head in Islington, London, the Bush in Shepherd's Bush, the Battersea Arts Centre, the Donmar Warehouse, and the Orange Tree in Richmond (all in London) operate without subsidy. Many operate in the informality of a room above a pub, seating an audience of only 50 or 70 people, and with the actors often receiving little more than their travelling expenses. Why do actors work for so

The Millennium Dome at Greenwich in London, designed by the Richard Rogers Partnership for a great exhibition in the year 2000.

little or no money? Partly they like to keep in practice in the sometimes long periods between other engagements, but a more serious reason is that many actors can only earn a living in film or television by performing meaningless and unrewarding roles in thrillers and so forth. Many want to perform serious drama. If they cannot do it for a living, they do it when they are free for little or no money. Some do it purely out of artistic commitment, some because it is the only work they can get, and many because they know that many of the best directors visit pub or fringe theatre in search of talent.

Since the 1960s Britain has achieved a special position in music. While Britain's operatic, dance and classical music performances compare well with top international standards, it is in the field of popular music that Britain achieved a particular pre-eminence. Britain remains at the forefront of pop music.

At the start of the 1990s, British pop music seemed to be rediscovering the spirit of the 1960s. Liverpool and London had been the musical powerhouses then, but in the 1990s the new pop generation took root in Manchester's clubland, the birthplace of acid house music. Why Manchester? According to one commentator, 'Large enough to support a culture infrastructure, yet small enough to form a community, the city has fused the styles of Ibiza, Chicago, Detroit and London into something recognisably, tantalisingly, new.' The new music marks a departure from the unrelaxed mood of the 1980s, and is a declaration of freedom. By 1997 easily the most successful Manchester group was Oasis, which consciously likened itself to the Beatles. Its lead performer, Noel Gallagher, hardly noted for his modesty, had this to say: 'When it's all done and dusted, our band will go down in history as one of the greatest of all time.' Other famous bands of the mid-1990s included Blur and Pulp, and also the Welsh bands Super Furry Animals, Manic Street Preachers and Catatonia. Ironically, the greatest danger such groups face is the pressure of success and the destructive media attention which accompanies it. That was the fate awaiting the Spice Girls, who attracted enormous coverage in 1996–98.

In the mid-1990s, a replica of Shakespeare's Globe theatre was built upon the original site.

One of Britain's more modern buildings: the Scottish Exhibition and Conference Centre in Glasgow, designed by Norman Foster and completed in 1997, is reminiscent of the Sydney Opera House.

Culture for the community

On the south bank of the Thames, opposite Whitehall, stands the South Bank Centre, the capital of Britain's cultural life, with three concert halls, the National Theatre (containing three theatres), the National Film Theatre and the Hayward Art Gallery. A 1980s addition is the lively Museum of the Moving Image. The South Bank receives two and a half million paying visitors each year, while many others come to see free exhibitions and use its restaurant facilities. The buildings, by leading architects of the 1950s, 1960s and 1970s, are in the bare and uncompromising concrete so favoured in the period.

On the South Bank one can hear the greatest sounds of classical music, and some of the finest acting in the world. But for artistic vitality one may be more successful in a fringe theatre or pub. For it is the level of popular participation which makes British artistic life so distinctive. All over the country there are millions of people engaged in amateur music, art and theatre. For example, for more than 200 years the Royal Academy in London has held an annual Summer Exhibition, for which any painter or sculptor may enter their work. Each year thousands of works are submitted, but little more than a thousand are actually exhibited. Virtually every town and suburb has some form of amateur music group, a choir, an orchestra or even neighbours who form a string quartet. All over the country there are amateur choral groups, ranging from the local village church choir through to highly selective and internationally known choirs, like the Bach Choir. Then there are all the amateur dramatic groups across the country. There are an estimated 6,500 separate amateur companies, involving roughly 75,000 aspiring actors. Such local activities take place everywhere.

Take Stranraer, as an example, a town with a population of 15,000, on the south-west tip of Scotland. Its amateur drama and opera groups put on a major opera and a play each year, plus a pantomime and one or two minor productions. It has youth choirs based in local schools, a youth brass band and two pipe bands, one for

A juggler at the Edinburgh International Festival where, alongside such street entertainment, the very finest high and radical cultural events are enjoyed each August.

entertainment and one for bagpipe competitions. It also has an annual dance festival. Stranraer may be geographically far from the mainstream of national life, but such activities suggest real community participation.

In many market towns and cities all over Britain, roughly 200 cultural festivals are held each year. The choice of what music or drama to perform may not always be very adventurous, nor the quality very high, but these festivals provide a lively forum in which local people can celebrate not only their own local arts and culture, but also invite visiting performers of national standing. Ludlow, a Shropshire market town with a population of 9,000, for example, started having an annual festival in 1960. It is entirely the result of local initiative and effort. The main event each year is a Shakespearean play staged against the castle walls. Local singers perform in the parish church, and there are cricket matches, jazz bands, string quartets and a fair. Fundamentally, such festivals are really celebrations of community.

People do these things for fun. But there are more serious conclusions to draw. In the words of the Director of the National Theatre, 'The arts help us to make sense of the world, they help us to fit the disparate pieces together; to try to make form out of chaos.'

The National Lottery

Making form out of chaos costs money, whether one is speaking of a voluntary association or a theatrical company. In 1994 the government established a national lottery with the intention of providing substantial funds for what it described as 'good causes'. It appointed a private operator to administer the project. Half the proceeds were to be given away as prizes, but 28 per cent was designated for the 'good causes', divided equally between five fields: sport, charities, the arts, heritage and millennium projects. The British took to the National Lottery with great enthusiasm, with thirty million adults regularly buying tickets, and it rapidly became the largest lottery in the world, with a weekly turnover of at least £80 million. There is a weekly jackpot usually in the order of £10 million, and plenty of smaller prizes. The private operator made enormous profits, proving the British were a nation of gamblers. Over 5,000 projects benefited from £1,200 million available in the first year of operation. The lottery provided great benefits for myriad worthy ventures across the country but some, including the Church, questioned the moral worth of an exercise which stimulated greed.

Further information

WEBSITES

The Design Council — www.design-council.org.uk
Fashion — www.fashionweb.co.uk
National Lottery — www.national-lottery.co.uk
The Arts Council — www.artscouncil.org.uk
The FA Premiership — www.fa-premier.com
Green Net — (website for myriad voluntary organisations and lobby groups) www.gn.apc.org
The National Trust — www.ukindex.co.uk/nationaltrust
Football 365 — www.football365.co.uk
Rugby Football Union — www.rfu.com

PRINTED MATERIAL

Adonis, Andrew and Pollard, Stephen 1997 *A Class Act: The Myth of Britain's Classless Society* Chapter 8 Hamish Hamilton
Bracewell, Michael 1997 *England is Mine: Pop Life in Albion, from Wilde to Goldie* HarperCollins
Haseler, Stephen 1996 *The English Tribe: Identity, Nation and Europe* Macmillan
Hebdige, Dick 1988 *Subculture: The Meaning of Style* Routledge
Hewison, R. 1987 *The Heritage Industry* Methuen
Leonard, Mark 1997 *Britain™: Renewing Our Identity* Demos
Polhemus, Ted 1994 *Street Style: From Side Walk to Catwalk* Thames and Hudson
Wiener, Martin 1985 *English Culture and the Decline of the Industrial Spirit, 1850–1980* Penguin
McKay, George (ed.) 1998 *DIY Culture: Party and Protest in the Nineties* Verso

QUESTIONS

Section analysis

1 **The community and the individual** List eight examples of the type of voluntary activities in which many ordinary British people engage.

2 **The fine distinctions of speech** Some people want to encourage different dialects of English because they admire their richness. Other people think they are socially divisive and should be abandoned. Based on the discussion in the text argue in favour of one point of view.

3 **The rural ideal** Is Britain's nostalgia for life in the countryside beneficial or damaging? State your opinion and support it with evidence from the text. Is there an equivalent nostalgia in your own country?

4 **Dress codes** How does fashion reflect the British character?

5 **Nostalgia and modernity** 'Tradition and creativity are in conflict (in Britain).' Give examples from the text to support this view.

6 **Urban sub-cultures** Why do young people join sub-cultures? What sub-cultures exist in your own country?

7 **The culture of sport** In what ways has the character of football as a national sport changed in the last 40 years?

8 **The arts** Why are many of the best British theatrical productions to be found in the smallest theatres?

9 **Culture for the community** What, if anything, strikes you as distinctive about artistic life in Britain?

Chapter analysis and discussion

1 William Beveridge remarked that the vigour and abundance of voluntary action 'are the distinguishing marks of a free society'. Do you agree? Is it true of Britain? Is it true of your country? Give reasons for your opinions.

2 British society is strongly individualistic. Find examples of the ways in which this individualism is expressed in the following areas: dress; urban sub-cultures; the theatre; and voluntary activities.

3 The National Lottery provides much-needed financial help to many 'good causes'. Should one, therefore, be concerned by the claim that it encourages personal greed and a gambling habit?

Textual interpretation

Consider the following four quotations. How far do they complement each other? Can you find evidence from the chapter to support the views they express?

Britain has finally rediscovered the stylishness and excitement of the Swinging Sixties, at least according to foreigners … The buzz, exemplified by the present London Fashion Week, is attracting a new type of visitor, interested not only in Big Ben and Shakespeare country but the club scene, street markets and a cool urban style previously associated with Paris or New York.

(Louise Jurer and Simon Calder, *The Independent*)

This culture – the culture of tradition – was expressed in emblems such as the telephone box, tall policeman's helmet and red London bus. These symbols were unique; yet any expression of regret at their passing is regarded as laughable. Foreign visitors must think we are mad.

(Clive Aslet, *Country Life*)

Rather than striking out in a new direction of their own, today's teenagers are characterised by a lack of interest in anything outside the parameters determined by the need to get a job … Far from subscribing to the celebrated axiom of hippie youth – 'never trust anyone over 30' – today's teenagers are rather keen on taking the advice of their parents.

(Paul Vallely and Glenda Cooper, *The Independent*)

There are two things that London girls have going for them that I don't think you find anywhere else in Europe. First she's got this quirky English style which is so easy for photographers and editors to visualise in the pages of a magazine. The other thing is that England is such a melting pot, you get more mixed backgrounds and more interesting looks.

(Tyler Brule, *The Independent on Sunday*)

9 The importance of not being English

A Canadian recently touring Britain discovered, in his own words, 'There's no such thing as the British, only English, Irish, Welsh and Scots.' Ethnic minority communities apart, there is considerable truth in his remark. The sense of difference is more than 1,000 years old and dates from when Anglo-Saxon invaders from the European continent drove the Celtic people out of what we now call England and into what we now call Ireland, Scotland and Wales. In fact, almost one in five of today's British is not English.

The English habit of considering Wales and Scotland to be extensions of England is an old one. In the sixteenth century William Shakespeare spoke of England as 'This royal throne of kings, this scepter'd isle', even though much of this isle was not English. Since 1945 there has been a growing dislike in the Celtic countries of the habit of defining the 'island race' as English, a growing sense of difference, and a desire to have more control over their own affairs. The English, for their part, have sometimes felt resentful that, as the wealthiest member of the United Kingdom, England subsidises the others.

Northern Ireland

Nowhere has the sense of conflict with the English been stronger than in Northern Ireland, where the population is composed of Protestants and Catholics. The Protestants do not feel English, though some would call themselves British and almost all claim Ulster (as most Protestants prefer to call Northern Ireland) as an integral part of Britain. They are known as 'Unionists' or 'Loyalists', a more militant term implying support for a paramilitary group. The Catholic population feels more Irish than British and most, calling themselves Nationalists, would prefer to be more clearly separate from Britain, or at any rate with closer links with the Irish Republic. Some call themselves Republican, implying support for Sinn Fein (pronounced 'shin fayn') and the IRA (the Irish Republican Army). Today there are approximately 900,000 Protestants and 680,000

The haunting beauty of the coastline of Northern Ireland's County Antrim: White Park Bay.

Catholics in Northern Ireland. There are 3.5 million Irish south of the border, in the Republic, with whom many Catholics feel an affinity. Both communities, and the people of the Republic, have felt great frustration with British policy.

England's involvement with Ireland has been an unhappy one. English adventurers colonised parts of Ireland over 800 years ago. In the sixteenth century England brought Ireland under systematic rule. When England became Protestant, Ireland did not. In order to strengthen its hold on the most rebellious part, Ulster, London encouraged English and Scottish Protestant settlers, or 'Planters'. These took the best land and soon outnumbered the indigenous people of Ulster. The English deliberately tried to destroy Irish language, culture and Catholicism.

Inspired by the American and French Revolutions, the Irish began their long struggle to be free. The majority of Protestants, particularly in Ulster, reacted to this struggle by forming the Orange Order, a solidarity association of 'lodges', or branches. The title refers to the Dutch Protestant, William of Orange, who seized the English throne from the Catholic King James II in 1688, and who defeated an Irish rebellion at the River Boyne in 1690.

The Irish finally forced England to concede independence in 1921. Ulster's Protestants warned that they would fight rather than be part of a Catholic-dominated Irish state. Partly to avoid that risk, but also because of its strong political and economic interests in Ulster, London persuaded the Irish to accept independence with the exception of six of the nine counties of historic Ulster where the Protestants were 67 per cent of the population.

London allowed the Northern Irish to govern themselves, wishing to benefit economically while being rid of the 'Irish problem'. It was a profoundly short-sighted arrangement, and neglected the fact that every generation since the Planters had seen outbreaks of sectarian violence. Northern Ireland became controlled by a Protestant oligarchy. Every election for the Northern Irish government at Stormont was about Ulster's future – whether it should remain part of the United Kingdom. The Protestants excluded the Catholic minority from political power, gerrymandering the electoral system when necessary. They also excluded them from local government and exercised gross discrimination in housing and employment. London ignored these glaring abuses of basic rights.

With the decline of shipbuilding in the early 1960s, Northern Ireland became one of the poorest parts of the United Kingdom. The poverty was not equally shared. Catholics were significantly disadvantaged and their anger grew. In the autumn of 1968 Catholics, supported by many Protestants, demonstrated on the streets, demanding civil rights, basically fair participation in political and economic life. Ulster Loyalists confronted them and the police, who were overwhelmingly Protestant, failed to act impartially or keep order. The violence soon resulted in deaths, some caused by the police, but most by paramilitary groups that rapidly grew in each community. The IRA, a small fringe group in 1968, sought to persuade Catholics that the issue was not civil rights but national self-determination. Many Loyalists were suspicious that Britain intended to weaken the Protestant hold on the Province and formed two main groups, the Ulster Defence Association and the Ulster Volunteer Force.

A Loyalist mural invokes Ulster's past defenders.

A Nationalist mural charged with heroic emotion.

At first there was popular sympathy in Britain for the Catholic population, in view of the grossly unfair system in Northern Ireland. When Loyalist riots persuaded London to deploy the army in the summer of 1969, many hoped that this action and popular sympathy in Britain would reassure the Catholic population. But the honeymoon did not last long, and the disorders increased with a disastrous chemistry at work. Stormont was too slow in introducing the necessary reforms, the security forces acted heavy-handedly, thus acquiring a reputation for brutal behaviour. Then London introduced internment without trial, aimed at crushing the IRA. It probably did more to alienate the Catholic population than any other single act. It accelerated a rapid erosion of civil rights at the very moment when such rights urgently needed to be affirmed.

In January 1972 British troops shot dead 13 unarmed demonstrators. 'Bloody Sunday' confirmed in many minds that Britain was basically hostile to the Catholic community, especially when an official enquiry exonerated those responsible. It was a gift to the revived IRA, known at the time as the Provisionals or 'Provos'. Later that year the Stormont government was suspended and the province brought under direct rule from London. This was a victory for the Catholic population, since it was now free from rule by Ulster Unionists. The IRA now concentrated on its main aim, to drive 'the Brits' out of Ireland altogether. Almost 500 people died in 1972 as a result of sectarian violence. Troop violence and confrontations, IRA bombs, sectarian killings, and intercommunal tension leading to the flight of minority groups from mixed areas all helped to make the ordeal appear intractable.

A British soldier patrols past a Republican demonstration.

The IRA evolved from a fringe group into a sophisticated fighting force able to sustain their war almost indefinitely. They also established a political wing, Sinn Fein, which would accept nothing short of a united Ireland. Nationalist splinter groups also formed, and there were short periods of killings between them. However, the majority of Catholics supported the Social Democratic Labour Party (SDLP), seeking a united Ireland only by non-violent democratic process.

On the Protestant side the Ulster Unionist Party (UUP) had always dominated the Unionist position. But it faced competition when a Presbyterian minister, Dr Ian Paisley, formed the Democratic Unionist Party (DUP), which was strongly anti-Catholic. Later on, two smaller parties formed, the Progressive Unionist Party (PUP) and the Ulster Democratic Party (UDP), both close to the Loyalist paramilitaries. This left the Unionists fragmented.

While the IRA was determined that Ulster should become part of the Republic, Loyalists resisted any measure that allowed the Catholics to share power, or implied recognition of Dublin's interest in the fate of Ulster. Unionists had understandable reasons for hostility to Dublin. Constitutionally the Irish Republic claimed the Province as its own: 'The national territory consists of the whole island of Ireland.' Furthermore, the Catholic Church, which many Unionists find repugnant, was highly influential in the affairs of the Republic.

From 1972 until 1985 London tried to foster the middle ground among the peaceable majority of both communities. But its efforts were undermined by the ease with which hard-liners could outflank the more conciliatory politicians, playing upon sectarian fears or pointing to British incompetence and duplicity. By 1985 London had abandoned its 'middle ground' policy. Nothing showed the weakness of the middle ground more clearly than the fortunes of the Alliance Party, committed to a non-partisan formula of reconciliation and full civil rights. It never attracted more than 10 per cent of the vote and by 1997 attracted less than 7 per cent.

The position of the Dublin government was not easy either. It naturally felt compelled to be supportive to the Catholic community, especially in the early days when dispossessed Catholic families fled in their hundreds to the border. It repeatedly criticised British policy and practice, in particular its wrongful imprisonment of innocent people, its physical and psychological abuse of arrested Republican suspects, and an undeclared (and denied) shoot-to-kill policy in security operations. Yet it also felt caught between its historical aspiration for a united Ireland, and reluctance to inherit either the sectarian conflict or a Protestant population deeply hostile to Irish rule. Any prospect of Britain abandoning Northern Ireland posed a political and economic nightmare for Dublin, but one it could hardly admit to.

London had grounds for irritation with Dublin, though on a lesser scale. It was angry at the apparent unwillingness of Dublin to hand over some terrorist suspects. There was also a feeling that Dublin only became cooperative after the Republic had experienced the unpleasant impact of a few Loyalist bombs. London resented the ease of Irish criticism when it faced a situation where the choice of what to do lay less between right and wrong than between bad and worse, and because of the huge financial cost of the situation. It also, perhaps, was expressing the prickliness of historic guilt.

However London and Dublin recognised a growing need to cooperate politically. In 1981 several IRA prisoners went on hunger strike to obtain political status. Thatcher refused to concede, and several strikers, most famously Bobby Sands, died. Thatcher's perceived stubbornness and their martyrdom created widespread sympathy that Sinn Fein had not before enjoyed. Sinn Fein now participated in elections, receiving one-third of the Nationalist vote. The lack of political progress by London slowly made Sinn Fein more popular with the Nationalist community, particularly young people who preferred its assertive message to the democratic and more conciliatory approach of the SDLP. Fear of growing support for Sinn Fein and frustration at Unionist refusal to allow power sharing or other meaningful compromise with the Catholic community persuaded the British government to negotiate an agreement with Dublin. By this stage Dublin's sympathy for the Nationalists was mixed with a vehement dislike of IRA violence and a reluctant recognition of the need for British troops to keep order in the Province.

The Anglo–Irish Agreement of 1985 sent a deliberate message to the IRA and to the Unionists: 'If in the future a majority of the people of Northern Ireland clearly wish for and formally consent to the establishment of a united Ireland, they (the London and Dublin governments) will introduce and support in the respective parliaments legislation to give effect to that wish.' London was thus no longer determined to keep Northern Ireland in the United Kingdom if a majority of its people wished it to become part of

a united Ireland, but Dublin was willing to abandon its claim to Ulster until its people were themselves ready for union. This weakened the position of the IRA/Sinn Fein, which argued for immediate withdrawal of British troops and unification with the south, and that of the Unionists, by warning them that Dublin had a legitimate interest in the Province which justified formal consultation.

In the late 1980s quiet developments took place on the Nationalist side. Sinn Fein's leader, Gerry Adams, became increasingly sceptical that IRA terrorism could eject Britain from the Province. It was increasingly apparent that neither the IRA nor the British government could defeat the other. Terrorist violence was now counterproductive. But it was difficult for Adams to persuade the IRA, fearful of appearing to surrender, that diplomacy might be more fruitful. In the meantime, the SDLP's leader, John Hume, despite his horror at IRA violence, became convinced that without Sinn Fein's involvement any possible peace discussions would prove ineffectual. In 1988 he began secret talks with Adams with a view to achieving a shared approach, one that fell short of Sinn Fein's final aim of Irish reunification, but which could be seen as a staging post on the road to a truly democratic province no longer subject to British dictation. Both men required great political skill in order to persuade their respective parties of the wisdom of what they were doing. Hume also worked closely with Dublin in the belief that together they might persuade London to show enough flexibility to obtain an IRA cease-fire.

London's ability to take a bold initiative was fatally compromised by the general election of 1992 which left the government with a slim majority. It was the Conservatives who had originally ensured that the six counties were excepted from Irish self-determination. There were still Tory MPs determined to frustrate any weakening of the Union, quite apart from the Unionist MPs. Thus, when the government announced in 1993 that it sought all-party talks on the basis of 'no predetermined outcome except the right of the Northern Ireland people to democratic self-determination' it found its position in the Commons threatened by both Tory and Unionist MPs.

In December 1993 Dublin finally secured London's agreement to a conciliatory joint governmental statement that 'it was their aim to foster agreements and reconciliation, leading to a new political framework founded on consent and encompassing arrangements within Northern

David Trimble, the leader of the Ulster Unionist Party.

Gerry Adams, the leader of Sinn Fein.

John Hume, the leader of the Nationalist SDLP.

Ian Paisley, leader of the Democratic Unionist Party.

Ireland, for the whole island, and between these islands'. The intention of the 'Downing Street Declaration' was to persuade the IRA to announce a cease-fire. However, both Sinn Fein and the DUP rejected the statement, while the IRA continued its bombing activities. In resisting this overture the IRA was now widely perceived as the single greatest obstacle to peace talks.

In August 1994 the IRA finally announced a cease-fire, an acknowledgement of growing pressure for peace within Republican ranks. A wave of euphoria swept across the Province. In October the two main Loyalist paramilitary groups also announced a cease-fire. US President Bill Clinton visited Belfast, putting the US seal of approval on the forthcoming process. London needed to use this cease-fire to get talks started. It had made a cessation of violence the only precondition to talks. However, as a result of Unionist pressure on its slim majority in the Commons it now demanded that the IRA 'decommission' its weapons as a sign that the cease-fire was permanent. The IRA viewed this as a demand for a symbolic surrender and refused. Neither side gave way, and the IRA continued to recruit and prepare for a resumption of war. An international commission, established under US leadership and headed by US Senator George Mitchell, worked unsuccessfully to break the impasse. Under strong Unionist pressure, London refused to agree to a proposal to start the decommissioning process *after* the commencement of talks.

In early 1996 the IRA abandoned its cease-fire and resumed its bombing campaign. Its most spectacular explosion caused £500 million worth of damage in London's Docklands. The targeting was deliberate. Many Republicans were convinced that, in the words of one man, 'The only time the Brits listen to us is when we give them grief. 'The IRA kept Northern Ireland high on Britain's political agenda but the Tory government was too weak and too beholden to the Unionists in the Commons to be capable of transacting negotiations. Everyone awaited the expected new Labour government.

Within five weeks of his election victory Blair conceded to Sinn Fein the unmet demands on which the cease-fire had foundered: guaranteed entry to peace talks six weeks after a renewal of the cease-fire, a brisk timetable for negotiations beginning in September and ending in May 1998, and the abandonment of prior decommissioning as an entry qualification. But Blair also warned that peace talks would not be delayed for Sinn Fein if it could not persuade the IRA to abandon violence.

Sinn Fein and the IRA accepted Blair's challenge and announced a new cease-fire. They knew that the Nationalists of the Province were, like the Unionists, sick of a war that could not be won. Now every party felt the challenge, whether or not to participate in difficult discussions based on the idea that the existing constitutional status of the Province was most unlikely to change in the short

Mo Mowlem, Britain's able Northern Ireland Secretary with John Hume and Gerry Adams.

term, but allowing for the possibility of future democratic change, and attempting within that framework to identify an acceptable form of executive government by the people of the Province. On the Unionist side, the DUP refused to do so, and the UUP expressed great reluctance. Remarkably, it was the smaller parties representing the Loyalist paramilitaries which were most willing to negotiate.

The negotiations proved extremely difficult. Both Nationalists and Unionists held to cherished principles regarding the solution they sought. In addition, both Republican and Loyalist paramilitaries carried out killings, leading to the temporary exclusion of their political representatives from the negotiations, until they pledged themselves once again committed to the process. With symbolism for the devout among both the Catholic and Protestant communities, a peace plan was finally agreed by the leaders of the participating parties on Good Friday, 10 April 1998.

The key points of the agreement were:
1 the establishment of a Northern Ireland assembly, composed of 109 members elected by proportional representation, with an executive committee of 12 members, thereby ensuring cross-community representation at both levels.
2 the assembly to have the power to legislate, with its first task to establish a North-South ministerial council to develop cooperation on all-island and cross-border issues.
3 the amendment by the government of Ireland of those articles of its constitution which laid claim to the six counties, and the replacement by the London government of the 1920 Government of Ireland Act which established the separate status of the six counties. These measures thus render both governments agnostic concerning the future.
4 the establishment of a Council of the Isles, as a forum for discussion of issues of interest to the South and North of Ireland, England, Scotland and Wales, and possibly even the Isle of Man and the Channel Islands which already enjoy their own governments for internal affairs.

Inevitably, reaching agreement proved extremely stressful for both Gerry Adams of Sinn Fein and David Trimble, leader of the Ulster Unionist Party. Both succeeded in persuading the majority of the respective parties to support the deal. Yet many also rejected it. On the Republican side, the IRA refused to 'decommission' its weapons, while three splinter groups, the Irish National Liberation Army (INLA), Continuity IRA and the Real IRA, decided to continue the armed struggle, as they described their actions. In August 1998 the Real IRA detonated a bomb in Omagh, a mixed town in County Tyrone, killing 29 people mainly women and children. It was the worst single outrage since the 'Troubles' began in 1969. In addition Dr Paisley's Democratic Unionist Party and the 60,000-strong Orange Order both rejected the agreement. In a referendum in May 1998 71 per cent of the people of Northern Ireland supported the peace agreement. While Catholics

The so-called 'Peace Wall' was constructed to keep the warring Protestant and Catholic inhabitants of West Belfast apart.

overwhelmingly voted in favour, however, only very slightly more than half the Protestants did so. For the very first time, however, Catholics felt they belonged to a majority viewpoint. (In the Republic over 90 per cent supported the agreement.) In the Assembly elections one month later, the pro-agreement vote slightly increased. The result for the main parties was: the UUP 28 seats, the SDLP 24, Dr Paisley's (anti-agreement) DUP 20 seats and Sinn Fein 18. David Trimble of the UUP was appointed First Minister of the new Northern Ireland Executive, with Seamus Mallon of the SDLP as his deputy. However, the UUP was deeply split and Trimble's political credibility seemed likely to come under greater pressure within the Unionist community over the participation of Sinn Fein in the Executive.

Even with a majority, led by the political parties, now committing themselves to peace, it is inevitable that factions on both sides will continue the conflict. So long as the troubles continue, the combined cost to both governments will probably be about £500 million each year. Furthermore, there is an estimated loss of a similar sum in terms of potential business and tourism in the Province, let alone the potential to create an estimated 20,000 jobs.

Behind the historical record, social and economic factors continue to influence events. One of the most important of these has been the voluntary and involuntary segregation of the two communities. Within a year of the outbreak of the troubles, walls and wire-mesh fences were erected to separate the warring communities. Mixed communities separated as the pressures of sectarian identity outweighed individual neighbourliness. In many cases mixed areas became battlegrounds for the youths of both groups. Many threatened families and individuals fled their homes out of fear, a process still happening in 1997, making intercommunity reconciliation much harder. However, much of the segregation is also voluntary. Where Catholics become a majority, for example in Derry and also central Belfast, Protestants tend to leave, feeling more secure in still predominantly Protestant areas. Yet housing in mixed middle-class areas of Belfast is in great demand by both communities.

Education has always been segregated, and barely 10 per cent of children attend integrated schools. Much of the resistance to integration has been because the Catholic Church has strong views regarding education. Yet generally speaking Catholic children tend to perform more poorly than their Protestant counterparts. Integration might remove this difference, thereby improving parity of career opportunity. As importantly, if Catholics and Protestants do not learn to relate to each other creatively as children, they are almost bound to develop and perpetuate entrenched sectarian loyalties. Continued segregation militates against forging a spirit of reconciliation. According to opinion polls, more than half of both communities believe that integrated schooling and residential areas should be encouraged by government. But what most people wish and what they do remains in contradiction.

The Orange Order marching at Drumcree in 1998.

Another crucial factor has been the high level of unemployment, affecting the Catholic community most. In 1976 London legislated against employment discrimination. Within the public sector (apart from the security forces) Catholics are now proportionately represented. The police force remains 92 per cent Protestant. But in the private sector the situation reflects continuing disparity. Progress can be slow. Unemployment remains about twice as high among Catholics than among Protestants. In 1995 unemployment stood at 18 per cent for Catholics and 8 per cent for Protestants, but male unemployment revealed a sharper disparity, 23 per cent for Catholics and 9 per cent for Protestants.

Unemployment in both communities has a political as well as an economic consequence. Young men with few prospects, little education and peer group or gender pressure are the easiest to recruit into paramilitary forces. In the words of one young man, 'In riots, people say you're a coward if you wouldn't throw a brick.' Throwing stones or bricks becomes meaningful in terms of male identity. Some start as early as eight or nine years old.

July each year has become a moment of tension, when the 'lodges' (or local branches) of the Orange Order organise parades to celebrate the Battle of the Boyne. Some of these marches go through Catholic areas. What Orangemen see as a celebration of community identity, Catholics see as an unacceptable humiliation and provocation. They expect government to protect their rights as a minority, but the Orangemen assert their right to march 'the Queen's highway', as a form of freedom of assembly. If thwarted, they can create enough disorder to bring Northern Ireland to a virtual standstill. That is what they did in 1996 when the government tried to reroute the first march of the season to avoid the Catholic Garvaghy Road at Drumcree, near Portadown. The government gave way. Nationalists were furious. In 1997, having failed to obtain any form of compromise from community leaders, the government again allowed the Drumcree march to go down the Garvaghy Road. It believed that, if frustrated, the Loyalists planned a wave of sectarian killings. This decision caused great Nationalist bitterness and rioting. The government used this anger to warn the Orange Order that it was unable to police all its planned marches sufficiently, and that the Order risked unrestrained and unpoliced civil conflict. This held severe political, economic and social consequences, and the Orange Order decided to reroute its more contentious marches. Growing recognition of the great damage these marches inflict on the whole

community may lead to their modification. It was a senior Orangeman who admitted of the Loyalist rioting in the 1996 Drumcree crisis, 'For 26 years the IRA bombed us and for 26 years the people were defiant and stood up to them. But today the country's being ruined: we're going to lose tourists; our businesses are failing; it's bad for everybody. It is worse than all the damage the IRA has done.' (David McKittrick, *The Independent*) However, until the Orange marchers and Catholic residents can agree mutually acceptable ground rules for marches, July each year will remain a very tense time. In July 1998 the Orangemen were forbidden to march down the Garvaghy Road at Drumcree. A major trail of strength, clearly also about the new political settlement, seemed inevitable. However, the savage killing of three young Catholic children living in a Protestant area caused a major crisis of confidence within Orange ranks, and many deserted them. This crisis may prove decisive in undermining the long-term influence of the Orange Order.

While political leaders struggle to find a mutually acceptable and durable political settlement, another dynamic is at work. Less than a decade ago the higher Catholic birth rate seemed offset by higher Catholic emigration, and any decisive demographic change seemed half a century away. That equation has radically changed, although at first this was unnoticed. In fact the Catholic population has increased from 34 per cent in 1969 to approximately 43 per cent by the early 1990s. The Catholic population is also significantly younger, and 52 per cent of under-16-year-olds in the Province are now Catholic. Meanwhile the Protestant community is ageing, with over 30 per cent of them over the age of 70. Part of this accelerating change has been caused by the relatively recent flight of the young Protestant middle class to England, for both work and also for university study, after which few return. Queen's University once had a substantial Protestant majority. Today, however, Catholics form 65 per cent of the student body.

The shifting balance is already evident from election results. Sixty per cent of the territory of the Province, virtually all the territory west of Lough Neagh, is now under Nationalist (SDLP or SF) control. Protestants tend to move eastwards. But they have also lost local government control of two traditional bastions of Unionism, Londonderry (Derry) and Belfast. Protestants have a sense of diminishing political power. This may partly explain Loyalist sectarian killings and also the assertiveness of the Orange Order marches, a form of defiance as electoral power slowly drains away.

Today Catholics feel more confident. In the words of the 1993 Opsahl Report, published by an international commission which investigated the feelings and aspirations of the ordinary people of Northern Ireland, 'The Catholic political future is vibrant, active, with a dynamic civil society – they have, for example, a profusion of political groups. The Protestant community, by comparison, is apolitical. Outside the public life of the churches, civil society barely exists.' Indeed, the Protestant community faces critical weakness. It is used to civic passivity because political and institutional authority has always been mainly Protestant. The shifting electoral balance demands strong Unionist leadership, if it is to secure the Unionists' best interests in any settlement. Yet they lack an outstanding political leader, lack a vision beyond clinging onto membership of the United Kingdom, and lack unity. The Unionist parties are distracted from these crucial issues by inter-party rivalry. David Trimble may prove able to provide the leadership the Unionists have previously lacked.

If the Catholic population was openly determined upon integration with the Republic, Unionists might have greater grounds for fear. However, it is uncertain what the Catholic majority really wants. Catholic opinion has always been a spectrum from those concerned solely with civil rights to those wanting union with the Republic. This ambivalence about a desirable outcome also exists in the Republic. It is also true that the decline in influence of the Catholic Church in the Republic makes the idea of a united Ireland seem less threatening to most Protestants than it did. Thus, while remaining part of the United Kingdom for the time being, an increasing degree of Irishness is more acceptable than it once was. Given the way in which the European Union has developed, the way forward may be for a political entity independent of, but in close relationship with, both the United Kingdom and also the Republic.

Wales

Wales was conquered by the English 700 years ago and incorporated into a single political and administrative system with England in the sixteenth century. However, the Welsh sense of difference survived. A cultural self-consciousness was awakened in the mid-nineteenth century, through a revival of literature in Welsh and the literary and music festivals, eisteddfods, for which Wales became famous. It was also awakened through higher education which emphasised Welsh identity. From 1900 onwards identity was also expressed through rugby football, which became a sport of national importance.

Welsh society in the nineteenth century was divided between the dominant Anglo–Welsh culture of the rich land-owning class, and the culture of the ordinary, mainly Welsh-speaking people. Dissent from the Anglo–Welsh and from mainstream English life has remained a vital aspect of Welsh identity. Until the Second World War its religious expression was through 'non-conformism', attendance at Methodist and Baptist chapels rather than at Anglican churches. Political dissent was expressed through support for Labour.

Rugby is still the national game of Wales, but the team no longer dominates the rugby world.

Mining communities were once a vital element in Welsh culture. However, most of the coal mines were closed in the 1980s.

There had been a short-lived autonomy campaign in the 1890s which shrank, and did not revive again until the 1960s, when there was growing disappointment with both the Conservatives and Labour on account of the recession which hit the industrial region in South Wales. Between 1957 and 1959 23 Welsh coal mines stopped production. The closure of mines led to a collapse of valley communities. In the words of one Welsh historian: 'The neighbourliness of old communities gave way to the alien impersonality of housing estates or commuter suburbs. Much of the vital culture of the Welsh heartland disappeared with them.' One veteran nationalist wrote in 1968, 'We Welsh are not just being denied self-expression as a nation today … we are fighting in the last ditch for our very identity.'

The London government responded by delegating some administrative responsibility, with the appointment in 1964 of a Secretary of State for Wales. It also used the Royal Family as a symbol of British unity. In 1969 Prince Charles was invested as Prince of Wales at a ceremony in Caernarfon Castle. The ceremony had been invented in 1911 to channel Welsh national feeling back to loyalty to the United Kingdom. The castle, however, had been built by the English King Edward I in his conquest of the Welsh, and inside its walls he had proclaimed his own baby son Prince of Wales in 1284. Not surprisingly, some Welsh found the ceremony symbolic of English rule, not Welsh identity.

The following year Plaid Cymru, the Welsh National Party founded in 1925, attracted 11 per cent of the Welsh vote and won three parliamentary seats in the 1974 election. Yet when asked by referendum in 1979 whether they wanted the proposed legislative devolution and the creation of a Welsh Assembly in Cardiff, the Welsh overwhelmingly rejected it – only 11.8 per cent were for it, and 46.5 per cent against. Plaid Cymru lost credibility and declined in popularity as a result. However, during the 1980s closures in both the coal and steel industries resumed and deep alienation from the Conservative government took place. In 1987 the Conservatives won only eight out of the 38 Welsh seats and appointed Englishmen as Welsh Secretaries of State. They lost two more seats in 1992, and lost the remaining six in 1997. Plaid Cymru won and kept four seats, but remained confined to the rural periphery.

Labour dominates Wales politically. As part of its strategy for devolved government, in 1997 Labour held a referendum in Wales on the proposed establishment of an elected Welsh assembly. This time the vote was in favour, but only by a fraction and only 50 per cent of the electorate bothered to vote. Nevertheless, the assembly will be formed. It will have 40 directly elected members using the traditional FPTP system, and 20 additional members elected by PR. The Welsh Assembly, to be located in Cardiff, will not be a law-making body, but will enjoy the powers already delegated by Westminster to the Secretary of State for Wales.

There are only 2.9 million Welsh, and they have struggled to maintain their identity in the second half of the twentieth century. They have had to do this not only against the political might of London but also the erosion of Welsh culture through English radio and television. Take, for example, the use of the Welsh language. At the end of the nineteenth century over 50 per cent still spoke Welsh as their first language. Since then the decline has been dramatic:

Speakers of Welsh as a first language	
1911	44 per cent
1931	37 per cent
1951	28 per cent
1971	20 per cent
1991	19 per cent

Because of fears that the language might disappear completely, Welsh language study has become compulsory in Welsh schools, and there is now Welsh medium radio and television. As a result 19 per cent still use Welsh, mainly in the north west and mid-Wales and many more over a wide area now understand it. The survival of the Welsh language is the most notable way in which the Welsh keep their special identity.

The cultural divide between Anglo–Welsh and Welsh Wales a century ago has been replaced by new divides (see map):
1 'Welsh-speaking Wales', those parts of western Wales which still retain the Welsh language as a living culture. It is only in Welsh-speaking Wales that Plaid Cymru candidates have been elected to Westminster.
2 'Radical Wales', the southern industrial valleys of Wales, where Welsh is no longer spoken but Welsh identity is still expressed through dissent, by voting for Labour within the wider context of Britain.
3 'English Wales', the far south-west tip (Pembrokeshire) and a broad belt of Wales adjacent to England, which have been heavily settled by the English, and where about half the population no longer think of themselves as Welsh. It is only in English Wales that the Conservative Party remains a significant political force.

In the 1997 referendum, 'Welsh-speaking' and 'Radical' Wales tended to vote for devolution while 'English' Wales voted mainly against. In that sense Wales remains a divided country.

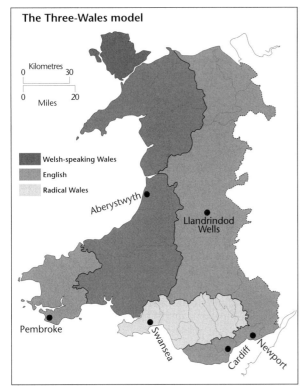

The Three-Wales model

Kilometres
0   30

0   20
Miles

- Welsh-speaking Wales
- English
- Radical Wales

Aberystwyth

Llandrindod Wells

Pembroke

Swansea

Cardiff   Newport

Welsh nationalism remains essentially a cultural movement. The language, eisteddfods, male-voice choirs, chapel attendance and rugby football were all traditional symbols of Welsh identity and pride. Yet apart from the language and rugby football the rest have either disappeared or are in rapid decline, leaving high unemployment and low morale in much of southern Wales. Yet Wales attracts more foreign investment than most other parts of Britain, and is largely free of English class consciousness. In the words of Martin Skipton of the newspaper *Wales on Sunday*: 'People in Wales don't have the same sort of deference you might get among the middle classes in, say, south-east England toward people regarded as higher up the scale.' Yet a new élite has emerged, a highly educated Welsh-speaking élite, nicknamed the Crachach ('upstarts' or 'snobs') who are resented by many Welsh who speak only English. In the words of the Welsh film maker Karl Francis, 'the Welsh-speaking mafia exclude English-speaking Welsh people: they don't want us in Wales. The Welsh-speaking mafia regards the culture heritage as being its own property.' However, for both groups it is difficult to resist the waves of homogeneous culture from England and further afield, and many Welsh have a sense of retreat.

Scotland

Scotland has stronger feelings than Wales about its overbearing neighbour, yet it was never conquered by England. But English attacks were so bad that in 1320 the Scottish clergy declared: 'For as long as even one hundred of us remain alive, we shall never consent to subject ourselves to the dominion of the English.' Scottish nationalism was born. In fact, when the English Queen Elizabeth I died childless in 1603, the Scottish king James VI inherited the English throne. London was politically and economically more powerful than Edinburgh, and he and his successors ruled from London, effectively becoming English. In 1707 England and Scotland were formally united as Great Britain. The government in London insisted on this union for political reasons, and the Scots could not refuse for economic reasons. The Scottish Parliament was suspended, and the new Parliament of Great Britain assembled in Westminster.

After 1707 Scotland kept three distinctive institutions: its own legal and education systems and its own church, or 'Kirk', the Presbyterian Church of Scotland. All three are important symbols of national identity. In part they reflect Scotland's closer relationship to continental Europe. Scottish law is discussed in Chapter 4. The Scottish universities were closer to the European model, and still have a four- rather than three-year undergraduate course.

However, the most important of Scotland's distinctive institutions is the Kirk, which is closely identified with national feeling. This is because of its role in national life since the Reformation in the late sixteenth century. The Kirk at that time insisted that all adults in Scotland should be literate, so as to read the Bible themselves. This laid the foundations for strong educational and democratic traditions. The head of the Kirk, or Moderator, is still elected by the General Assembly each year. The Kirk never allowed the monarch to interfere in the life of the Kirk or to become its head as happened in England. Even in a secular age, the Kirk remains an important focus for national feeling. Approximately 20 per cent of Scots are practising members of the Church of Scotland.

The thought of England unites Scotland, but the image of Scotland as one nation can be misleading. Scotland 'has no unity except upon the map' the nineteenth-century Scottish novelist, Robert Louis Stevenson, wrote. 'Two languages, many dialects, innumerable forms of piety, and countless local patriotisms and prejudices,' he

Scotland's capital, Edinburgh, is one of the most beautiful cities of Europe. The castle dominates the city's skyline.

continued, 'part us among ourselves more widely than the extreme east and west of that great continent of America.'

Even allowing for some exaggeration, there indeed is a big cultural as well as geographical divide between the Lowlands and Highlands. The Lowlanders are thought of as quiet, moral and hard-working, the Highlanders as exuberant, carefree and unreliable. If there is some truth in this, it is to be seen in another division, that between Scotland's two great and rival cities, Edinburgh and Glasgow. In the words of one writer, 'For all her elegance and lofty-mindedness, Edinburgh is a reserved, plain, cautious and thrifty city. She is more Lowland, in these respects, than Highland. Glasgow is ... an expansive, extravagant, romantic, less tight-laced city.' Edinburgh thrives as Scotland's capital, as the venue for the world-famous festival, and because it is the most handsome city in Britain. Glasgow, despite its exuberant spirit, struggles with high unemployment, poor health and low morale.

As in Wales, there has long been resentment at the concentration of political power in London and the sense of economic neglect. To offset this feeling, the government in Whitehall established a Scottish Office in 1885. From 1945 education, health, agriculture, roads, transport, planning, housing and public order were handled within the Scottish Office. From 1945 onwards the Scots saw the giants of their economy, particularly shipbuilding on the River Clyde, disappear. In 1913 Clyde shipbuilding employed 60,000 men. Today the industry barely exists. The closure of Scottish shipyards, coal mines and steel mills, and the

consequent high levels of unemployment in Scotland are, in the popular view closely associated with London government. By 1979 60 per cent of Scots in manufacturing were working for English, American, Japanese or other foreign-owned enterprises. The Scots were especially hard hit by Thatcher's economic restructuring. In the years 1979–81 alone, there was a fall of 11 per cent in Scottish industrial production, and a 20 per cent drop in manufacturing jobs. Two steel mills, Gartcosh and Ravenscraig, the 'flagships' of Scottish industry, were closed in 1986 and 1992 with a loss of at least 11,000 jobs. For Scots these closures symbolised the attitude of an ultra-English Conservative government.

During the 1980s and the 1990s Scotland's economy changed and partly revived. Scotland could boast one of the largest electronics industry concentrations in Western Europe. Whisky distilleries in the north east accounted for 20 per cent of Scottish manufactured exports. There are 100,000 jobs in North Sea oil. Edinburgh has become the fourth financial centre of Europe, with important fund management and insurance services.

Yet the new service industries could not help those who had worked in the old heavy industries. One consequence of the 'progressive loss of morale' has been a worse state of health in Scotland and a higher rate of heart disease, smoking, alcohol and drug abuse than elsewhere in Britain. Another consequence was emigration which has been a long-standing feature. Throughout the nineteenth century the Highland chiefs allowed the communal clan lands to be cleared of people. Between 1871

Glasgow is Scotland's business and manufacturing capital. What it lacks in style to its rival, Edinburgh, it makes up for in the zest of its inhabitants.

Fair Isle, between the Orkney and Shetland Islands off the north coast of Scotland. The Scottish highlands and islands are places of the most compelling beauty in all of Britain.

and 1901 half a million Scots emigrated. Other highlanders moved to Glasgow. Emigration still offsets natural increase. The population has remained static at 5.1 million in the decade 1986–96.

The Highlands, the greater part of Scotland, are now largely deserted. Once the Highlands were stripped of their inhabitants, the great landowners set aside their estates for sport: the hunting of deer. Most great landowners do not live on their estates, and many neither live in Scotland nor are Scottish. The reality of day-to-day life in the Highlands stands in cruel contrast with the tourist picture of jolly kilted Highlanders playing bagpipes or participating in Highland Games.

By the 1960s there were fewer than 300,000 people living in this large area which, in the words of one Highland land expert, John McEwen, 'suits absentee landlordism admirably'. Since the 1960s the Highland population has grown by about 50,000 people. The question of who owns Scotland has become a national issue. McEwen found that no official land register had been made in Scotland since the nineteenth century. In 1977, at the age of 90 and after much obstruction by landowners, he published his research which showed that of Scotland's 19 million acres (7.6 million hectares) only 2.5 million acres belonged to the state, and only 4.5 million acres were in private estates of 1,000 acres or less. Two-thirds of all Scotland, 12 million acres, was in private estates of over 1,000 acres in size. Half of Scotland is still owned by only 500 people, some of whom are actually Scots, but most of whom are absentee land lords.

Dismay at the progressive integration with England has led to growing cultural expression. Gaelic, still spoken by about 70,000 people chiefly in the Hebrides, has attracted the interest of a growing number of students. Between 1986 and 1996 Gaelic-medium schools increased from two to 50. Ironically the Gaelic revival is partly the result of enthusiastic incoming English families. Pride in the Scots dialect of English is also expressed in the translation of the Bible into Broad Scots – part of a resurgence of Scottish identity against the authority wielded by Standard English.

Scottish political feeling has also grown since 1945. In the late 1960s the Scottish National Party (SNP) began to attract serious support, and in 1974 won 11 of Scotland's 71 seats. Yet in 1979 Scotland failed to vote decisively for devolution, 32.9 per cent in favour (less than the required 40 per cent), 30.8 per cent against. Margaret Thatcher and John Major were consistently hostile to devolution, unlike their predecessor, Edward Heath, who had proposed devolution in 1968. The facts speak for themselves. In 1955 Conservatives won 36 of the then 71 Scottish seats in the Commons, the last time they had a Scottish majority. In the 1979 election the Conservatives won 23 seats, but declined dramatically thereafter. In 1987 they kept only 10, compared with Labour's 50 Scottish seats. Scots deeply resented being governed by a party unable to attract even one-sixth of the Scottish vote. In 1989 50 Scottish Labour and Liberal Democrat MPs, leading churchmen and other community leaders met, significantly, in the Church of Scotland's General Assembly buildings in Edinburgh. Here they unanimously signed a 'Claim of Right' to a parliament of their own. In 1997 the Conservatives lost every seat in Scotland. The Scottish National Party won six seats, but attracted 22 per cent of the national vote. The Liberal Democrats took 10 seats but with only 13 per cent of the vote, and Labour took the remaining 56 seats.

Even after their defeat, the Conservatives opposed devolution for Scotland, warning that it would weaken the Union. Whether this turns out to be true or not, Scots did not like being 'lectured' by the English. Of the 62 per cent of the electorate who voted in the devolution referendum in September 1997, 75 per cent voted in favour of a Scottish parliament, and 63 per cent favoured this new parliament enjoying tax raising powers.

The new Scottish parliament will have 73 directly elected members (by the FPTP system) and 56 additional members elected by proportional representation on an electoral district basis. The higher proportion of additional members will make this parliament more representative of public opinion than the Welsh Assembly. This should weaken the dominance of the leading party and, ironically in view of its opposition to devolution, it should give the Conservatives a chance to recover in Scotland. If proportional representation works in Scotland, it will make its introduction into the rest of the United Kingdom more likely. In the meantime, the Scots and Welsh will continue to be represented in Westminster.

The Scottish parliament will be able to make binding laws without seeking permission from Westminster except in areas retained by Westminster: the UK constitution; foreign policy; border control; defence and national security; monetary and fiscal affairs, and common markets; and employment and social security. Scotland will have its own first minister and executive, formed from the leading party in its parliament. There is therefore the distinct prospect of Scotland being governed by one political party while the United Kingdom is governed by another.

Finally, there is one more possible influence that Scotland may have on constitutional development. The basis of the English constitution, as explained in Chapter 2, is the unlimited sovereignty and legal powers of the Crown in Parliament. This was the result of the Glorious Revolution of 1688, before the formal 1707 union with Scotland. In Scotland sovereignty resided in the community, in the will of the people. This was the great democratic achievement of the Kirk. The Scots have never been as fond of the Crown as the English have. If the British people decide they need a Bill of Rights, it is possible that Scotland's constitutional view may prove as influential as the English one of the Crown in Parliament.

Further information

WEBSITES

Northern Ireland

Government	www.nics.gov.uk
Northern Ireland Information Centre	www.nireland.com
Democratic Unionist Party	www.dup.org.uk
Progressive Unionist Party	www.pup.org.uk
Sinn Fein	www.irlnet.com/sinnfein
Social Democratic Labour Party	www.sdlp.ie/sdlp
Ulster Democratic Party	www.udp.org.uk
Ulster Unionist Party	www.uup.org.uk
Belfast Telegraph	www.belfasttelegraph.co

Wales

Plaid Cymru	www.plaidcymru.org
Wales	www.netwales.co.uk
Wales	www.open.gov.uk (functional index 'Wales')

Scotland

Scottish National Party	www.snp.org.uk
Scotland	www.open.gov.uk (functional index 'Scotla

PRINTED MATERIAL

Northern Ireland

Coogan, Tim Pat 1996 *The Troubles: Ireland's Ordeal and the Search for Peace, 1966–96* Arrow

McGarry, J. and O'Leary, B. 1995 *Explaining Northe Ireland: Broken Images* Blackwell

O'Leary, B. and McGarry, J. 1996 *The Politics of Antagonism: Understanding Northern Ireland* Athlone Press

Wilson, Tom 1989 *Ulster: Conflict and Consent* Blackwell

Wales

Morgan, Kenneth O. 1988 *Rebirth of a Nation: Wale 1880–1980* Oxford University Press

Scotland

Finlayson, Iain 1988 *The Scots* Oxford University Pre

QUESTIONS

Section analysis

1 **Northern Ireland** List what you think Unionist and Republican leaders have each most feared in trying to negotiate a compromise. What do you think they fear most from their own side?

2 **Northern Ireland** Why does the Protestant community have a sense of receding power?

3 **Northern Ireland** Has your view of the Northern Ireland problem been modified by reading this section, and if so, in what ways has your view changed?

4 **Wales** How has Welsh cultural identity weakened over the second half of the twentieth century?

5 **Wales** Why do you think the devolution referendum of 1997 had such a close result, compared with that in Scotland?

6 **Scotland** Scotland has always retained its own distinctive institutions. What are they and how do they differ from similar institutions in England?

7 **Scotland** Why do you think many Scots resent the concentration of political power in London?

Chapter analysis and discussion

1 Do the nationalist movements in Northern Ireland, Wales and Scotland result from similar or different causes? Are they expressed in similar or different ways? Find evidence from the text to support your views.

2 Which of the following statements refers to Northern Ireland, which to Scotland and which to Wales? Find evidence from the text to support your choice.
   a Nationalism is mainly expressed in cultural and linguistic terms.
   b Nationalism has increased the divisions between communities, making the gaps harder to bridge.
   c Nationalism has increased as industrial power has declined, and nationalists have clear economic as well as political goals.

3 In what ways do you think membership of the European Community could affect the nationalist aspirations of Northern Ireland, Wales and Scotland?

4 Are there regions of your country with strong nationalist feeling? If so, are their aspirations expressed in political parties? How do these parties compare with Sinn Fein, Plaid Cymru or the SNP?

Visual interpretation

In what ways do Catholic and Protestant views expressed in this survey give grounds for both hope and anxiety for the future?

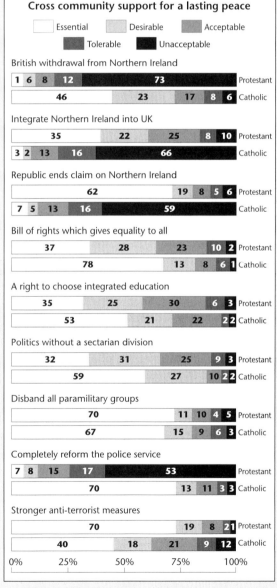

Source: *Colin Irwin, The Search for a Settlement* 1998

10 *A view of Europe and the world*

Foreign policy dilemmas

All countries foster myths about themselves, for they are essential to a national self-image. One of Britain's myths is to do with its world position, based on the lingering afterglow of a bygone glory. For 200 years, until the 1950s, Britain's view of the world was dominated by its overseas territorial possessions and trade. Britain was reluctantly involved in continental Europe, usually only when its own security was directly threatened. Since the disappearance of its empire and the comparative decline in its power, Britain has adjusted its world view with difficulty. In 1959 the Prime Minister asked his intelligence services to review the likely world position of Britain by 1970. This review challenged the maintenance of a nuclear weapons programme, foresaw that the Commonwealth would become increasingly useless as an economic unit, and forecast that Britain would be dwarfed politically and economically by the new European Common Market. But the conclusions were watered down by senior civil servants before they reached the Prime Minister. They contradicted too many assumptions of Britain's world position. There are still occasions when Britain acts as if it were of greater importance than it is. In the words of one retired diplomat, once ambassador to Paris and then to Washington, 'We don't brag as some countries do, but we do tend to assume we'll be treated as a great power.'

As a result, Britain's foreign policy has tended to lag behind the reality of its world position and to conflict with its true economic interests. It has repeatedly adjusted its overseas political and military commitments since 1945, by troop reduction or political withdrawals, but after, rather than before these had become a burden. The legacy of empire has distracted Britain from concentrating on its economic and political future. During the 1970s Britain was dogged by a sense of economic and political weakness, and by the apparent inevitability of post-imperial decline. During the 1980s Prime Minister Thatcher sought to reverse the process, and claimed, 'Once more

Britain is confident, strong, trusted … Strong, because our economy is enterprising, competitive and expanding. And trusted, because we are known to be a powerful ally and a faithful friend.' Not everyone agreed with such an assessment. Britain's military strength (discussed below) was achieved at the expense of the civil economy. Furthermore, even with economic prosperity, Britain's comparative world position remained bound to decline on account of the rise of the Pacific and Latin American economies.

Britain found it difficult to adjust following the loss of its colonial territories in the 1960s. For approximately 25 years Britain seemed uncertain where its primary interests lay, whether it was with the United States, its most important military ally, or with the European Community, its most important economic arena. It found it difficult to decide which was the more important politically. Because of this uncertainty it was slower than its European allies to invest economic and political effort in the newly free countries of Eastern Europe, and more anxious than others that America's involvement in Europe should not decline. It remained a keen advocate of the North Atlantic Treaty Organisation (NATO), in which it plays a leading role. Behind its strategic concerns lay another fear, that without the role it plays in NATO, it might return to what it was until the seventeenth century, an offshore island on the edge of European affairs.

Armoured troops on exercise in Germany. British troops are still stationed in Germany despite the Cold War having ended.

In 1945 Britain had been a founder member of the United Nations. By dint of its international importance it became one of the five permanent members of the Security Council and found itself playing two implicitly contradictory games. On the one hand, as a NATO member it was an ardent participant in the Cold War contest. On the other, it paid lip service to the peaceful and conciliatory criteria, declarations and treaties of the UN. With the end of the Cold War, but also with its comparative decline, Britain faces another dilemma. Should it hang onto its permanent seat in order to maximise its influence at the UN, or should it resign it in favour of a Security Council more representative of UN global membership? And if it chose to resign its seat, should it be as willing as it has been in the past to provide troops for UN peace-keeping missions? During the 1990s Britain seemed increasingly to act as the junior partner of the United States in ensuring that US policy prevailed in the Security Council, particularly with regard to the Middle East.

Ever since the Second World War, Britain has believed in a 'special relationship' with the United States. This relationship is based upon a shared language and Anglo-Saxon culture, and particularly strong relationships between Churchill and Roosevelt during the war, and between Thatcher and Reagan during the 1980s and between Blair and Clinton at the end of the century. For Britain the relationship was vital to its own world standing after 1945. For the United States it was useful for strengthening the European commitment to NATO. But the United States has seldom valued the special relationship as highly as Britain has done, and it can only last if both have something to gain from it. In spite of Britain's difficult relations with other members of the European Union, there were signs in the 1990s that its relationship with the United States was weakening, as the implications of growing political and economic unity in Europe became harder to ignore.

In 1997 Labour dramatically announced that human rights considerations would become central to British foreign policy. All governments pay lip service to human rights requirements but few honour them. In stating its position so firmly, Labour's record was bound to be judged by this difficult standard it had set itself. Sceptics believed it would only occasion embarrassment as Labour discovered the irreconcilable clash of interests, particularly with regard to arms sales.

Britain has encouraged the development of a strong arms industry to supply the armed forces

Tony Blair and Bill Clinton at Downing Street. Blair and Clinton have forged a very close bond, like Churchill and Roosevelt and Thatcher and Reagan before them.

and also to make profitable sales internationally. During the 1980s it became the second largest arms trader internationally. In 1996 it took 25 per cent of the total world market in weaponry. No other export sector achieves anything like the same proportional value. Critics claim that well over half British arms sales go to states with bad human rights records. In the mid-1990s the Conservative government was gravely embarrassed by the Scott Inquiry when it emerged that it had secretly condoned the sale of arms to Iraq during the late 1980s, in contradiction of its own public prohibition of such sales to Iraq. The export of arms is an area in which the sincerity of Labour's foreign policy will be severely tested.

Britain in Europe

In the long term Britain is bound primarily to Europe, despite its sometimes unenthusiastic view of the European Union (EU), as the Community became in 1992. Britain did not share the same passion to create an economic and political network as the founder members of the Community. It had not experienced foreign European armies on its soil, and relied economically on trade with Commonwealth members and colonies.

Britain joined the Community in 1973, but it remained diffident, with several MPs of both main parties believing membership to be a mistake, and demands for conformity irksome. In 1980 it was still possible that Britain could leave the European Community. British resentment at interference from Brussels was well expressed by one Conservative MP: 'Almost overnight and largely unnoticed by our fellow citizens, Britain's right to decide many practical matters, even her own destiny, is being surrendered to the majority vote and the interests of other nations, not all of whom share our parliamentary traditions.' Against such an attitude a British Commissioner to the European Community argued the harsh pragmatic case that, 'Only on a European rather than a national basis can we hold our own in the world.' By 1990 few could disagree with this assessment, and although it remained the most argumentative member of the Community, there was no longer any question of it leaving. But it continued to show it was less enthusiastic than other major members about accepting the implications of membership.

Britain's economy is closely interrelated with the other members of the Community. By 1995 57 per cent of UK exports and 15 per cent of GDP were accounted for by the EU market. Moreover, most large companies now operate across frontiers. With progressive economic integration, national political sovereignty has reduced meaning.

Yet the question of Europe and national sovereignty produced the crisis within government which led to the downfall of Margaret Thatcher in November 1990, and to the split in Conservative ranks which made defeat for the subsequent Major administration inevitable. Britain's relations with Europe deteriorated further under Major. In 1992 he agreed to the Treaty of Maastricht with two important provisos. He declined to sign the Social Chapter safeguarding minimal employment conditions throughout the Union, on account of the strong Conservative belief in a free market economy with an unregulated labour force. He also insisted on Britain's right to opt out of the planned single currency for the Union. Later the same year apprehensions concerning the dangers of a single currency were confirmed in many British minds when Britain was forced out of European Exchange Rate Mechanism (ERM) by intense speculation on the pound sterling. Yet it was the crisis over contaminated British beef, so-called 'mad cow disease', in 1995–6 which brought British relations with the rest of the Union to an unprecedented low point. Britain did everything it could to avoid the Union's safety requirements, with its behaviour, according to one British journalist, 'a mixture of lofty abuse and abject whining'.

Labour adopted the few more positive European policies of its predecessor, urging rapid completion of the single market for every sector of economic activity, and also advocating the progressive enlargement of the Union to include Central and Eastern European states. It also immediately signed the Social Chapter, and indicated that it would make membership of the single currency contingent on a referendum. It recognised more readily than the Conservatives that the question was not whether to join the single currency but when.

Europe occupies two extreme positions on the spectrum of popular esteem. For a long time there has been strong middle-class support for membership of the European Union, based not only upon Britain's pragmatic interests, but also upon interest in European culture. Many middle-class Britons take their holidays exploring different parts of Europe. They are largely pan-European in outlook. However, there is also another, smaller, category of British visitor to the Continent. These are the young holidaymakers who drink heavily and sometimes become violent, for example, on Spain's Mediterranean coast, or following English football teams. Their behaviour is not solely to do with social problems in Britain. It also reflects a contemptuous attitude for those who are not British. Many other British people, while not behaving in such anti-social ways, do not yet feel culturally European.

The Commonwealth

Beyond its immediate foreign policy priorities, its ties with Europe and the United States, Britain has important relations across the rest of the world, primarily through the Commonwealth. The Commonwealth is a voluntary association of members of the former British Empire and Colonies, which allows for a new relationship between Britain and its former possessions. Its purpose is the promotion of international understanding and cooperation by working in partnership with each other. It is as much an association of peoples as of states, with a plethora of informal non-governmental links. There were only 11 members in 1960, which grew to 21 by 1965, when Britain resigned the permanent chairmanship in favour of an international secretariat, and then 53 in 1998. Some have resigned, for example Ireland, others have been suspended, like Fiji and Nigeria, while others which withdrew to avoid expulsion have returned to the fold, like Pakistan and South Africa. Recent admissions have included countries with no previous connection with Britain, for example in 1995 the ex-Portuguese territory of Mozambique. Yemen and the embryo state of Palestine have both expressed interest in membership. The Queen is titular head of the Commonwealth, even though half the member states are republics. She remains an ardent supporter of the Commonwealth idea.

Heads of State at the Commonwealth Conference held at Holyroodhouse, the Queen's residence in Edinburgh. The Royal Family still tends to dominate the formalities of the event.

Why is the Commonwealth so popular? A chief reason is that it is an international forum that lacks the formality and pomposity of the United Nations. In the words of Peter Lyon, head of the Institute for Commonwealth Studies, 'It is a comfortable form of international cooperation where people can talk confidentially without feeling threatened. It hasn't got a centre or periphery. All have equal status.' One of the major attractions for the prime ministers of the member states is that at the conferences they have direct personal contact with each other, frequently without any officials present. The Commonwealth also operates by consensus rather than by voting. This allows for a more gradualist approach to problems than is possible in the United Nations. The heads of government of member states meet every two years to consider current issues, and sometimes to make declarations on agreed principles. For example, in 1971 the Singapore Declaration stated: 'We believe in the liberty of the individual, in equal rights for all citizens regardless of race, colour, creed or political belief, and in their inalienable right to participate by means of free and democratic political processes in framing the society in which they live.' As with the United Nations, many members fall short of their undertakings.

It is easy to think of the Commonwealth as a cosy association. In fact it has times of great stress, three of which were a direct consequence of British policy. When Britain refused to send troops to restore Rhodesia to British rule in 1964, the Commonwealth came close to disintegration. Its

entry into the European Community greatly damaged relations with Commonwealth trading partners in the 1970s, and its refusal to apply economic sanctions against South Africa nearly resulted in the relocation of the Secretariat to Toronto. Meanwhile a number of Conservative MPs openly expressed the view that the Commonwealth was no longer worth having. It was the quiet diplomacy of the Queen herself which healed this rift.

The current popularity and growth of the Commonwealth may signal its success. Yet the great virtue of the Commonwealth in the 1960s and early 1970s was the intimacy of this varied club. The larger the Commonwealth becomes, the harder it is to ensure it remains a place for the uninhibited exchange of views and to achieve consensus.

The end of Empire?

In 1997 Britain relinquished sovereignty of Hong Kong. Under the 1984 accord with Beijing, Hong Kong is designated a Special Administrative Region with its own government and legislative council composed of Hong Kong people. But it is less democratic than the last British governor had wanted. The existing elected legislative council was replaced with an appointed provisional legislature by the Chinese government, followed by fresh elections for a legislative council in 1998 with a severely reduced franchise. Of the six million people in Hong Kong, just over three million are British passport holders, but only 50,000 of these have rights of residence in Britain. Britain retains a strong interest in Hong Kong, partly because of the embarrassment it will feel if Beijing does not honour its obligations, but also because Hong Kong remains Britain's second largest export market in Asia.

Many viewed the loss of Hong Kong as the final end of empire, but in fact Britain retains another 16 'dependent' territories, with a total population of about 200,000. The largest is Bermuda, with 60,000 inhabitants, which, like most of the others, is British by choice. Britain claims all these territories may freely exercise self-determination, but there is one glaring exception. In the early 1970s Britain removed the 1,800 or so islanders from the Indian Ocean island of Diego Garcia to Mauritius in order to make it a base for US forces. They have not been allowed back or allowed to determine their future. Government conduct contrasts with its willingness to fight for the self-determination of the Falklands/Las Malvinas which Argentina occupied in 1982. Although ejected by British forces, Argentina continues to claim the Falklands, South Georgia and the Sandwich Islands. Gibraltar, acquired in 1713, is claimed by Spain, which from time to time has tried to pressure this territory into accepting Spanish sovereignty. In the latter two cases the inhabitants strongly wish to remain under British rule.

In 1981 the British Nationality Act stripped the people of these dependent territories, including Hong Kong, of full British citizenship with the exception of the Falklands and Gibraltar whose citizens are largely of European origin. Many believed this to be overtly racist. The other area of discontent concerns a sense of under-representation in London and a desire for direct representation in the Commonwealth.

Since 1990 British troops have been used increasingly in peace-keeping operations, particularly in Bosnia.

The 1997 ceremony whereby Britain handed Hong Kong back to China.

The armed forces

The British have mixed feelings about their armed forces. There is pride in their abilities and bravery, and in the history and traditions of the Royal Navy, the Royal Air Force and the regiments of the Army, many of which are over 250 years old. On the other hand the authority required in, and imposed by, an army is deeply disliked by a nation of individualistic and anti-authoritarian people. Any use of the armed forces in mainland Britain to maintain order would provoke a major popular protest.

After 1945 it was clear that Britain was no longer the foremost power it had been previously. In order to secure 'the right to sit at the top of the table', as one Prime Minister put it, Britain invested in the development and deployment of

nuclear weapons. It soon found it could not afford the production costs and became dependent on US-supplied weapons. Whether Britain needs a nuclear deterrent for security rather than to increase its political influence has always been a matter for debate. During the 1980s Britain upgraded its nuclear capability with US Trident missiles. These came into service in the 1990s and will last until about 2020. Trident gives Britain a nuclear capacity greatly in excess of its deterrent requirement. Each of four submarines will carry eight missiles with each missile capable of carrying fourteen independent warheads. Supporters of nuclear deterrence speak of Britain being able to 'punch above its weight'. Critics point to what the enormous sum of money could buy in terms of the civil economy, education or health.

As in the political sphere, Britain has adjusted too slowly to its changing status as a military power, and failed to anticipate the need to contract from widespread commitments in good time.

In response to the collapse of the Warsaw Pact there has been a 30 per cent reduction in the size of the armed forces since 1990. Yet Britain still spends proportionately more on defence than other NATO members. In 1997 it spent £22 billion to maintain a force of 214,000 service personnel. This was 2.8 per cent of its gross domestic product compared with the NATO average of 2.3 per cent, an extraordinary fact for one of the poorer members of NATO which faces no major military threat. How does one rate value for money? Take, for example, the cost of its fleet. A report in 1990 showed that out of the 20-year life expected of the average naval vessel, only five years were spent at sea and that the total maintenance bill might well be two or three times the initial purchase price. Or look at the Air Force. In 1998 it was admitted that half its war planes were unfit to fly.

The continuing pressure to reduce significantly both the size and cost of Britain's armed forces cannot be ignored. Labour undertook the third major review in a decade when it came to power. But any government faces a dilemma. Should it maintain an integrated force, which will require maintenance of tanks, heavy artillery and the equipment necessary for a major war or radically reduce these, in favour of more helicopters and transport planes to produce a highly versatile rapid deployment force which can be used anywhere in the world? Or should it reduce its already small navy, or alternatively abandon development of the warplane Eurofighter, to which the Conservative government pledged over £15 billion?

Flight Lieutenant Sarah Hancock, the first woman to captain a Nimrod patrol aircraft. She is symbolic of the changes slowly taking place in the armed forces.

The Army, more than the Navy or Air Force is a deeply 'tribal' institution. Infantry regiments, with 200 or more years of history, regard themselves as families. Many officers are the sons or grandsons of men who also served in the same regiment. The officer culture tends to be old-fashioned and conservative in its values and political outlook. It is also, particularly in the 'smarter' regiments, like the Guards, cavalry, Highland and rifle regiments, distinctly upper class in a way seldom found outside the Army. The sons of great landowners sometimes pursue an army career, for example in a Guards regiment, until they inherit the family estate. It almost goes without saying that most officers in such regiments were educated at public schools.

The Guards may represent the upper-class élite in the Army, but the Special Air Service (SAS) represents the tough operational élite. It was established during the Second World War to work behind enemy lines. Since then it has continued to exist, but is deliberately hidden from publicity. Men may only join the SAS from other army units after the most rigorous selection procedure for physical and mental ability. They sometimes operate in other countries to support regimes considered friendly to Britain. They also operated in Northern Ireland, though it was years before the government admitted to this. Their image of a tough, 'go anywhere', secret élite has stimulated much interest.

It is, perhaps, inevitable that no army is likely to be described as liberal. But the frank statement of one officer, 'You're training people to be aggressive. The kind of guy that's going to leap into a trench and kill someone is probably not going to help some nice Indian chap across the road' says much about the state of mind in the British army. Fewer than 1 per cent of the armed forces belong to an ethnic minority, and those with the courage to enlist often complain of racism. There is also strong official prejudice against homosexuality, and several men and women in the armed forces have been discharged for being of homosexual orientation. With the intended incorporation of the European Convention on Human Rights into British law, it would no longer be possible to forbid homosexuals to serve in the armed forces, but the prejudice is likely to linger on.

The question of security

Britain is possibly the most secretive of all parliamentary democracies. The air of mystery surrounding the intelligence services fascinates the public, both in Britain and elsewhere. The success of Ian Fleming's hero James Bond, the novels of Len Deighton and also John Le Carré owes much to this fascination.

Secrecy may be romantic but it has serious implications in a democracy. Parliament is unable to know what is undertaken by Britain's intelligence services, on the grounds that some parliamentarians would be a security risk. It is a strange argument for a parliamentary democracy to use, since it implies that neither Parliament nor people are sovereign, and that someone else, whose identity we cannot be sure of, knows best.

Fantasy rather than fact: Pierce Brosnan plays James Bond, the mythical hero of MI6.

Secrecy provides a protection against public accountability. It also gives the intelligence services a powerful hold on the country. Two main intelligence organisations exist: MI5, which deals with internal security and countering espionage, and MI6, Britain's spy network abroad.

In the past MI5 threatened or used smear campaigns to undermine Labour politicians of whom it did not approve. In 1997 it was revealed that MI5 had once monitored the activities of ex-Prime Minister Edward Heath, and also of two Labour politicians who became senior members of Blair's administration. One, embarrassingly for MI5, was the Home Secretary, responsible for overseeing MI5's activities. Indeed, it is the Home Secretary, not a law officer, who grants approval to tap telephones, intercept mail or break into property.

Since the decision for such normally illegal measures is essentially a political one, there is no legal protection for the citizen. It is estimated that 35,000 telephone lines are tapped yearly.

In spite of government silence, the existence of MI5 and MI6 was common knowledge for years.

Both services received considerable public exposure during the 1980s because of open discussion in the press. MI5 was officially acknowledged in 1989 and MI6 (also known as the Secret Intelligence Service (SIS)) only in 1992 when denial became increasingly untenable since MI6 and the identity of its director had become such public knowledge. British diplomats, however, are still coy. They refer to MI6 simply as 'the Friends'. Although it is unlikely that MI6 has entirely abandoned watching its old adversaries of the Eastern Bloc, its greatest effort is now on monitoring drugs trafficking. It has also increased intelligence gathering in the Islamic and Arab worlds.

MI5 has made a virtue of its new public persona. It has even advertised publicly for recruits. Greater openness indicates a shift of emphasis since the end of the Cold War. Since 1990 two-thirds of its effort has been directed to counter-terrorist intelligence gathering, particularly in Northern Ireland, and it has a growing role in combatting organised crime. Peace in Northern Ireland would probably not lead to a reduction in MI5's activities and personnel but greater concentration on combatting organised crime.

MI5, MI6, the police Special Branch and Signals Intelligence (which monitors international radio and satellite communications) are all coordinated by the Joint Intelligence Committee (JIC), which is composed of senior civil servants and intelligence chiefs responsible to the Cabinet Secretary (see p.144) and the Prime Minister. The rivalry between these intelligence networks is most in evidence, it is said, at meetings of the JIC.

During the 1980s several important incidents occurred which demonstrated the government's obsession with secrecy. The government forbade the publication of an intelligence officer's autobiography, protected the anonymity of some SAS men who killed three unarmed members of the IRA in Gibraltar, and brought a police investigation into the activities of MI5 and the Special Branch in Northern Ireland to a swift and unresolved end. In another incident, a senior civil servant believed his minister was deliberately concealing information from Parliament. He revealed this information to an interested MP. His argument was that concealment had taken place not on the grounds of secrecy but because it would embarrass the government since it had already been deliberately misleading Parliament for two years. He was prosecuted for violating the Official Secrets Act, but the jury found him not guilty. It decided he had acted in the public interest and that his disclosure was justified. The government angrily introduced a new Official Secrets Act in 1989 which specifically stated that the disclosure of secrets 'in the public interest' was no defence.

The Government Communications Headquarters (GCHQ) in Cheltenham operates one of the most important parts of the security apparatus, Signals Intelligence, known as SIGINT. The system is linked to similar operations in the United States, Canada, Australia and New Zealand. As with other aspects of its intelligence services, the government is shy about its existence.

Conservative governments, 1979–97, championed secrecy more than their predecessors but almost every government this century has acted undemocratically in areas of national security. There have been repeated evasions by government from telling the truth to Parliament on sensitive issues, for example the costs involved in nuclear weaponry. Too often the need for state security has been invoked merely to save the government from embarrassment, either for having deliberately misled Parliament or the public, or for having wasted large sums of money or some other kind of glaring incompetence. The trouble is that the desire for secrecy in British government goes beyond the need to protect national security to the protection of politicians in power from embarrassment. Whitehall's standard security handbook reads: 'Precautions are needed ... to prevent foreign powers and subversive organisations from obtaining unauthorised information and to avoid disclosures which would cause embarrassment hampering good government ... .' However, secret government is usually bad government as well as undemocratic. The ability to conceal the truth is an irresistible temptation for a government under attack from the opposition. Yet the process is corrupt and undermines the democratic principle. In 1980 the Civil Service set out regulations (known as the 'Osmotherly Rules') for civil servants appearing before the new select committees (see p.45) which state, 'Any withholding of information should be limited to reservations that are necessary in the interests of good government or to safeguard national security.' The explanatory notes following this rule effectively deny MPs any real knowledge of the inside workings of Whitehall, thus preventing Parliament or the electorate making government truly accountable for its conduct.

Labour came into office in 1997 pledged to establish the principle of accountability. It promised a Freedom of Information Act designed to give citizens a right of access to government information including the right to challenge any government refusal to disclose material. It also promised to reintroduce the 'public interest' principle which the Conservatives removed. In short, it promised 'a change in the culture of government'.

It is, perhaps, never possible to strike a final balance between secrecy in the interests of national security or good government, and openness in the protection of democratic values. It is only by constant challenge and debate that the public (and Parliament) can keep governmental secrecy within reasonable limits.

Further information

WEBSITES

Armed Forces

Army	www.army.mod.uk
Royal Air Force	www.open.gov.uk/raf
Royal Navy	www.royal-navy.mod.uk

International relations

Foreign & Commonwealth Office	www.fco.gov.uk
The Commonwealth	www.thecommonwealth.org
MI5	www.mi5.gov.uk

PRINTED MATERIAL

Austin, Dennis 1988 *The Commonwealth and Britain* Routledge

Byrd, P. (ed.) 1991 *British Defence Policy: Thatcher and Beyond* Philip Allan

Clarke, M. 1992 *British External Policy-Making in the 1990s* Macmillan/RIIA

Coxall, Bill and Robins, Lynton 1994 *Contemporary British Politics* Chapter 7 (European Union), 18 (The secret state) and 30 (Foreign and defence policy) Macmillan

Cradock, Percy 1997 *In Pursuit of British Interests: Reflections on Foreign Policy under Margaret Thatcher and John Major* John Murray

Dorreil, S. 1992 *The Silent Conspiracy, Inside the Intelligence Service in the 1990s* Heinemann

QUESTIONS

Section analysis

1 **Foreign policy dilemmas** Which of the following sentences do you think best illustrates the basic problems of British foreign policy?

   a Britain still cannot abandon a self-image of imperial greatness.

   b Britain has always been late in scaling down its foreign policy commitments in line with its real political and economic power.

   c Britain's fundamental problem is whether to back the European Union fully or to pursue a wider role as a junior partner of the United States.

2 **Britain in Europe** Why does Britain have such ambiguous feelings about the European Union?

3 **The Commonwealth** Why is the Commonwealth popular with its membership?

4 **The armed forces** Why has Britain had difficulty in reducing military expenditure?

5 **The question of security** In what ways is Britain's preoccupation with secrecy bad for democracy? Do you think officials should legally be able to disclose secrets 'in the public interest'? How does the British government's attitude to secrecy compare with that in your own country?

Chapter analysis and discussion

1 Do you think the following reflect a particular state of mind?

   a Britain's concern to 'sit at the top table'

   b Its reluctance to reduce its armed forces as much as its European allies have done

   c Its ambiguous attitude to Europe and its concern with secrecy

   Do you think these characteristics are more to do with:

   i a sense of superiority

   ii fear of the future

   iii pragmatic realism

   iv a lack of self-confidence?

2 Think about basic British attitudes regarding Britain's international role, its relations with the United States and Europe, and the use of its armed forces and intelligence services. What broad changes would you propose if you were Prime Minister?

Textual interpretation

Consider this statement in the Labour Party manifesto for the 1997 General Election:

With a new Labour government, Britain will be strong in defence; resolute in standing up for its own interests; an advocate of human rights and democracy the world over; a reliable and powerful ally in the international institutions of which we are a member; and will be a leader in Europe.

Are these empty words, or do you think the Labour administration is putting these commitments into practice? Can you find evidence in this chapter, or from the press, to make a judgment?

11 *Educating the nation*

Education has been a controversial issue periodically since 1945, and subject to major changes as successive governments have tried to improve it. Government policy (both Conservative and Labour) has been bitterly criticised for providing a system which is either too élitist or insufficiently so, which is wasteful of human resources, which is insufficiently demanding of the nation's children, or which simply fails to compete with the education systems of other industrialised countries. During their long period of government, 1979–97, the Conservatives sought to eliminate some of these criticisms in accordance with their political philosophy. The results have been mixed and controversial. On coming into office Labour made education its priority for fundamental transformation. It said it wished to avoid the ideological warfare of previous administrations. But its insistence on 'serving the many, not the few' indicated that its broad position was similar to previous Labour governments in wishing to improve the mass, rather than emphasise high standards for an intelligent élite. The controversy surrounding education results partly from particular historical developments, briefly described below, but also from awareness that the broad mass of schools perform less well than their counterparts in other industrialised countries.

Primary and secondary education

Schooling is compulsory for 12 years, for all children aged five to 16. There are two voluntary years of schooling thereafter. Children may attend either state-funded or fee-paying independent schools. In England, Wales and Northern Ireland the primary cycle lasts from five to 11. Generally speaking, children enter infant school, moving on to junior school (often in the same building) at the age of seven, and then on to secondary school at the age of 11. Roughly 90 per cent of children receive their secondary education at 'comprehensive' schools (see below). For those who wish to stay on, secondary school can include the two final years of secondary education, sometimes known in Britain (for historical reasons)

as 'the sixth form'. In many parts of the country, these two years are spent at a tertiary or sixth-form college, which provides academic and vocational courses.

School should be fun: children at primary school.

Two public academic examinations are set, one on completion of the compulsory cycle of education at the age of 16, and one on completion of the two voluntary years. At 16 pupils take the General Certificate of Secondary Education (GCSE), introduced in 1989 to replace two previous examinations, one academic and the other indicating completion of secondary education. It was introduced to provide one examination whereby the whole range of ability could be judged, rather than having two classes of achievers; and also to assess children on classwork and homework as well as in the examination room, as a more reliable form of assessment. During the two voluntary years of schooling, pupils specialise in two or three subjects and take the General Certificate of Education (always known simply as 'GCE') Advanced Level, or 'A level' examination, usually with a view to entry to a university or other college of higher education, discussed later. New examinations, Advanced Supplementary (AS) levels, were introduced in 1989, to provide a wider range of subjects to study, a recognition that English education has traditionally been overly narrow. The debate about the need for a wider secondary level curriculum continues, and Labour is likely to introduce more changes at this level. These examinations are not set by the government, but by independent examination boards, most of which are associated with a particular university or group of universities. Labour may replace these boards with one national board of examination.

A new qualification was introduced in 1992 for pupils who are skills, rather than academically, orientated, the General National Vocational Qualification, known as GNVQ. This examination is taken at three distinct levels: the Foundation which has equivalent standing to low-grade passes in four subjects of GCSE; the Intermediate GNVQ which is equivalent to high-grade passes in four subjects of GCSE; and the Advanced GNVQ, equivalent to two passes at A level and acceptable for university entrance.

The academic year begins in late summer, usually in September, and is divided into three terms, with holidays for Christmas, Easter and for the month of August, although the exact dates vary slightly from area to area. In addition each term there is normally a mid-term one-week holiday, known as 'half-term'.

Scotland, with a separate education tradition, has a slightly different system. Children stay in the primary cycle until the age of 12. They take the Scottish Certificate of Education (SCE) usually at the age of 16 and, instead of A levels, they take the Scottish Higher Certificate which is more like continental European examinations since it covers a wider area of study than the highly specialised A level courses. Many take their 'Highers' aged 17 rather than 18, with some opting to take a further examination later, the Certificate of Sixth Year Studies (CSYS).

The story of British schools

For largely historical reasons, the schools system is complicated, inconsistent and highly varied. Most of the oldest schools, of which the most famous are Eton, Harrow, Winchester and Westminster, are today independent, fee-paying, public schools for boys. Most of these were established to create a body of literate men to fulfil the administrative, political, legal and religious requirements of the late Middle Ages. From the sixteenth century onwards, many 'grammar' schools were established, often with large grants of money from wealthy men, in order to provide a local educational facility.

Pupils at a comprehensive school learning sewing.

From the 1870s local authorities were required to establish elementary schools, paid for by the local community, and to compel attendance by all boys and girls up to the age of 13. By 1900 almost total attendance had been achieved. Each authority, with its locally elected councillors, was responsible for the curriculum. Although a general consensus developed concerning the major part of the school curriculum, a strong feeling of local control continued and interference by central government was resented. A number of secondary schools were also established by local authorities, modelled on the public schools (see below).

The 1944 Education Act introduced free compulsory secondary education. Almost all children attended one of two kinds of secondary school. The decision was made on the results obtained in the '11 plus' examination, taken in the last year of primary school. Eighty per cent of pupils went to 'secondary modern' schools where they were expected to obtain sufficient education for manual, skilled and clerical employment, but where academic expectations were modest. The remaining 20 per cent went to grammar schools. Some of these were old foundations which now received a direct grant from central government, but the majority were funded through the local authority. Grammar school pupils were expected to go on to university or some other form of higher education. A large number of the grammar or 'high' schools were single sex. In addition there were, and continue to be, a number of voluntary state-supported primary and secondary schools, most of them under the management of the Church of England or the Roman Catholic Church, which usually own the school buildings.

By the 1960s there was increasing criticism of this streaming of ability, particularly by the political Left. It was recognised that many children performed inconsistently, and that those who failed the 11 plus examination were denied the chance to do better later. Early selection also reinforced the divisions of social class, and was wasteful of human potential. A government report in 1968 produced evidence that an expectation of failure became increasingly fulfilled, with secondary modern pupils aged 14 doing significantly worse than they had at the age of eight. Labour's solution was to introduce a new type of school, the comprehensive, a combination of grammar and secondary modern under one roof, so that all the children could be continually assessed and given appropriate teaching. Between 1965 and 1980 almost all the old grammar and secondary modern schools were replaced, mainly by coeducational comprehensives. The measure caused much argument for two principal reasons. Many local authorities, particularly Conservative-controlled ones, did not wish to lose the excellence of their grammar schools, and many resented Labour's interference in education, which was still considered a local responsibility. However, despite the pressure to change school structures, each school, in consultation with the local authority, remained in control of its curriculum. In practice the result of the reform was very mixed: the best comprehensives aimed at grammar school academic standards, while the worst sank to secondary modern ones.

One unforeseen but damaging result was the refusal of many grammar schools to join the comprehensive experiment. Of the 174 direct-grant grammar schools, 119 decided to leave the state system rather than become comprehensive, and duly became independent fee-paying establishments (see below). This had two effects. Grammar schools had provided an opportunity for children from all social backgrounds to excel academically at the same level as those attending fee-paying independent public schools. The loss of these schools had a demoralising effect on the comprehensive experiment and damaged its chances of success, but led to a revival of independent schools at a time when they seemed to be slowly shrinking. The introduction of comprehensive schools thus unintentionally reinforced an educational élite which only the children of wealthier parents could hope to join.

Comprehensive schools became the standard form of secondary education (other than in one or two isolated areas, where grammar schools and secondary moderns survived). However, except among the best comprehensives they lost for a while the excellence of the old grammar schools.

Alongside the introduction of comprehensives there was a move away from traditional teaching and discipline towards what was called 'progressive' education. This entailed a change from more formal teaching and factual learning to greater pupil participation and discussion, with greater emphasis on comprehension and less on the acquisition of knowledge. Not everyone approved, particularly on the political Right. There was increasing criticism of the lack of discipline and of formal learning, and a demand to return to old-fashioned methods.

From the 1960s there was also greater emphasis on education and training than ever before, with many colleges of further education established to provide technical or vocational training. However, British education remained too academic for the less able, and technical studies stayed weak, with the result that a large number of less academically able pupils left school without any skills or qualifications at all.

The expansion of education led to increased expenditure. The proportion of the gross national product devoted to education doubled, from 3.2 per cent in 1954, to 6.5 per cent by 1970, but fell back to about 5 per cent in the 1980s. These higher levels of spending did not fulfil expectations, mainly because spending remained substantially lower than that in other industrialised countries. Perhaps the most serious failures were the continued high drop-out rate at the age of 16 and the low level of achievement in mathematics and science among school-leavers. By the mid-1980s, while over 80 per cent of pupils in the United States and over 90 per cent in Japan stayed on till the age of 18, barely one-third of British pupils did so.

The educational reforms of the 1980s

The Conservatives accused Labour of using education as a tool of social engineering at the expense of academic standards. The dominant right wing of the party argued that market forces should apply, and that the 'consumers', parents and employers, would have a better idea of what was needed than politicians or professional educationists who lived in a rarefied and theoretical world. They also condemned low teaching standards and poor performance by many pupils. Through the Education Act (1986) and the Education Reform Act (1988) the Conservatives introduced the greatest reforms in schooling since 1944.

A science class at a comprehensive school.

Most educational experts saw good and bad features in these reforms. A theme running through most of them was the replacement of local authority control with greater central government power combined with greater parental choice, based on the philosophy of freedom of choice for the 'consumer'.

The main reforms included the introduction of a National Curriculum making certain subjects, most notably science and one modern language, compulsory up to the age of 16. These had previously often been given up at the age of 13. But there was also unease that the compulsory curriculum, taking up over 70 per cent of school time, would squeeze out important wider areas of learning. Periodic formal assessments of progress, at the ages of seven, 11, 14 and 16 were also introduced. Independent fee-paying schools (see below), to which most Conservative government ministers sent their children, were exempted from teaching according to the National Curriculum. Critics questioned why these schools did not have to follow the same national objectives.

In keeping with its philosophy of consumer choice, the government gave parents the right to enrol their children – given appropriate age and aptitude – at any state school of their choice, within the limits of capacity. Parents already sent their children to the local school of their choice. The decision to publish schools' examination results, however, gave parents a stark, but not necessarily well-informed, basis on which to choose the most appropriate school for their child. Increasingly parents sought access to the most successful nearby school in terms of examination

results. Far from being able to exercise their choice, large numbers of parents were now frustrated in their choice. Overall, in 1996 20 per cent of parents failed to obtain their first choice of school. In London the level was 40 per cent, undermining the whole policy of 'parental choice' and encouraging only the crudest view of educational standards. Schools found themselves competing rather than cooperating and some schools, for example in deprived urban areas, faced a downward spiral of declining enrolment followed by reduced budgets. Thus the market offered winners and losers: an improved system for the brighter or more fortunate pupils, but a worse one for the 'bottom' 40 per cent. Schools in deprived parts of cities acquired reputations as 'sink' schools. As one education journalist wrote in 1997, 'There is a clear hierarchy of schools: private, grammar, comprehensives with plenty of nice middle-class children, comprehensives with fewer nice middle-class children and so on.'

In 1988 schools were given the power to opt out of local authority control, if a majority of parents wanted this. The government hoped that many schools would opt for this new 'grant-maintained' status, and that local education authorities would be marginalised. In fact far fewer schools opted for grant-maintained status than the government had hoped or the public had expected. By 1997 only 18 per cent of English secondary schools had opted for it, and only 5 per cent in Wales. The few that opted out tended to be in the wealthier middle-class areas with a large measure of parental support and ambition. Most schools valued the guidance and support of the local education authority.

Secondary schools and larger primary schools were also given responsibility for managing their own budgets. Each school board of governors, composed of parents and local authority appointees, was given greatly increased responsibility, including the 'hiring and firing' of staff. Once again, schools with support from highly educated parents did better than those in deprived areas. The additional work added greatly to the load carried by the school principals, while still denying them full executive powers over their staff. By 1996 head teachers were resigning in record numbers as a result of stress. Inner London schools, for example, were notorious for discipline problems. In 1995 40 per cent of inner London headships were readvertised.

These reforms were insufficient to change the face of British education. Too many children left school with inadequate basic skills, specifically weakness in literacy, numeracy, science and technology. Although A level science pupils are among the best internationally, they are a small group. Internationally Britain's standard of science at primary level remains an embarrassment. One reason is that British children, along with American children, spend a lot of time watching television or playing computer games, and there is an established negative association between these habits and high achievement in science and mathematics. The teaching cadre suffered from low morale, discipline problems, poor pay, inadequate training and the increased workload resulting from the reforms. Many teachers took early retirement or sought alternative employment. The wastage rate had become so high that by 1989 there were as many trained teachers not teaching as teaching. Inadequate pay resulted in teachers avoiding posts in areas where housing was expensive, particularly in the south east. By the 1990s teacher vacancies in London primary schools were twice as high as the national average. The worst shortages were in the subjects identified as of greatest national importance: mathematics and science. But perhaps this was not surprising. Public funding per student had fallen by 25 per cent between 1987 and 1997. Britain still spent less of its gross domestic product on education than other industrialised countries, had one of the highest pupil–teacher ratios, was one of the poorest providers of nursery education, and boasted one of the lowest proportions of young people going on to full-time tertiary education. Indeed the steep drop in enrolment at the end of the compulsory cycle told its own story. In 1996 71 per cent of 16-year-olds, 59 per cent of 17-year-olds and only 40 per cent of 18-year-olds were still in full time education. It was therefore probably true that Britain suffered from a much stronger anti-education culture than its European competitors.

Education under Labour

Education was the central theme of the new Labour government. It promised a huge range of improvements: high-quality education for all four-year-olds whose parents wanted it and lower pupil–teacher ratios, in particular that children up to the age of eight children would never be in classes of over 30 pupils. It also declared that all children at primary school would spend one hour each day on reading and writing, and another hour each day on numeracy, the basic skills for all employment. When Labour took office only 57 per cent of children reached national literacy targets by the time they left primary school, and only 55 per cent reached similar targets in maths. The

government pledged to raise these proportions to 80 per cent and 75 per cent respectively. It also established a new central authority responsible for both qualifications and the curriculum, to ensure that these were, in the government's own words, 'high quality, coherent and flexible'. It warned that it intended to evolve a single certificate to replace A levels and vocational qualifications, and possibly to reflect a broad range of study rather than the narrow specialism of the A-level system. Because 30 per cent of students who started A-level courses failed to acquire one, it also wanted to create a more flexible system that would allow students still to attain recognised standards of education and training on the road to A levels. However, unlike France or Germany, an increasing proportion of those taking exams at this standard were actually passing.

Boys generally have greater difficulty than girls with literacy.

The government also promised to improve the quality of the teaching staff, with a mandatory qualification for all newly appointed heads of schools, to improve teacher training, to establish a General Teaching Council, which would restore teacher morale and raise standards, and to introduce more effective means of removing inefficient teachers. It also promised to look at the growing problem of boys underachieving at school compared with girls. Finally, Labour asked for its record to be judged at the end of its first term in office, in 2002.

The private sector

By 1997 8 per cent of the school population attended independent fee-paying schools, compared with under 6 per cent in 1979, and only

5 per cent in 1976. By the year 2000 the proportion may rise to almost 9 per cent, nearly back to the level in 1947 of 10 per cent. The recovery of private education in Britain is partly due to middle-class fears concerning comprehensive schools, but also to the mediocre quality possible in the state sector after decades of inadequate funding.

Although the percentage of those privately educated may be a small fraction of the total, its importance is disproportionate to its size, for this 8 per cent accounts for 23 per cent of all those passing A levels, and over 25 per cent of those gaining entry to university. Nearly 65 per cent of pupils leave fee-paying schools with one or more A levels, compared with only 14 per cent from comprehensives. Tellingly, this 8 per cent also accounts for 68 per cent of those gaining the highest grade in GCSE Physics. During the 1980s pupils at independent schools showed greater improvement in their examination results than those at state schools. In later life, those educated at fee-paying schools dominate the sources of state power and authority in government, law, the armed forces and finance.

The 'public' (in fact private, fee-paying) schools form the backbone of the independent sector. Of the several hundred public schools, the most famous are the 'Clarendon Nine', so named after a commission of inquiry into education in 1861. Their status lies in a fatally attractive combination of social superiority and antiquity, as the dates of their foundation indicate: Winchester (1382), Eton (1440), St Paul's (1509), Shrewsbury (1552), Westminster (1560), The Merchant Taylors' (1561), Rugby (1567), Harrow (1571) and Charterhouse (1611).

The golden age of the public schools, however, was the late nineteenth century, when most were founded. They were vital to the establishment of a particular set of values in the dominant professional middle classes. These values were reflected in the novel *Tom Brown's Schooldays* by Thomas Hughes, written in tribute to his own happy time at Rugby School. Its emphasis is on the making of gentlemen to enter one of the professions: law, medicine, the Church, the Civil Service or the colonial service. The concept of 'service', even if it only involved entering a profitable profession, was central to the public school ethos. A career in commerce, or 'mere money making' as it is referred to in *Tom Brown's Schooldays*, was not to be considered. As a result of such values, the public school system was traditional in its view of learning and deeply

Bastion of privilege: boys at Harrow School, one of Britain's most prestigious public schools.

resistant to science and technology. Most public schools were located in the 'timeless' countryside, away from the vulgarity of industrial cities.

After 1945, when state-funded grammar schools were demonstrating equal or greater academic excellence, the public schools began to modernise themselves. During the 1970s most of them abolished beating and 'fagging', the system whereby new boys carried out menial tasks for senior boys, and many introduced girls into the sixth form, as a civilising influence. They made particular efforts to improve their academic and scientific quality. Traditionally boarding public schools were more popular, but since the 1970s there has been a progressive shift of balance in favour of day schools. Today only 16 per cent of pupils in private education attend boarding schools, and the number of boarders declines on average by 3 per cent each year.

Demand for public school education is now so great that many schools register pupils' names at birth. Eton maintains two lists, one for the children of 'old boys' and the other for outsiders. There are three applicants for every vacancy. Several other schools have two applicants for each vacancy, but they are careful not to expand to meet demand. In the words of one academic, 'Schools at the top of the system have a vested interest in being élitist. They would lose that characteristic if they expanded. To some extent they pride themselves on the length of their waiting lists.' This rush to private education is despite the steep rise in fees, 31 per cent between 1985 and 1988, and over 50 per cent between 1990 and 1997 when the average annual day fees were £5,700 and boarding fees double that figure. Sixty per cent of parents would probably send their children to fee-paying schools if they could afford to.

In order to obtain a place at a public school, children must take a competitive examination, called 'Common Entrance'. In order to pass it, most children destined for a public school education attend a preparatory (or 'prep') school until the age of 13.

Independent schools remain politically controversial. The Conservative Party believes in the fundamental freedom of parents to choose the best education for their children. The Labour Party disagrees, arguing that in reality only the wealthier citizens have this freedom of choice. In the words of Hugh Gaitskell, the Labour leader in 1953, 'We really cannot go on with a system in which wealthy parents are able to buy what they and most people believe to be a better education for their children. The system is wrong and must be changed.' But since then no Labour government has dared to abolish them.

There can be no doubt that a better academic education can be obtained in some of the public schools. In 1993 92 of the 100 schools with the best A-level results were fee-paying. But the argument that parents will not wish to pay once state schools offer equally good education is misleading, because independent schools offer social status also. Unfortunately education depends not only on quality schools but also on the home environment. The background from which pupils come greatly affects the encouragement they receive to study. Middle-class parents are likely to be better able, and more concerned, to support their children's study than low-income parents who themselves feel they failed at school. State-maintained schools must operate with fewer resources, and in more difficult circumstances, particularly in low-income areas. In addition, the public school system creams off many of the ablest teachers from the state sector.

The public school system is socially divisive, breeding an atmosphere of élitism and leaving some outside the system feeling socially or intellectually inferior, and in some cases intimidated by the prestige attached to public schools. The system fosters a distinct culture, one based not only upon social superiority but also upon deference. As one leading journalist, Jeremy

Paxman, himself an ex-public schoolboy remarked, 'The purpose of a public school education is to teach you to respect people you don't respect.' In the words of Anthony Sampson, himself an ex-pupil of Westminster, the public school élite 'reinforces and perpetuates a class system whose divisions run through all British institutions, separating language, attitudes and motivations'.

Roedean School, one of Britain's most famous girls' schools, has staff and facilities that most state-funded schools can only dream of.

Those who attend these schools continue to dominate the institutions at the heart of the British state, and seem likely to do so for some time to come. At the beginning of the 1990s public schools accounted for 22 out of 24 of the army's top generals, two-thirds of the Bank of England's external directors, 33 out of 39 top English judges, and ambassadors in the 15 most important diplomatic missions abroad. Of the 200 richest people in Britain no fewer than 35 had attended Eton. Eton and Winchester continue to dominate the public school scene, and the wider world beyond. As Sampson asks, 'Can the products of two schools (Winchester and Eton), it might be asked, really effectively represent the other 99.5 per cent of the people in this diverse country who went to neither mediaeval foundation?' The concept of service was once at the heart of the public school ethos, but it is questionable whether it still is. A senior Anglican bishop noted in 1997, 'A headmaster told me recently that the whole concept of service had gone. Now they all want to become merchant bankers and lawyers.'

There are two arguments that qualify the merit of the public schools, apart from the criticism that they are socially divisive. It is inconceivable that the very best intellectual material of the country resides solely among those able to attend such schools. If one accepts that the brightest and best pupils are in fact spread across the social spectrum, one must conclude that an élitist system of education based primarily upon wealth rather than ability must involve enormous wastage. The other serious qualification regards the public school ethos which is so rooted in tradition, authority and a narrow idea of 'gentlemanly' professions. Even a century after it tried to turn its pupils into gentlemen, the public school culture still discourages, possibly unconsciously, its pupils from entering industry. 'It is no accident,' Sampson comments, 'that most formidable industrialists in Britain come from right outside the public school system, and many from right outside Britain.'

Britain will be unable to harness its real intellectual potential until it can break loose from a divisive culture that should belong in the past, and can create its future élite from the nation's schoolchildren as a whole. In 1996 a radical Conservative politician argued for turning public schools into centres of excellence which would admit children solely on ability, regardless of wealth or social background, with the help of government funding. It would be a way of using the best of the private sector for the nation as a whole. It is just such an idea that Labour might find attractive, if it is able to tackle the more widespread and fundamental shortcomings of the state education system.

Further and higher education

Further education has traditionally been characterised by part-time vocational courses for those who leave school at the age of 16 but need to acquire a skill, be that in the manual, technical or clerical field. In all, about three million students enrol each year in part-time courses at further education (FE) colleges, some released by their employers and a greater number unemployed. In addition there have always been a much smaller proportion in full-time training. In 1985 this figure was a meagre 400,000, but by 1995 this had doubled. Given Labour's emphasis on improving the skills level of all school-leavers, this expansion will continue. Vocational training, most of which is conducted at the country's 550 further education colleges is bound to be an important component.

Higher education has also undergone a massive expansion. In 1985 only 573,000, 16 per cent of young people, were enrolled in full-time higher education. Ten years later the number was 1,150,000, no less than 30 per cent of their age group.

Further education: young women learning to be hairdressers.

This massive expansion was achieved by greatly enlarging access to undergraduate courses, but also by authorising the old polytechnics to grant their own degree awards, and also to rename themselves as universities. Thus there are today 90 universities, compared with 47 in 1990, and only seventeen in 1945. They fall into five broad categories: the medieval English foundations, the medieval Scottish ones, the nineteenth-century 'redbrick' ones, the twentieth-century 'plate-glass' ones, and finally the previous polytechnics. They are all private institutions, receiving direct grants from central government.

Oxford and Cambridge, founded in the thirteenth and fourteenth centuries respectively, are easily the most famous of Britain's universities. Today 'Oxbridge', as the two together are known, educate less than one-twentieth of Britain's total university student population. But they continue to attract many of the best brains and to mesmerise an even greater number, partly on account of their prestige, but also on account of the seductive beauty of many of their buildings and surroundings.

Both universities grew gradually, as federations of independent colleges, most of which were founded in the fourteenth, fifteenth and sixteenth centuries. In both universities, however, new colleges are periodically established, for example Green College, Oxford (1979) and Robinson College, Cambridge (1977).

Scotland boasts four ancient universities: Glasgow, Edinburgh, St Andrews and Aberdeen, all founded in the fifteenth and sixteenth centuries. In the Scottish lowlands greater value was placed on education during the sixteenth and later centuries

The seductive charm of a Cambridge college.

than in much of England. These universities were created with strong links with the ancient universities of continental Europe, and followed their longer and broader course of studies. Even today, Scottish universities provide four-year undergraduate courses, compared with the usual three-year courses in England and Wales.

In the nineteenth century more universities were established to respond to the greatly increased demand for educated people as a result of the Industrial Revolution and the expansion of Britain's overseas empire. Many of these were sited in the industrial centres, for example Birmingham, Manchester, Nottingham, Newcastle, Liverpool and Bristol.

With the expansion of higher education in the 1960s 'plate-glass' universities were established, some named after counties or regions rather than old cities, for example Sussex, Kent, East Anglia and Strathclyde. Over 50 polytechnics and similar higher education institutes acquired university status in 1992. There is also a highly successful Open University, which provides every person in Britain with the opportunity to study for a degree, without leaving their home. It is particularly designed for adults who missed the opportunity for higher education earlier in life. It conducts learning through correspondence, radio and television, and also through local study centres.

University examinations are for Bachelor of Arts, or of Science (BA or BSc) on completion of the undergraduate course, and Master of Arts or of Science (MA or MSc) on completion of postgraduate work, usually a one- or two-year course involving some original research. Some students continue to complete a three-year period of original research for the degree of Doctor of Philosophy (PhD). The bachelor degree is normally classed, with about 5 per cent normally gaining a First, about 30 per cent gaining an Upper Second, or 2.1, perhaps 40 per cent gaining a Lower Second, or 2.2, and the balance getting either a Third, a Pass or failing. Approximately 15 per cent fail to complete their degree course.

In addition there are a large number of specialist higher education institutions in the realm of the performing and visual arts. For example, there are four leading conservatories: the Royal Academy of Music, the Royal College of Music, Trinity College of Music and the Royal Northern College of Music. There are a large number of art colleges, of which the most famous is the Royal College of Art, where both Henry Moore and David Hockney once studied. Other colleges cater for dance, film-making and other specialist areas of artistic study.

In spite of the high fees, Britain's universities, FE colleges and English language schools host a large number of foreign students, in 1996 there were no fewer than 158,000.

Female undergraduates have greatly increased proportionately in recent years. In the mid-1960s they were only 28 per cent of the intake, became

A group of international students on graduation day at Coventry University, one of the new universities established in the 1990s.

41 per cent by the early 1980s, and were 51 per cent by 1996. There is still an unfortunate separation of the sexes in fields of chosen study, arising from occupational tradition and social expectations. Caring for others is still a 'proper' career for women; building bridges, it seems, is not. Unless one believes women's brains are better geared to nursing and other forms of caring and men's to bridge-building, one must conclude that social expectations still hinder women and men from realising their potential. Students from poorer backgrounds are seriously underrepresented in higher education. Although more in social categories C, D and E (see p.93) are now enrolled, it is the more prosperous social categories A and B which have benefited most from university expansion. For Labour there are two issues here: equality of opportunity, and maximising all of society's intellectual potential. Ethnic minorities' representation is growing: 13 per cent in 1996 compared with only 10.7 per cent in 1990. It is noteworthy that their university representation exceeds their proportion within the whole population, a measure of their commitment to higher education.

In 1988 a new funding body, the University Funding Council, was established, with power to require universities to produce a certain number of qualified people in specific fields. It is under the UFC's watchful eye that the universities have been forced to double their student intake, and each university department is assessed on its performance and quality. The fear, of course, is that the greatly increased quantity of students that universities must now take might lead to a loss of academic quality.

Expansion has led to a growing funding gap. Universities have been forced to seek sponsorship from the commercial world, wealthy patrons and also from their alumni. The Conservative Party also decided to reduce maintenance grants but to offer students loans in order to finance their studies. However, the funding gap has continued to grow and Labour shocked many who had voted for it by introducing tuition fees at £1,000 per annum in 1998. Although poorer students were to be exempted it was feared that, even with student loans, up to 10 per cent of those planning to go to university would abandon the idea. One effect of the financial burden is that more students are living at home while continuing their studies: about 50 per cent at the ex-polytechnics, but only 15 per cent at the older universities.

Today many university science and technology departments, for example at Oxford, Cambridge, Manchester, Imperial College London, and Strathclyde, are among the best in Europe. The concern is whether they will continue to be so in the future. Academics' pay has fallen so far behind other professions and behind academic salaries elsewhere, that many of the best brains have gone abroad. Adequate pay and sufficient research funding to keep the best in Britain remains a major challenge.

As with the schools system, so also with higher education: there is a real problem about the exclusivity of Britain's two oldest universities. While Oxbridge is no longer the preserve of a social élite, it retains its exclusive, narrow and spell-binding culture. Together with the public school system, it creates a narrow social and intellectual channel from which the nation's leaders are almost exclusively drawn. In 1996 few people were in top jobs in the Civil Service, the armed forces, the law or finance, who had not been either to a public school or Oxbridge, or to both.

The problem is not the quality of education offered either in the independent schools or Oxbridge. The problem is cultural. Can the products of such exclusive establishments remain closely in touch with the remaining 95 per cent of the population? If the expectation is that Oxbridge, particularly, will continue to dominate the controlling positions in the state and economy, is the country ignoring

equal talent which does not have the Oxbridge label? As with the specialisation at the age of 16 for A levels, the danger is that Britain's governing élite is too narrow, both in the kind of education and where it was acquired. It is just possible that the new Labour government, which itself reflects a much wider field of life experience in Britain, will mark the beginning of significantly fuller popular participation in the controlling institutions of state.

Further information

WEBSITES

State education   www.dfee.gov.uk
Private education   www.isis.org.uk

PRINTED MATERIAL

Chitty, C. 1992 *The Education System Transformed* Baseline Books
Walden, George 1996 *We Should Know Better: Solving the Education Crisis* Fourth Estate
The Times Educational Supplement (weekly)
The Times Higher Education Supplement (weekly)

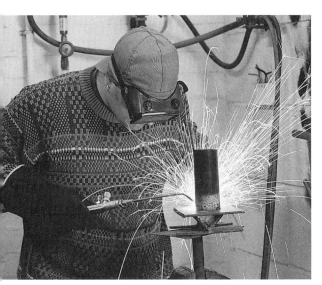

Vocational training: a young man learns how to be a welder.

QUESTIONS

Section analysis

1 **Primary and secondary education**
   a Name the three levels of school at which most children receive their education from the age of five to 16. How do they equate with the school system in your country?
   b Name the two basic public academic examinations to assess English and Welsh pupils first at the age of 16 and then after another two voluntary years of schooling. Name the similar two for Scotland. How do they equate with the examination system in your country?

2 **The story of British schools** After 1944 almost all children attended one of two kinds of school. What were they called? What was the difference between them? In the 1960s this system was changed. What kind of school was introduced? What effects did the change have?

3 **The educational reforms of the 1980s** What was the basic philosophy of the Conservatives' reforms? How did they put this into practice?

4 **Education under Labour** What were the broad problems facing Labour in the field of education when it came to office? How did it propose to resolve them?

5 **The private sector** Why does the author suggest that the public school system is socially divisive?

6 **Further and higher education** Is higher education free for all in Britain? Will the systems of funding tuition and day-to-day expenses for students lead to greater or lesser equality of opportunity, in your opinion? How do these systems compare with those in your own country?

Chapter analysis and discussion

1 Do you accept the author's contention that élitism is a major problem in the British education system? Is there any textual evidence to suggest that state education can be as good as the private system?

2 Compare what you believe to be the strengths and weaknesses of Britain's education system with your own. Make a comparative list of the respective strengths and weaknesses.

Visual interpretation

1 Examine the following table and discuss how these statistics indicate not only different standards between state and private sector education, but some of the reasons behind them.

Figures for state and private schools		
	State	*Private*
Number of UK schools	31,000	2,540
Number of pupils	8,883,000	610,000
The yearly cost per secondary pupil	£2,250	£3,600–£8,700 (day)
Pupil–teacher ratios	18:4	9:8
A-level results % of all A grades, 1994	59	41
Entry to higher education (%)	27	88
Oxbridge: % of all entrants, 1994	54	46

Source (adapted from): George Walden, *We Should Know Better*, 1996, p 43.

2 What do the following graphs say about Britain's higher education record, compared with other countries? Is there any reason to be cautious about the implications of the table?

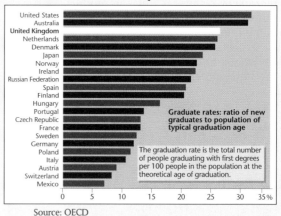

Source: OECD

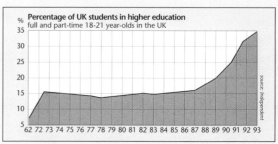

Source: *The Independent*

12 *The media:*
the press, radio and television

The press

Britain's first newspapers appeared over 300 years ago. Now, as then, newspapers receive no government subsidy, unlike in some other European countries today. Advertising has always been a vital source of income. As long ago as 1660, King Charles II advertised in a newspaper for his lost dog. Today, income from advertising is as crucial as income from sales. In 1995, for example, £5,465 million was spent on press advertising, making the press by far the largest advertising medium in Britain.

There are approximately 130 daily and Sunday papers, 1,400 weekly papers and over 6,500 periodical publications. More newspapers, proportionately, are sold in Britain than in almost any other country. On average, two out of three people over the age of 15 read a national morning newspaper. National newspapers have a circulation of about 13 million on weekdays and 17 million on Sundays, but the readership is twice this figure. At first glance, therefore, the British press seems in good health.

National newspapers		
Title	*Owner*	*Circulation 1996 (1000s)*
National dailies		
Populars		
Daily Mirror (1903)	Mirror Group	2,475
Daily Star (1978)	United News & Media	669
Sun (1964)	News International	4,049
Daily Express (1900)	United News & Media	1,245
Daily Mail (1896)	Associated Newspapers	2,058
Qualities		
The Financial Times (1888)	Pearson	302
The Daily Telegraph (1855)	Telegraph Group	1,044
The Guardian (1821)	Guardian Media Group	398
The Independent (1986)	Mirror Group Consortium*	279
The Times (1785)	News International	685
National Sundays		
Populars		
News of the World (1843)	News International	4,608
Sunday Express (1918)	United News & Media	1,259
Sunday Mirror (1963)	Mirror Group	2,426
Mail on Sunday (1982)	Associated Newspapers	2,108
People (1881)	Mirror Group	2,049
Qualities		
The Sunday Telegraph (1961)	Telegraph Group	667
The Observer (1791)	Guardian Media Group	453
The Sunday Times (1822)	News International	1,299
The Independent on Sunday (1990)	Mirror Group Consortium*	304

* Owned by Independent Newspapers since 1998

Source: Central Office of Information, *Britain 1997 An Official Handbook*

The national newspapers, both on weekdays and on Sundays, fall into two broad categories: the 'popular' and 'quality' press.

Ownership of the press, as can be seen, is in the hands of a few large publishing groups. The most significant of these are News International, owned by the Australian-born press tycoon Rupert Murdoch, and the Mirror Group. Although the law provides safeguards against undue concentration of control in one company, the acquisitions of News International have caused concern. Its purchase of *The Times* in 1981 marked the beginning of a shift in that paper from an establishment view, politically slightly right of centre but independent, to a more openly right-wing position, in line with the right-wing flavour of the Conservative governments in the 1980s. It also acquired *The Sunday Times*, and two popular papers, the *Sun*, a daily, and the *News of the World*, a Sunday paper, both of which it successfully turned into the two largest circulation newspapers. Thus News International owns the papers read by over one-third of the newspaper-reading public. In 1989 it entered the television market by launching a satellite television network, now known as BSkyB Television.

Private ownership affects the political viewpoint of most newspapers. Most proprietors, or owners, are more sympathetic to a right of centre political viewpoint. Until the 1990s it could be claimed that 70 per cent of the newspapers sold supported a Conservative viewpoint. Among the populars, only the *Daily* and *Sunday Mirror*, and the *People*, express a left of centre view, while among the qualities *The Guardian*, and its sister Sunday paper, the *Observer*, reflect a moderate left-of-centre

view. *The Independent* and *The Financial Times* tend to be left of centre on social issues while right of centre on economic ones, but would prefer to be viewed as non-aligned. In fact several right-of-centre papers supported a Labour victory in 1997, partly because of Conservative disarray, and partly because of Labour's perceived shift to the right.

The table above categorises newspapers as either popular or quality. All the popular papers, with the exception of the *Sunday Express*, are 'tabloid' in format. The tabloids are essentially mass entertainment. They are smaller than the other papers, and are distinguished by large illustrations, bold captions and a sensational prose style. In the words of one ex-editor of *The Times*:

> *The values of mass journalism are the traditional romantic values of energy, intuition, personality, sexuality, excitement and myth. The romantic element in the mass mind responds instinctively to the energy in the mass newspaper. Readers are presented with an exciting world of demons and temptresses, a flickering and exotic fairy tale … By contrast the values of the serious press are those of analysis, rationality, truth, lucidity, balance, reality and, I would hope, compassion.*

The result is that the tabloids' news content is minimal and their emphasis is on gossip, emotion and scandal. By contrast quality newspapers, known as 'broadsheets' on account of their larger, rather cumbersome format, emphasise news coverage, political and economic analysis and social and cultural issues.

Since 1971 over three million readers have been lost, mainly from the populars. A fundamental reason lies with television becoming the main medium for news. Consequently all newspapers now give more attention to sports results, city finance and entertainment, but this has failed to halt the decline in readership.

Sunday readers have also declined. Since 1991 there has been a drop of one million in the number of populars sold each Sunday. Sunday quality papers have become fatter as the market competition increased during the 1980s. No Sunday quality paper can afford a circulation of less than about 400,000 without serious difficulty in attracting enough advertising. *The Independent on Sunday* (1990) was integrated with the daily *The Independent* in order to reduce production costs, but both seriously need to increase their circulation if their future is to be assured.

The British are avid newspaper readers, especially while travelling to and from work.

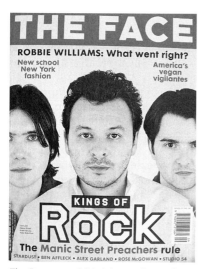

The Face, *one of Britain's most innovative magazines about popular culture.*

During the 1980s virtually every paper was radically affected by new printing technology. Bitter conflicts were fought between management and the unions as the new technology was introduced. Almost every newspaper left its historic home in Fleet Street, known colloquially as 'the Street of Shame', the centre of the British press for over a century. Some went to new sites in London's Docklands, while others moved elsewhere. New technology increased the profitability of the press, and this in turn allowed the creation of new newspapers. Some of these flopped. The most important new paper was *The Independent*. Established in 1986, it rapidly seized the centre ground vacated by *The Times*, which had moved to the right following its purchase by Murdoch's News International. By 1990 its circulation was only slightly behind its two main competitors, *The Times* and *The Guardian*, and it rivalled *The Times* as 'the newspaper of the establishment'. However a sustained price war by *The Times* from 1993 seriously damaged *The Independent*'s sales and by the mid-1990s, its future looked uncertain. Circulation of *The Times*, however, increased from 350,000 in 1993 to 680,000 as a result of what its critics would describe as 'predatory' pricing.

Britain has a substantial number of regional newspapers also. Of these the two Scottish ones, *The Scotsman* (Edinburgh) and the *Herald* (Glasgow) are the most important, since they are also national papers. They each sell about 750,000 copies daily. But others with a large circulation include the *Birmingham Evening Mail* (200,000), the *Wolverhampton Express and Star* (208,000), the *Birmingham Sunday Mercury* (145,000), and the *Leeds Yorkshire Post* (75,000). These, too, are all in numerical decline.

Britain's ethnic minority communities also produce their own papers, both in English and in the vernacular languages. The oldest of these is the *Jewish Chronicle*, founded in 1841. But there are Asian, Caribbean and even Arabic newspapers published in Britain.

Finally, there are over 800 free newspapers, popularly known as 'freebies', almost all of them weekly and financed entirely by advertising. They achieve a weekly circulation of over 40 million. They function as local noticeboards, where local events are advertised, and anyone can advertise in the 'for sale' or 'wanted' columns.

The best-selling weeklies are those giving details of the forthcoming week's television and radio programmes, *What's On TV*, the *Radio Times* and *TV Times*, with circulations in 1996 of 1.6 million, 1.4 million and 1 million, respectively. Second to them in popularity are women's magazines, of which easily the best-selling is *Take a Break*, with a weekly sale of almost 1.5 million, and *Woman's Weekly*, *Woman's Own*, *Woman*, *Woman's Realm*, which sell between 300,000 and 800,000 copies each week. During the early 1990s some recently established men's magazines, *Loaded*, *GQ* and *Esquire*, became popular with circulations of 100,000 to 240,000. The leading opinion journals are *The Economist*, a slightly right-of-centre political and economic weekly, the *New Statesman and Society*, a left-of-centre political and social weekly, the *Spectator*, a right-of-centre political weekly, and *Private Eye*, a satirical fortnightly with a reputation for devastating attacks on leading personalities, and some libel suits against it in the law courts.

Inside a newspaper office.

With almost 1,500 staff in 91 countries, no newspaper anywhere can compete with Britain's formidable news agency, Reuters. Across the world its name has become an assurance of objectivity, accuracy and reliability. Although run from London, Reuters deliberately avoids any image of being a British institution with English news values. As the day progresses, its world news file is edited from three different cities, switching time zones from Hong Kong to London to New York. Its reports are filed in French, German, Japanese, Arabic and Spanish, as well as English. Reuters also owns Reuters Television (RTV), the largest international television news agency in the world, providing news video to broadcasters in 89 countries.

Radio and television

In 1936 the government established the British Broadcasting Corporation (BBC) to provide a public service in radio. It also began broadcasting that year on the recently invented television. At first solely through its agency, television and radio changed the entertainment habits and the culture of the nation. In 1955, however, the establishment of independent and commercial television and radio removed the BBC's broadcasting monopoly.

In spite of its much reduced evening audience, BBC radio still provides an important service. Its five radio stations (BBC Radio 1–5) provide: (1) non-stop pop music; (2) light entertainment; (3) minority interests, e.g. classical music, arts programmes and academic material (some for Open University courses); (4) news and comment and discussion programmes; (5) sport. The BBC additionally runs 38 local radio stations, providing material of local interest.

Commercial radio offers three nationwide services: Classic FM, which broadcasts mainly classical music; Virgin 1215, broadcasting popular music; and Talk Radio UK, a speech-based service.

In addition there are 180 independent local radio stations which provide news, information, music and other entertainment, coverage of local events, sports commentary, chat shows and 'phone-in' programmes. The latter provide an important counselling service to isolated, aggrieved or perplexed people.

A disc-jockey inside a college radio station.

An important but separate part of the BBC's work is its 'external services'. The BBC World Service broadcasts by radio in English and 43 vernacular languages. The service is funded separately from the rest of the BBC, by the Foreign Office. Although the BBC has freedom in the content of what it broadcasts, the government decides in which foreign languages it should broadcast, and the amount of funding it should receive. As such, the service is a promotional part of British foreign policy. The BBC World Service reaches an audience of approximately 140 million listeners, who are predominantly young (aged between 25 and 35) and male. The strength of the BBC's external services has been the provision of relatively objective and impartial news and comment to listeners in countries where local censorship exists.

In 1991 the BBC also commenced a commercial operation called Worldwide Television, which provides 24-hour news coverage and entertainment to broadcast networks in 80 countries and reaches an estimated 45 million homes. BBC World has only one rival, the American network, CNN. Where CNN has three times as many camera crews, the BBC has almost twice as many correspondents.

Television is the single most popular form of entertainment in Britain. In the mid-1990s viewers spent on average over three and a half hours daily in front of the television set. Until 1997 they had four terrestrial channels to choose from: BBC1 and BBC2, ITV (Independent Television) and Channel 4. Channel 4, which was established in 1982, specialises in minority interest programmes, but has proved highly successful. A third commercial channel, Channel 5, began broadcasting in 1997 and terrestrial broadcasting is likely to expand further. In 1996 legislation provided for transition of all broadcasting and telecommunications services from analogue frequency to digital transmission, probably early in the twenty-first century. Satellite broadcasting has been available since 1989. The major provider of satellite programmes is BSkyB. Cable television was introduced in 1993 and currently has 1.3 million subscribers.

A television drama being filmed.

An airport official in a popular television 'docu-drama' which dramatises real lives and occupations.

BBC television and radio derives its income from an annual licence fee for television, while ITV and Channel 4 are financed solely through advertising. The question of financing by licence fee was strongly challenged by the Conservative government which argued that the BBC had to demonstrate its ability to operate with commercial efficiency in order to continue to enjoy public funding. As a consequence the BBC underwent a radical restructuring in the mid-1990s, with six separate components: BBC Broadcast, which schedules and commissions services for audiences; BBC Production, which develops in-house radio and television production; BBC News which provides an integrated national and international news operation; BBC Worldwide, to be responsible for generating income in Britain and abroad, and for the World Service; BBC Resources, to provide support and expertise to programme-makers; and BBC Corporate Services, to provide strategic services to the BBC as a whole. The danger, however, is that the drive for managerial efficiency will undermine the high quality of individual programmes. Take, for example, the new news operation. All news is now centrally gathered rather than by particular programmes. Leading BBC journalists protested strongly that this would threaten the distinctive ethos of particular news and current affairs programmes with a growing, and possibly bland, homogeneity. A compromise was struck, but the danger remains. In the words of one retired World Service director:

> *The tragedy is that a once great organisation – one of the finest creations of the liberal mind, one dedicated to an open and humane dialogue with its listeners and viewers, one that could carry out such dialogue because it conducted it internally first – has been subjected to such brutalising so-called 'managerialism'.*

(John Tusa, *The Independent*)

The fear is that the BBC's wonderful variety will be replaced by a unified and homogenised service, in news, sport, and other areas.

Since 1991 ITV has been governed through the Independent Television Commission, which is empowered to give regional franchises for a 10-year period to a number of different companies. There are 15 such companies, providing programmes many of which are sold or broadcast on other regional networks. When commercial television commenced in 1955 there had been fears that advertising would erode the high standards already set by the BBC. In fact ITV became fiercely competitive with the BBC in the production of high-quality programmes which, like the BBC's, were sold profitably to many foreign networks. Channel 4 provides an alternative service with more documentary, cultural and informative programmes. Channel 5 aspires to the same standards of quality as ITV, but has yet to achieve this. In Wales there is a special fourth channel, S4C (Sianel Pedwar Cymru) which provides a minimum of 32 hours of Welsh-medium broadcasting weekly. Since 1993 there has also been a Gaelic TV fund to assist the provision of Gaelic broadcasting on commercial television and radio.

The strength of British television lies in its high quality. 'Go anywhere in the world,' one leading political journalist has written, 'and British television is an object of envy and admiration ... . The foundation of Britain's excellence in the field of television is the tradition of public service broadcasting as upheld by the BBC.' Many involved in television, including foreigners living in Britain, claim that British television is the best in the world. Its export record and high audience ratings certainly suggest it is among the best. The reason lies in the quality of its innovation and its willingness to experiment. For example, British television enthusiastically took *The Muppet Show*, when its creator, Jim Henson, had been rejected by the American networks. In the fields of documentary, comedy and satire, or drama, British television is a world leader.

In 1990 the government passed the Broadcasting Act, which promised to change the basis of television from 1992 onwards. This act was inspired by two factors: the Conservative government's free-market ideology and the reality that satellite television would make it possible for viewers to receive programmes transmitted from outside Britain, which would effectively destroy the regulatory controls previously applied by government. In order to prepare Britain's own commercial television for the 'white heat' of competing with satellite television for audiences, and thus for advertisers, the intention of the Act was to open British commercial television to genuine and open competition. In 1992, an Independent Television Commission (ITC) replaced the Independent Television Authority and auctioned television transmission licences. It had the authority to use its discretion in awarding franchises on the basis of high quality, not merely to the top financial bidders. It is a recognition that there cannot be a wholly free market in television. As a result of the auction two major networks, Thames Television and also the morning service, TV-AM, both lost their franchises. The ITC also planned for a fifth television channel. But the danger remains that a larger number of channels will not, as is argued, provide greater choice. The greater the number of transmitting channels, the smaller the audiences will be for each individual channel. The smaller the audience, the less will be the advertising revenue possible, and if less advertising revenue is expected the production budget will be proportionately smaller. This is bound to hit hard a wide range of programmes, particularly minority ones.

It remains to be seen how this affects television in the long term. By the late 1990s it seemed that companies were generally less willing to invest heavily in the origination of expensive new programmes unless they were assured they would enjoy a franchise long enough to recoup their investment. Television is still unquestionably something Britain does really well. It remains to be seen whether the Broadcasting Act supports Britain's leading position, or weakens it.

Ever since the beginning of the 1980s there has been growing anxiety concerning pornographic and violent programmes. The Broadcasting Act provides for increased censorship. Any policeman of superintendent rank or above may demand access to any untransmitted material under the obscenity or public order laws. In addition, the Broadcasting Standards Council, created in 1989, is empowered to veto transmission of any programme it considers indecent. It is also empowered to censor imported material, although this is made meaningless by the high number of joint ventures in which British television is now engaged. Many parents have expressed considerable concern at the amount of sex and violence portrayed on television, particularly before 9 p.m., the time when younger children are expected to have gone to bed. On the other hand many journalists were suspicious of the Conservative government's intentions and, in the

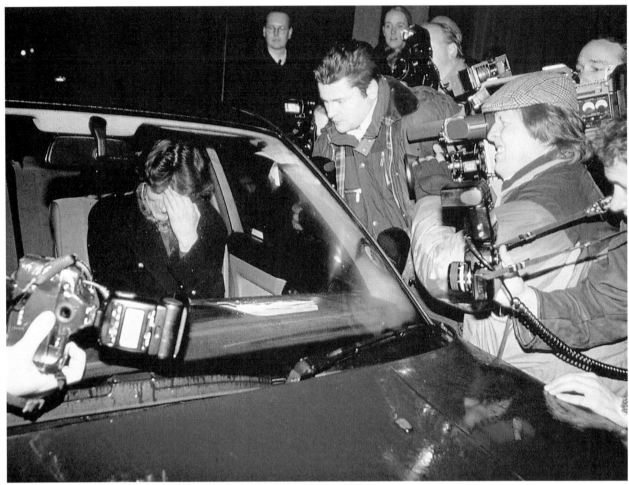

The intrusion of privacy by the press: paparazzi go to work on someone in the news.

words of one of them, '[found] it hard to separate zeal for market-led reform from a desire to destabilise a system capable of delivering tough and challenging programmes.' They are likely to watch Labour policy towards the media very closely.

Government and the media

Writing in 1741, the philosopher David Hume praised press freedom in Britain with the words: 'Nothing is more apt to surprise a foreigner, than the extreme liberty which we enjoy in this country, of communicating whatever we please to the public, and of openly censuring every measure entered into by the King or his ministers.' Is such a boast still justified? The relationship between government and the media is bound to be an uneasy one in any democracy. Governments are concerned with maintaining their own authority. The media must watch the exercise of that authority, and criticise when they feel it is wrongly used.

The British obsession with secrecy has already been discussed in Chapter 10. For over 50 years the government has had an arrangement for the protection of national security in the media. Its Defence, Press and Broadcasting Committee has agreed that in some circumstances the publication of certain information might endanger national security. In such cases a 'D (Defence) Notice' is issued. A D Notice does not quite have the force of law, but no newspaper editor would ignore a D Notice without incurring major penalties. Over the past 25 years there has been increasing criticism of the apparent abuse of the D Notice system in order to conceal not matters of national security but potentially embarrassing facts.

During the 1980s the government frequently tried to prevent discussion of sensitive issues. In 1989 the new Official Secrets Act greatly strengthened the government's ability to prevent disclosure of sensitive information. Any revelation of material obtained in any unauthorised way from a government source would make a journalist liable to prosecution. Not surprisingly, this provoked strong criticism from journalists. As the Deputy Director General of the BBC wrote in 1989:

Only a threat to vital interests should prevent disclosure by journalists. Those interests include the safety of the realm: they do not include the sensitivities of foreign leaders or the avoidance of embarrassment to the United Kingdom government. A journalist who discovers – say from a confidential Foreign Office document – that a foreign government is using torture faces a dilemma. He or she will wish to publish. The journalist is aware that the regime concerned may respond by refusing contracts to British firms. The story would 'jeopardise' UK interests abroad; and the journalist would face criminal sanction. But at a trial he or she would not be able to argue that the benefit that may result from the revelation of torture outweighs the loss of business.

(John Birt, *The Independent*)

Nowhere is the issue of journalistic freedom more sensitive than in the case of the BBC, for it occupies a curious position. It is generally regarded as admirably independent of government. But is this really true? It is controlled by a board of 12 governors appointed by the government. They are answerable to the government for all aspects of BBC broadcasting, and in the end the Home Secretary has the authority to replace them. In 1986 the governors came under intense pressure from the government on account of certain programmes which angered the government. One senior Cabinet minister publicly referred to the BBC as the 'Bashing Britain Corporation'. The BBC's Director General was sacked on account of two programmes that angered the government, an act which suggested that the BBC had less independence than many thought.

Nevertheless, the BBC is freer today than in the 1950s when its sense of national loyalty was defined in terms of loyalty to the state rather than the people. There has been a subtle change in vocabulary. Forty years ago, people would have asked of a controversial programme, 'Was it in the national interest?' Today, people are more likely to ask whether it is 'in the public interest'.

There was another way in which the government exercised a hold on the media in order to reduce its true independence. This was through the 'Lobby', a system whereby government ministers and MPs made disclosures to certain accredited journalists on the understanding that it was 'off the record'. The Lobby system began in 1884. The advantage to journalists was that they learnt many things officially not admitted. The advantage to politicians was that they could make things public in an anonymous or deniable way. Officially such meetings between journalists and politicians 'never took place'. Typical newspaper reports begin, 'Senior government sources are saying …' or, 'Sources close to the Prime Minister … '. Politicians used this method for various purposes, often to attack a colleague in a way they could not possibly do publicly. Prime Ministers, for example, used this technique to undermine a minister's public standing before sacking him or her. Or it was a way of manipulating information to mislead, possibly to attract attention to one issue in order to avoid press attention on something else.

Journalists found it useful, but as a result of the increased use of the Lobby system in the 1980s for the disclosure of sensitive or damaging material, two newspapers, *The Guardian* and *The Independent* refused to accept anything from government ministers which they were not prepared to state 'on the record', and withdrew from the Lobby. After it came to power, Labour announced the appointment of an official spokesperson, and the end of the Lobby system.

Privacy and self-regulation of the press

It might seem that in the face of government secrecy, journalists must be allowed the fullest investigative powers. But how free should the press be? During the 1980s there was growing popular disgust at the way in which some newspapers, most notably the *Sun*, attempted to investigate the private lives of well-known people. Many had their careers ruined or damaged when their sexual activities were made public. The prime targets have been, of course, members of the Royal Family who found it increasingly difficult to escape from the voyeurism of the popular press. The dramatic death of Princess Diana while being chased by paparazzi is unlikely to bring press intrusion to an end. Admittedly Diana was a unique phenomenon. As she said of herself, 'You see yourself as a good product that sits on a shelf and sells well, and people make a lot of money out of you.' Only a few days before their death, the blurred pictures of Diana supposedly embracing her friend Dodi al Fayed, sold an extra 175,000 copies of the *Sun*. Little wonder the editor of the *Sun* said at the time: 'There is an absolute fascination with her that never wanes from our readers' point of view.' It was not only newspapers. Magazines with a picture of Diana on the front could see their circulation leap by as much as 30 or 40 per cent.

Diana may have been unique, but other public figures will also fascinate the public. In the end the voyeuristic appetite of the public is an inevitable component in the struggle between the tabloids for a greater share of the market. The tabloids will do whatever is necessary to maintain or increase their share of the market.

Diana was a highly public figure who often courted the press. Many people, however, feel that the press has no right to publicise personal matters when they have no relevance to any public issue, and that the victims of inaccurate reporting are entitled to a right of reply. As a result of public anger at the end of the 1980s, most newspapers appointed an ombudsman to deal with individual complaints. As one correspondent noted, however, 'Most of the ombudsmen are from inside the papers that have appointed them. Not all are experienced in journalism. Almost the only thing they have in common is that they are (all) men.'

Beyond each newspaper is a final court of appeal for outraged members of the public. This is the Press Complaints Commission established at the beginning of 1991. The Commission replaced a previous body, the Press Council, which progressively lost its authority since its own establishment in 1953. If the new Commission cannot convince the public that press self-regulation can be made to work, the government may bring in legislation to control the worst excesses of the press.

Further information

WEBSITES

BBC	www.bbc.co.uk (use search facility)
Daily Express	www.research.expressnewspapers.co.
The Daily Telegraph	www.telegraph.co.uk
The Economist	www.economist.com
The Financial Times	www.ft.com
The Guardian	www.guardian.co.uk
The Independent	www.independent.co.uk
The Observer	www.observer.co.uk
The Times	www.the-times.co.uk
Reuters	www.online.reuters.com
The Press Association	www.pad.press.net

PRINTED MATERIAL

Coxall, Bill and Robins, Lynton 1994
   Contemporary British Politics Chapter 16 Macmillan
Curran, J. and Seaton, J. 1990
   Power without Responsibility: The Press and Broadcast in Britain Routledge
Recent editions of any of the above daily and weekly newspapers

QUESTIONS

Section analysis

1 The press Consider this list of the characteristics of British newspapers:
a dependent on advertising revenue
b separate Sunday papers
c format divided between quality broadsheets and popular tabloids
d ownership in the hands of a few large publishing groups
e variety of types of paper: national, regional, ethnic and local free ('freebie') papers.
Now check this list against what you consider are the essential characteristics of your own country's press. List the differences.

2 Radio and television What were the two basic reasons for the Conservative government's Broadcasting Act of 1990, and what were the provisions of that Act?

3 Government and the media In your opinion, should the media:
a represent the 'national' interest or the 'public' interest?
b be permitted to reveal embarrassing facts about the government which might jeopardise commercial or political interests?
c publish information gained secretly from politicians?

4 Privacy and self-regulation of the press What is the essential dilemma faced by the press concerning the respect of privacy?

Chapter analysis and discussion

1 Is the British press predominantly left or right of centre on the political scale? Do you think this balance truly reflects the balance of political views among the British people?

2 Do you agree or disagree with the following statements?
a The BBC World Service broadcasts the views of the British government.
b The media in Britain has to defend its independence in the face of pressure from the government.

3 Make predictions about the future. Do you think that:
a newspaper readership in Britain will increase or continue to decline?
b British television will maintain its world reputation for excellence?
c the British media will become more or less subject to government interference?

4 Make comparisons between the British media and the media in your country.
a Which newspapers are comparable to the main British tabloids and broadsheets?
b To what extent are newspapers, radio and television funded by advertising?
c Are there any limits to press freedom?

Textual interpretation

Consider the following excerpt from *The Independent* editorial following Princess Diana's death:

> … her (Princess Diana's) death ought to start a much-needed debate (which has to be international rather than just national) about the structure and appetites of this global industry of images and words which the public both adores and loathes. The media is omnipresent, and treated with the same mixture of enjoyment and dislike as other great powers. It was, of course, the reviled media to which people turned yesterday, unquestioningly, avid for the news.
>
> (From the Leader Page of *The Independent*)

Is there a balance between the public's right to know and the individual's right to privacy? If so, how do you think this should be achieved? By legislation or by a voluntary code as at present? Compare what happens in Britain with what happens in your own country.

13 *Religion in Britain*

Barely 16 per cent of the adult population of Britain belongs to one of the Christian churches, and this proportion continues to decline. Yet the regional variation is revealing. In England only 12 per cent of the adult population are members of a church. The further one travels from London, however, the greater the attendance: in Wales 22 per cent, in Scotland 36 per cent and in Northern Ireland no fewer than 75 per cent.

Today there is complete freedom of practice, regardless of religion or sect. However, until the mid-nineteenth century, those who did not belong to the Church of England, the official 'established' or state church, were barred from some public offices. The established church still plays a powerful role in national life, in spite of the relatively few people who are active members of it.

The Church of England

There are two established or state churches in Britain: the Church of England, or Anglican Church as it is also called, and the Church of Scotland, or 'Kirk'.

In 1533 the English king, Henry VIII, broke away from Rome and declared himself head of the Church in England. His reason was political: the Pope's refusal to allow him to divorce his wife, who had failed to produce a son. Apart from this administrative break, the Church at first remained more Catholic than Protestant. However, during the next two centuries when religion was a vital political issue in Europe, the Church of England became more Protestant in belief as well as organisation.

Ever since 1534 the monarch has been Supreme Governor of the Church of England. No one may take the throne who is not a member of the Church of England. For any Protestant this would be unlikely to be a problem, since the Church of England already includes a wide variety of Protestant belief. However, if the monarch or the next in line to the throne decided to marry a Roman Catholic or a divorcee, this might cause a constitutional crisis. It has always been understood that if such a marriage went ahead, the monarch or heir would have to give up their claim to the throne, and to being Supreme Governor of the Church. In 1936 Edward VIII, who had only just succeeded to the throne, abdicated in order to marry a divorcee. Today it is more likely that the monarch or heir would marry the person he or she loved, and would renounce the title of Supreme Governor of the Church. It might pose a constitutional crisis, but is less likely to be one for the Church. The monarch is crowned by the senior Anglican cleric, the Archbishop of Canterbury, but if the monarch renounced Supreme Governorship of the Church, this ceremony might be abandoned or radically changed.

As Head of the Church of England, the monarch appoints the archbishops, bishops and deans of the Church, on the recommendation of the Prime Minister, who might well not be an Anglican. The Prime Minister makes a recommendation from two nominee candidates, put forward by a special Crown Appointments Commission (composed of bishops, clergy and lay members of the Church). All Anglican clergy must take an oath of allegiance to the Crown, a difficult proposition for any priest who is a republican at heart. Thus Church and Crown in England are closely entwined, with mutual bonds of responsibility.

The most senior spiritual leaders of the Church of England are the Archbishop of Canterbury, who is 'Primate of All England', and the Archbishop of York, who is 'Primate of England'. They are head of the two ecclesiastical provinces of England, Canterbury and York. Both provinces are divided into dioceses, each under a bishop. Canterbury is the larger province, containing 30 dioceses, while York contains only 14. The choice of Canterbury and York is historical. Canterbury is the site of where St Augustine reestablished the Christian church in England at the end of the sixth century. The see of York was founded in the early seventh century by an envoy of St Augustine to this capital

George Carey, Archbishop of Canterbury.

of Northumbria. (The Celtic churches which survived in Ireland and Scotland were well established two centuries earlier.)

The senior bishops are those of London, Durham and Winchester, but there is no guarantee of promotion according to seniority. George Carey, for example, the present (103rd) Archbishop, was previously Bishop of Bath and Wells, no longer considered a senior bishopric. Because of the growth in population, some bishops are assisted by deputies assigned to a geographical part of the diocese. These are 'suffragan' bishops. Each diocese is composed of parishes, the basic unit of the Church's ministry. Each parish has a vicar, or sometimes a team of vicars, if it includes more than one church.

The Archbishop of Canterbury is head of the Anglican 'Communion'. This Communion is composed of the various independent churches which have grown out of the Church of England in various parts of the world. In fact England accounts for only two of the 28 provinces of the Anglican Church. In theory, about 40 per cent of the English might say they were members of the Church of England. Far fewer ever actually attend church and only one million regularly attend, a drop of over 13 per cent since 1988. It is also a small proportion of the 70 million active Anglicans worldwide. More Nigerians, for example, than

English are regular attenders of the Anglican Church. Within the worldwide Anglican Communion are some famous people, for example Desmond Tutu, head of South Africa's Truth and Reconciliation Commission and once Archbishop of Cape Town. It is said that most of the 'ruling establishment' of Washington belong to the Episcopal Church, the Anglican Church of the United States. The Scottish Episcopal Church, the Church in Wales and the Church of Ireland are members of the Anglican Communion but are not 'established' churches and have memberships of not more than about 100,000 each.

Once in every 10 years the Archbishop of Canterbury invites all the bishops of the Anglican Communion to a conference at Lambeth in London to exchange views and debate issues of concern. Rather like the Commonwealth Conference, the Lambeth Conference provides an opportunity for the sister churches from every continent to meet and share their different concerns and perspectives.

The Church of England is frequently considered to be a 'broad' church because it includes a wide variety of belief and practice. Traditionally there have been two poles in membership, the Evangelicals and the Anglo-Catholics. The Evangelicals, who have become proportionately stronger in recent years, give greater emphasis to basing all faith and practice on the Bible. There are over one million British evangelicals of different Protestant churches belonging to an umbrella group, the Evangelical Alliance. The Anglo-Catholics give greater weight to Church tradition and Catholic practices, and do not feel the same level of disagreement as many

An Anglican church service. In the countryside many church buildings, like this one, are over 500 years old.

Evangelicals concerning the teaching and practices of the Roman Catholic Church. There is an uneasy relationship between the two wings of the Church, which sometimes breaks into open hostility.

Yet most Evangelicals and Anglo-Catholics are united in their deeper dislike of the liberal theologians within the Church of England. These have challenged the literal validity of several beliefs of the Church, and have argued that reinterpretation must constantly take place, partly as a result of recent biblical scholarship, but also because they maintain that theological understanding changes as society itself changes and develops over the years. In that sense, one can divide the Church of England in a different way, into conservatives and modernists. It is estimated that 80 per cent of the Church of England are of evangelical persuasion, and the balance is divided almost equally between Anglo-Catholics and liberals.

However, a large number of church-goers either feel no particular loyalty to any of these traditions, or feel more comfortable somewhere between these poles. Since most bishops are theologians, the liberals are more strongly represented among the bishops than sheer numbers in church membership justifies.

The Church of England is above all things a church of compromise. It is, in the words of one journalist, 'a Church where there has traditionally been space on the pew for heretics and unbelievers, doubters and sceptics'. It takes a long view and distrusts zealous theological or ideological certainty. It prefers to live with disagreements of belief rather than apply authoritarian decisions. It fudges issues where it can, to keep its broad body of believers together. Most of its members are happy with the arrangement. In that sense the Church of England is profoundly typical of the English character. It distrusts the rigid logic of a particular tradition of theology and prefers the illogical but practical atmosphere of 'live and let live' within a broader church climate. Consequently there is always a concern to ensure that all wings of the Church are represented among the bishops, and that those appointed as archbishops shall be neither too controversial in their theology, nor too committed to one particular wing of the Church as to be unacceptable to others.

The Church is governed by its bishops. In that sense it is a hierarchical organisation. Nevertheless its regulating and legislative body is the General Synod, made up of three 'Houses', the House of

An Anglican woman priest celebrating the Eucharist. Women were first permitted to become priests in 1992.

Bishops (53 diocesan and suffragan bishops), the House of Clergy (259 representatives of the clergy) and the House of Laity (258 representatives of lay members of the Church). The General Synod meets twice yearly with two functions: (1) to consider matters concerning the Church of England, and to take any necessary steps for its effective operation; (2) to consider and express its opinion on any matters of religious or public interest. In order to reach agreement on any issue, General Synod requires a majority in each House, in the words of one religious commentator, 'a clumsy and largely ineffective cross between a parliament and a democracy. It is a typical Anglican compromise.'

This has been particularly true in the two areas of greatest controversy within the Church since the mid-1980s: the ordination of women and of homosexuals (and the acceptance of homosexuals already in the priesthood). In both cases the modernists are ranged against the conservatives. After a long and often contentious debate, the Church finally accepted the ordination of women in 1992, and the first were ordained in 1994, long after the practice had been adopted in other parts of the Anglican Communion. Some 200 clergy, fewer than expected, chose to leave the Church of England rather than accept women priests. They were almost all Anglo-Catholic. While great passion was aroused among some clergy and lay people on this issue, the large majority of church-goers did not feel strongly enough, either way, to force a decision. It is unlikely that any woman will become a bishop for some years. Having accepted women priests, a fresh controversy arose over the question of homosexuality with, if anything, even greater vehemence. This time the contest is primarily between modernists and evangelicals, but the essence of the debate is the same: biblical and traditional values versus contemporary social ones. The director general of the Evangelical Alliance claims that 'a vast number of churches stand by 2,000 years of biblical analysis which concludes that homosexual sex is outside the will and purpose of God'. The modernists argue that it is ludicrous to pick one out of many culturally specific prohibitions in the Old Testament, and that a judgmental posture excludes Christians who quite sincerely have a different sexual orientation and perspective from heterosexuals. Modernists say the church should listen and learn from them. It is a controversy likely to persist well into the twenty-first century.

The Church of England was traditionally identified with the ruling establishment and with authority, but it has been distancing itself over the past 25 years or so, and may eventually disengage from the state. 'Disestablishment', as this is known, becomes a topic for discussion each time the Church and state clash over some issue. Since 1979 the Church has been ready to criticise aspects of official social policy (see below).

Nevertheless, the Church of England remains overwhelmingly conventional and middle class in its social composition, having been mainly middle and upper class in character since the Industrial Revolution. Most working-class people in England and Wales who are religious belong to the nonconformist or 'Free' Churches, while others have joined the Catholic Church in the past 140 years.

Because of its position, the Anglican Church has inherited a great legacy of ancient cathedrals and parish churches. It is caught between the value of these magnificent buildings as places of worship, and the enormous cost of their upkeep. The state provides about 10 per cent of the cost of maintaining the fabric of historic churches.

The other Christian churches

The Free or nonconformist churches are distinguished by having no bishops, or 'episcopacy', and they all admit both women and men to their ministry. The main ones today are: the Methodist Union (400,000 full adult members); the Baptists (150,000); the United Reformed Church (110,000) and the Salvation Army (50,000). These all tend towards strong evangelicalism. In the case of the Methodists and Baptists, there are also smaller splinter groups. In addition there are a considerable number of smaller sects. Most of these churches are, like the Anglicans, in numerical decline.

In Scotland the Church, or Kirk, vehemently rejected the idea of bishops, following a more Calvinist Protestant tradition. Its churches are plain. There is no altar, only a table, and the emphasis is on the pulpit, where the Gospel is preached. The Kirk is more democratic than the Anglican Church. Although each kirk is assigned a minister, it also elects its own 'elders'. The minister and one of these elders represent the kirk at the regional presbytery. Each of the 46 presbyteries of Scotland elects two commissioners to represent it at the principal governing body of the Church, the General Assembly. Each year the commissioners meet in the General Assembly, and elect a Moderator to chair the General Assembly for that year. Unlike the Church of England, the Church of Scotland is subject neither to the Crown nor to Parliament, and takes pride in its independence from state authority, for which it fought in the sixteenth and seventeenth centuries. In keeping with its democratic nature, it admits women as well as men to the ministry.

Among all these Protestant churches, but particularly among the larger English ones, there has been a recent important development called the 'house church' movement. This began in the 1970s and has a membership of roughly 90,000, although attendance is far higher. This movement is a network of autonomous 'churches' of usually not more than 100 members in each. These churches meet, usually in groups of 15 or 20, in members' homes for worship and prayer meetings. Most of those joining such groups are in the 20–40 year-old age range and belong to the professional middle classes – solicitors, doctors and so forth – who have felt frustrated with the more

The Methodists tend to be far less formal in worship than Anglicans or Catholics.

ponderous style of the larger churches. They try to recapture what they imagine was the vitality of the early church. But it is doubtful how long these house churches will last. If they are anything like some of the revivalist sects of the nineteenth century, they in their turn will lose their vitality, and discontented members may return to the churches which their predecessors left, or drift away from the Christian church altogether.

The Protestant churches of Britain undoubtedly owe part of the revival taking place in some evangelical churches to the vitality of the West Indian churches. West Indian immigrants in the 1950s and 1960s were not welcomed into Anglican churches, and many decided to form their own churches. Their music and informal joyfulness of worship spread quickly in evangelical circles. As Philip Mohabir, a West Indian, describes:

Congregations that would have been cold, dull and boring, would now sing to guitar music, clap their hands, and even play tambourines. Those were things that only West Indian churches did ... . Now people would raise their hands in the air and clap and even dance. English, white, evangelical Christians dancing and clapping their hands, praising God. That in itself is a miracle we West Indian Christians never thought would happen.

The Roman Catholic Church only returned to Britain in 1850. During the preceding 300 years the few Catholic families which refused to accept the new Church were popularly viewed as less than wholeheartedly English. The English Protestant prejudice that to be Catholic is to be not quite wholly English only really disappeared in the 1960s.

The Roman Catholic Church grew rapidly after 1850, particularly among the industrial working class. By the mid-1980s it had about 5.7 million members, of whom 1.4 million were regular attenders. By the mid-1990s this had fallen to 1.1 million attenders, a decline of over 17 per cent. Alongside growing secularism in society, many have left the Catholic Church because of its authoritarian conservatism, particularly in the field of sexual mores. It is estimated that attendance will barely exceed 600,000 by the year 2005. The Catholic Church in England is composed of four main strands: immigrants from Ireland; working-class people in deprived areas among whom Catholic effort was concentrated in the nineteenth century; a few upper-class families; and finally

middle-class converts, for example a bishop of London and two government ministers who all left the Anglican church and became Catholics over the Anglican ordination of women in 1992. The senior English cleric is the Archbishop of Westminster.

All the formal churches are in numerical decline. Each time there is a census of church attendance and membership, the numbers in almost every church have fallen. In 1970 there were an estimated 8.6 million practising Christians. By 1994 the figure had fallen to 6.5 million. At Christmas, the major festival, perhaps 5 million will attend church, but on a normal Sunday it is barely half this figure. One must conclude that numerical decline will probably continue in an age when people feel no apparent need for organised religion. But the decline may not be as dramatic as the figures suggest. Many church-goers have ceased to be regular simply because they often go away at weekends. Within the Church the debate is bound to continue between the modernists who wish to reinterpret religion according to the values of the age they live in, and conservatives who believe it is precisely the supernatural elements which attract people in the age of science.

A Pentecostal service. Black Pentecostalists are known for their exuberance in worship.

On the national stage the Church has made its greatest mark in recent years in the area of social justice. In 1985 the Church of England produced a report, *Faith in the City: A Call for Action by Church and Nation*, which examined inner-city deprivation and decline, and recommended measures both by church and state to reverse the trends. The Roman Catholic and Free Churches showed similar concern at increased social deprivation in the 1980s. Today the Church is no longer seen as an integral part of the establishment but as possibly its most formidable critic.

Besides these 'orthodox' churches which accept the doctrine of the Trinity, there are others which have their own specific beliefs, and are consequently viewed as outside orthodoxy. The Mormon Church which is strong in the United States, has doubled its membership to about 200,000 in the past 20 years. Other non-Trinitarian churches have also grown, part of an alternative form of spirituality which has been attractive to many people since the 1960s.

Other religions

Apart from Christianity, there are at least five other religions with a substantial number of adherents in Britain. These are usually composed of either immigrants or the descendants of immigrants.

The oldest is the Jewish community, which now numbers barely 300,000, of whom fewer than half ever attend synagogue and only 80,000 are actual synagogue members. Today the Jewish community in Britain is ageing and shrinking, on account of assimilation and a relatively low birth rate, and is in rapid decline. A survey in 1996 revealed that 44 per cent of Jewish men under the age of 40 are married to or are living with a non-Jewish partner. Between 20 and 25 per cent of Jewish women in this age range also marry outside the community. Even so, it is the second largest Jewish community in Western Europe. Two-thirds of the community live in London, with another 9,000 or so in Manchester and Leeds respectively, and another 6,000 in Brighton.

Jews returned to England in the seventeenth century, after their previous expulsion in the thirteenth century. At first those who returned were Sephardic, that is, originally from Spain and Portugal, but during the last years of the nineteenth century and first half of the twentieth century a more substantial number of Ashkenazi (Germanic and East European) Jews, fleeing persecution, arrived. Ashkenazis form 70 per cent of British Jews.

As a result of these two separate origins, and as a result of the growth of Progressive Judaism (the Reform and Liberal branches), the Jews are divided into different religious groups. The largest group, approximately 120,000, are Orthodox and belong to the United Synagogues. They look to the Chief Rabbi of Great Britain for spiritual leadership. A much smaller number of Sephardic Orthodox still recognise a different leader, the Haham. The two Progressive groups, the Reform and Liberal Jews, which roughly equate with the broad church and modernists of the Anglican Church, have no acknowledged single leader, but they do have a number of rabbis who command a following among those who admire their wisdom. The Progressives account for 17 per cent of the entire community. Thirty-seven per cent of Jews claim no religious affiliation at all.

Orthodox Jewish worship. As in Islam, men and women are segregated for worship.

There is also a Board of Deputies of British Jews, the lay representation of Anglo-Jewry since 1760, to which 250 synagogues and organisations in Britain elect representatives. It speaks on behalf of British Jewry on a wide variety of matters, but its degree of genuine representation is qualified in two ways: fewer than half of Britain's Jews belong to the electing synagogues and organisations; and none of the community's more eminent members belongs to the Board. In fact many leading members of the community are often uneasy with the position the Board takes on issues.

As in the Christian church, the fundamentalist part of Jewry seems to grow compared with other groups, especially among the young, and causes similar discomfort for those who do not share its certainties and legal observances. The most obvious concentrations of orthodox Jews, who are distinguishable by their dress, are in the north London suburbs of Golders Green and Stamford Hill.

There are also more recently established religious groups: Hindus, Sikhs, Buddhists and Muslims. The most important of these, not only on account of its size, is the Muslim community. There are 1.5 million Muslims and over 1,000 mosques and prayer centres, of which the most important (in all Western Europe) is the London Central Mosque at Regent's Park. There are probably 900,000 Muslims who regularly attend these mosques. Most are of Pakistani or Bangladeshi origin, but there are also an increasing number of British converts. Apart from London, there are sizeable Muslim communities in Liverpool, Manchester, Leicester, Birmingham, Bradford, Cardiff, Edinburgh and Glasgow. Islam gives coherence and a sense of community to people of different ethnic origins. It also gives Britain informal lines of communication with several Muslim countries.

During the past quarter century, since large numbers of Muslims arrived in Britain, there has been a tension between those Muslims who sought an accommodation between Islam and Western secular society, one might call them modernists, and those who have wanted to uphold traditional Islamic values even when these directly conflicted with secular social values. The tension has been made worse by the racism Asian Muslims feel in British society. Until 1989 it might be said that those Muslims who were relatively successful economically and socially were the prevailing example of how Muslims could live successfully in the West. However, in 1988 many Muslims were deeply offended by the publication of Salman Rushdie's book *The Satanic Verses*, which they considered to be blasphemous.

Many Muslims were offended by the reaction they saw from the rest of society and from government. The blasphemy law, mainly on account of its age, only applied to Christianity, so they were unable to prosecute Rushdie. But perhaps what they found most offensive was the patronising attitude of non-Muslim liberals, who lectured them on the values of a democratic society in a way which was dismissive of Muslim identity and feeling. Muslims found themselves in conflict with those who had previously been perceived as their friends, those of the secular left who had championed immigrant rights and most strongly opposed racism.

Muslim worship in Britain. An increasingly 'British' form of Islam is emerging, especially among the younger generation.

After the Rushdie affair other external factors also stimulated a Muslim revival, including the Gulf War (1991) and also the suffering of Bosnian Muslims (1994–6).

Within the British Muslim community as a whole, which like Jewish and Christian communities, is divided into different sects and traditions, modernists lost influence to traditionalist leaders. Mosque attendance increased and religious observance became an outward symbol of Muslim assertion. In 1985 only about 20 per cent of Muslims were actually religiously observant. By 1995 that figure had risen to about 50 per cent.

Yet the Islam of young British Muslims is different from that of their parents. It is less grounded in the culture of the countries from which their parents came. Young Muslims come from several different ethnic origins but they all share their religion and their British culture and education. This is leading to a 'Britain-specific' form of Islam. As a result, in the words of one religious affairs journalist, 'For every child who drifts into the moral relativism of contemporary Western values, another returns home with a belief in a revitalised form of Islam. Many parents find the second just as difficult to come to terms with as the first.'

British Islam is sufficiently vibrant that a Muslim paper, *Q-News*, now appears regularly. One of its editors is a woman, Fozia Bora, itself a statement on the relatively liberal culture of British Islam. Indeed, a new sense of self-confidence emerged out of the initial feeling of alienation over *The Satanic Verses*. It is partly self-assertion against anti-Islamic prejudice, but it is also the comfort felt in a relatively tolerant environment. Fozia Bora believes that 'Britain is a good place to be Muslim. There is a tradition of religious and intellectual freedom.' In the opinion of Dr Zaki Badawi, one of Britain's foremost Muslims, 'Britain is the best place in the world to be a Muslim – most Muslim states are tyrannies and things are harder else-where in Europe.'

Anti-Islamic feeling, however, remains a factor in racial tensions in Britain. In the words of the Runnymede Trust, which concerns itself with race relations, 'Islamophobic discourse, sometimes blatant but frequently subtle and coded, is part of the fabric of everyday life in modern Britain, in much the same way that anti-Semitic discourse was taken for granted earlier this century.'

There are other areas of Muslim frustration. Some want Muslim family law to be recognised within British law, a measure which would allow Muslim communities in Britain to follow an entirely separate lifestyle governed by their own laws. Others want state-supported Muslim schools, where children, particularly girls, may receive a specifically Muslim education in a stricter moral atmosphere than exists in secular state schools. The state already provides such funding for Anglican, Catholic and Jewish schools within the state system. It was only in 1997 that the first Muslim school obtained financial support from the state.

Children in a traditional Quran school learning Arabic. British Muslims learn to function in two social cultures, British and Islamic.

Smaller communities include about 450,000 Sikhs who mainly originate in the Indian Punjab. They live mainly in London, Manchester and Birmingham. There are over 200 *gurdwaras* or temples in Britain. There are about 320,000 Hindus living mainly in Leicester, London and Manchester. There are about 150 *mandirs* in which Hindus worship, the largest, in Neasden, north-west London, is also the largest outside India.

Outsiders sometimes see possible tensions between one religion and another. They are less aware of the often greater tensions within each religion or sect between conservatives and liberals. In many religious groups there is a conservative wing which has little time for, or interest in, other religions and which disapproves of its own liberal co-religionists. By contrast, these liberals usually welcome dialogue and warm relations between religions, and enjoy the rich pluralism of a multi-faith society. But regardless of viewpoint, most people in Britain whether religious or not, consider the matter of faith to be a private and personal matter.

Further information

WEBSITES

The Church of England	www.church-of-england.org
The Church Times (Anglican)	www.churchtimes.co.uk
Church of Scotland	www.cofs.org.uk/3colcos.htm
Roman Catholic Church	www.tasc.ac.uk/cc/
United Synagogue	www.brijnet.org/us
Jewish Chronicle	www.jchron.co.uk
Q-News (Muslim)	www.aapi.co.uk/q-news

PRINTED MATERIAL

Graham, Y. M. 1993 *The Church Hesitant: A Portrait of the Church of England Today* HarperCollins
Harrison, Ted 1996 *Defender of the Faith: The Church and the Crisis in the Monarchy* Fount/HarperCollins

QUESTIONS

Section analysis

1 The Church of England In what way does the author believe that the Church of England is 'profoundly typical of the English character'?

2 The Church of England What are the two poles of the Anglican Church, and which theologians do they both distrust, and why?

3 The other Christian churches What are the essential differences between the Church of England and the Church of Scotland, the two 'established Churches' of Britain?

4 The other Christian Churches What is the 'house church' movement?

5 Other religions What are the main religious and secular institutions of the Jewish community in Britain?

6 Other religions Why do you think there has been a revival of religious observance among British Muslims during the 1990s?

Chapter analysis and discussion

1 Consider the following:

For the Church of England to be on its own, self-governing, free from parliamentary oversight, uninvolved in Prince Charles's affairs, would be a liberation. It could shake off its innate conservatism. Bishops could address their congregations and the wider world without inhibition. They would lose prestige but might, paradoxically, gain self-confidence and speak with greater conviction. The Church of England would be more of an adventure and all the better for it.
(Andreas Whittam Smith, *The Independent*)

What are your reactions to this point of view? Give your reasons.

2 Find evidence from the chapter both for and against this point of view:

We have a wonderful opportunity in a country like Britain. We have freedom of expression to develop our own thinking without oppression, in spite of Islamophobia. And we have the opportunity to live with Muslims from many parts of the world in a multifarious Islamic cultural mix.
(Paul Vallely and Andrew Brown, *The Independent*, Section Two)

3 Do you think that religious pluralism offers different communities a way to make sense of the world they inhabit? Or is it largely responsible for intercommunal discord? Which do you think is true of Britain? Which is true of your own country?

Textual interpretation

Unlike member-only denominations, the Church of England is broad enough to offer a spiritual home for those with almost diametrically opposing beliefs – practising gay clergy and those who regard them as sodomites, those who believe the ordination of women is heresy alongside a thousand woman priests. It is a Church where there has traditionally been space on the pew for heretics and unbelievers, doubters and sceptics. People who pray weekly sit next to people who haven't prayed since childhood. It is all part of what one bishop calls a 'grand compromise'.
(Martin Wroe and Andrew Adonis, *The Observer*)

1 Do you think this is a good formula for the established church, since it must remain at the service of every English person who wishes to join it?

2 Do you think this kind of approach to the questions of theology and belief could operate in your own society, or would the obvious contradictions be unacceptable?

14 *Transport:*
the threat of paralysis

Britain's transport and communications infrastructure is developing rapidly. The Channel Tunnel has linked the rail transport system of Great Britain to that of the European mainland. Britain's road network is being improved, with the emphasis on upgrading existing routes rather than building new motorways. Investment at seaports and airports and in air traffic control equipment is expanding capacity and easing the international movement of people and goods.

(HMSO, *Britain 1997*)

This comfortable claim, made in the official government handbook for 1997, belies the reality. Britain faces a growing crisis in its transport systems.

Rail

Britain pioneered the very first railway, in 1825. Today it has one of the least advanced systems in Western Europe. In 1948 the privately owned railway lines were nationalised and forged into one integrated system. The service was not good, partly because it was assumed that motor vehicles would finally make railways largely redundant. Investment was inadequate and the environmental advantages were ignored. By 1990 the railway system faced its most serious period of crisis since railways were first built.

During the 1980s it was part of the government's free-market philosophy that the rail service should operate on increasingly commercial lines, rather than as a public service. Government subsidy to the rail system was cut by 51 per cent during the years 1984–9, by which time it was the least subsidised rail system in Western Europe. In order to survive this stringent policy, services were reduced and fares increased substantially. By chance, this coincided with the biggest single increase in rail travel since the nineteenth century. Between 1984 and 1989 an extra 100,000

commuters started travelling into London by train, because of road congestion. Travel by British Rail became not only less reliable and more crowded, but also twice as expensive per mile as rail travel in Belgium and a third more expensive than Germany, France and the Netherlands. The boast that the railway's Intercity diesel trains were the fastest in the world, ignored the fact that increasingly electrification was recognised as the most effective power source for the railway. The explanation for the failure to convert to electrical power may lie in the fact that investment in rail by the mid-1990s was still about 30 per cent below the European average.

Virgin, one of the companies operating the rail system after the 1996 privatisation, quickly acquired a reputation for delays and break-downs.

The government decided to take its market philosophy further. It decided to privatise the rail system and to break it up into component parts. In 1996 it sold the track system to one company, Railtrack. Later that year it sold off 25 separate operating units to different companies. Those companies offered a franchise for a minimum of five years, undertook not to reduce services or increase fares unduly. In order to help the new companies the government increased its subsidy from £1.1 billion to £1.8 billion for the first two years of private operation. The public was very sceptical of the break-up of the old integrated system. By the end of 1997 it had yet to get what it had paid for in subsidies. More than two-thirds of the whole rail network suffered poorer punctuality than it had when in public hands. One operator admitted that one-quarter of all its trains ran late. Once the increased subsidy was reduced in 1998, the public also expected fares to be increased and services to be reduced as the operating companies came to terms with the real cost of running a rail service. The public also feared that staff would be reduced and safety compromised. Labour had opposed privatisation, but indicated it would not try to reverse legislation because of the enormous difficulty and costs involved. But it will almost certainly increase government regulations to ensure that the companies' motive, profit, is matched by the government's concern for a safe and effective public service.

The Channel Tunnel opened in 1994. A high-speed rail link from the tunnel to London (St Pancras) is planned to be in operation in 2003, by which time the tunnel may be carrying 17 million passengers and 800,000 tonnes of freight. Since between 17 and 30 per cent of trade with Europe (other than oil shipments) will in due course pass through the tunnel, there is still a need for high-speed rail beyond London to ensure that the Midlands, Wales, the north and Scotland can also benefit.

Congestion on Britain's motorways: the junction between the M4 and M25 in London is one of the busiest intersections in Europe.

The Shuttle arriving in France, following the opening of the Channel Tunnel in 1994.

Quite apart from the question of high-speed rail links, some transport experts argue that there is a fundamental need to convert the rail system to the continental Berne gauge, in order to enable the free flow of continental freight. In the meantime, work is being carried out to provide an improved freight facility whereby lorry trailers can be transported by rail between Glasgow and the Channel Tunnel, with the intention of reducing international road freight by up to 400,000 lorries a year by the year 2000.

Roads

The state of Britain's road system is hardly happier than the rail system. During the 1970s the new motorway system was quickly filled by new cars, as these became affordable to an increasing proportion of the population. Although the rate of car ownership is well below French or German levels, there are more cars than the road system of Britain can handle. In 1995 there were 21 million cars and 2.6 million light and heavy goods vehicles on 248,000 miles of road. Travel by car had increased by 35 per cent and road freight by 45 per cent in the preceding 10 years. One of the most significant areas of increased car use is in order to take children to school. In 1970 80 per cent of seven- and eight-year-olds went to school on their own. By the 1990s only 9 per cent did so, almost all the balance travelling by car, ironically because of the increased danger for children trying to cross busy roads.

During the first half of the 1990s a lively debate led to increasing doubts about the wisdom of building more motorways. It was increasingly felt that motorways simply encouraged more people to travel by car rather than by public transport, and the increase in traffic would rapidly prove unsustainable. The car itself began to be seen as the problem. There was increasing criticism of the two million 'company' cars, given to employees instead of direct money payment as a form of tax avoidance. By the mid-1990s the car accounted for 86 per cent of passenger mileage in Britain, buses and coaches for only 6 per cent and rail for only 5 per cent. It became increasingly obvious that travellers had to be persuaded to take public transport. Government road policy by the beginning of 1997, therefore, was simply to upgrade existing roads. Yet without rigorous discouragement the number of cars will still double by the year 2025.

There is also a serious underuse of buses and coaches. Public use of buses is half what it was in 1950, because people prefer to use cars. In 1986, as part of its market philosophy, the Conservative government deregulated bus services outside London, allowing private operators to abandon unprofitable routes. One consequence was that journeys by bus fell by 29 per cent in the decade up to 1996. By contrast, in London where regulation was maintained, passenger journeys increased by 5 per cent. Another consequence was that with more competition on popular routes overall bus mileage increased by 25 per cent in the same period, and operational costs fell by one-third, allowing the government to halve its subsidy. The challenge for government is to encourage both a more comprehensive bus service, and greater use of it, without pushing up the cost.

Air

By the mid-1990s there was also growing concern about the expansion of air traffic. The British Airports Authority (BAA) providing airport facilities argued that the airports were failing to meet the

Checking-in at Heathrow airport. The steadily increasing volume of passengers is evident to anyone who uses this airport.

rapidly growing demands placed upon them. In 1996 120 million passengers used UK airports. Although there are regional airports at Manchester, Glasgow, Birmingham, Belfast, Edinburgh, Aberdeen, Newcastle and in the East Midlands, the heaviest concentration is in the London area, primarily at Heathrow, but also Gatwick, Stansted and Luton. The annual rate of passenger increase has been about 6 per cent yearly for the past two decades. The rate will drop to about 4.5 per cent yearly until 2020, but still poses a formidable challenge. For many years Heathrow has been the busiest international airport in the world (and the fourth largest airport internationally), handling 55.7 million passengers in 1996. Since the end of the 1980s there has been a plan to enlarge Heathrow with a fifth air terminal that could double the airport's overall capacity. There is widespread resentment among the half million residents living within 10 miles of Heathrow. They strongly object to any increase in aircraft noise and air pollution, particularly as three out of 10 travellers are merely in transit to another destination. Furthermore, they are sceptical about BAA's motive, since it makes a greater profit from Heathrow's shops and carparks than from aircraft handling charges. Why should residents suffer for such a profit motive? There is also pressure to enlarge Gatwick, among the world's 30 largest airports, and Stansted.

Greater London

A major reason for delaying a decision on Heathrow's Terminal 5 has been the need to allow for vastly increased road traffic in the Heathrow area. Heathrow already lies at the heart of the busiest road system in Europe. Terminal 5 would require the M25 (London's orbital motorway) and the M4 (the principal western access road to London) to be virtually doubled in capacity, a massively expensive undertaking at a time when the wisdom of enlarging motorway capacity is already in doubt. Indeed, the M25 already illustrates Britain's acute transport dilemma. Opened in 1986, within two years it was experiencing serious traffic jams almost daily. It was intended as a bypass, but only one-third of vehicles used it as such. Most users were commuters going to and from work in the Greater London area. So the more heavily used parts of the motorway were widened to four lanes. Yet by 1996 there were on average 73 miles (117 km) of traffic jams daily on weekdays. The obvious conclusion is to widen the M25 again if it is inadequate for the amount of traffic. However,

Heavy demand on London's underground is largely a combination of commuter and tourist pressure.

there has been growing fear that bigger and better roads merely draw more cars onto the roads and lead to worse jams.

Greater London and its outlying commuter areas place a very high demand on transport services, and it is the failure of one system that leads to the heavy use of another. While the resident population of London has declined, each year more commuters enter the capital. More than 1.5 million vehicles enter or leave central London every working day. As a result, the critics of plans to enlarge the M25 argue that the real way to reduce traffic congestion throughout the Greater London area is not to build new roads or enlarge old ones, but to improve the speed, capacity, and regularity of mainline and underground trains.

In fact 85 per cent of commuters already travel on public transport. Almost 48 per cent of the one million commuters who work in central London travel in and out by rail. Yet, despite privatisation, the rail system remains seriously overcrowded and susceptible to train cancellations. The reason many people do not choose to drive to work is simple. By 1996 the average speed of traffic in London had fallen to 10 miles per hour (16 km per hour), equivalent to the speed of horse-drawn transport in the capital a century earlier. Car journey times increase by about 5 per cent each year. Bicycle is now the fastest means of transport in London. A five-mile journey will take 34 minutes by bicycle, 45 minutes by car or train and 64 minutes by bus. The city is also now very susceptible to 'gridlock', when a large segment of the entire system jams.

An increasing number of those who live in Greater London use the third main transport facility, the Underground, or 'Tube', train service, which was built from the mid-nineteenth century onwards. The London Underground is large, old and complex. Each day 2.7 million people use its 268 stations, and the number of users continues to climb. This added pressure requires replacement and expansion of infrastructure. Yet the government cut its subsidy in the 1980s and by the mid-1990s was providing about half what the Tube believed it needed. The reduction of subsidy has led inevitably to increased fares. Travel tickets cost twice as much as in Paris and five times as much as in Madrid. Failure to maintain and repair the infrastructure is also beginning to tell. By the mid-1990s the Conservative Government was beginning to plan the sale of the Tube to private operators. Labour may follow that plan reluctantly. It would prefer to keep the system publicly owned, but would find it difficult to finance the system as it deserves.

There is a further problem concerning Greater London's transport system. The capital acts as a major obstacle to traffic wishing to pass through the area but not wishing to enter it. This has major implications for increased traffic with continental Europe, and for the M25 orbital motorway. Systems need to be devised not only to facilitate movement within the region but also across or around it. Outside of London 10 cities, Birmingham (the largest city in Europe without a rapid transport system), Bristol, Sheffield, Cardiff, Edinburgh, Leeds, Portsmouth, Nottingham, Gloucester and Chester all plan to complete rapid light railway systems during the 1990s as an economic and environmentally sensitive solution to congestion problems. Newcastle and Glasgow already have one. As in London, such local solutions are unlikely to solve fundamental problems unless they are part of much wider planning.

The need for infrastructure

Without an integrated plan it is difficult to see how a national transport system in a modern economy can respond effectively and efficiently to the different demands placed upon it. Yet the provision and implication of such a plan have, for too long, been sacrificed to doctrinal arguments over free-market or nationalised services. The prospect is one of progressive failure.

As long ago as 1989 the Confederation of British Industry recognised that '... the nation's transport infrastructure is hopelessly inadequate. It is already costing £15 billion a year, or in excess of £10 per week for every household'. The problem is not, of course, merely a matter of inconvenience or of added expense. Britain is already disadvantaged within the European Union because of the additional transport costs of an offshore island. If it fails to offer investors standards of transport communications at least comparable to the European mainland, it will simply lose foreign and British business investment. In the words of the Director General of the CBI, 'We will force business to emigrate, especially to northern France where land is cheap, skills are available, and interest rates are lower; and where there is an excellent infrastructure into the rest of Europe.'

A major concern with both the road and rail system is its inadequate service to the country's peripheral regions. If the more distant parts of Britain are not to wither economically, it is vital that they are properly linked to the south east.

In 1997 the new Labour government began a major consultation in order to produce an integrated transport plan. It envisaged three basic elements: an integrated public transport system; environmentally more acceptable cars and car use; and more efficient and environmentally sustainable transport. It intended to put in place actual discouragements to vehicle use and incentives for public transport travel, and it hoped by such means to reduce car and lorry use, and to encourage the public to use public transport, to walk more and to bicycle. The secret to improved public transport, it believed, was the creation of efficient transport 'nodes', mainly railway stations where other services, bus, taxi and car hire, would be plentifully available. It also sought a comprehensive information system, and an integrated ticketing structure. But deregulation and privatisation of both bus and rail services by the previous Conservative administration looked likely to make the achievement of such aims difficult.

Further information

WEBSITES

Transport policy, etc. www.open.gov.uk
(functional index 'transport')

QUESTIONS

Section analysis

1 Rail Why did the Conservative government cut the subsidy to British Rail so severely in the 1980s?

2 Rail Why is Labour unlikely to reverse rail privatisation?

3 Roads What are the essential arguments in the debate over whether or not to build more motorways?

4 Air Who opposes the proposed Terminal 5 at Heathrow Airport and why?

5 Greater London List the basic problems of commuting into central London by a) car; b) rail; c) Tube.

6 The need for infrastructure What are the penalties for Britain's economy if an effective transport infrastructure is not created?

Chapter analysis and discussion

1 What do you think is the most serious problem with Britain's transport system?
a failure to modernise the railways
b an inadequate network of roads
c an unwillingness to subsidise public transport
d a lack of overall planning, especially in London
e inadequate integration with the European transport networks as part of the Channel Tunnel development

2 'There is still an island mentality at large in this country which is preventing us from seeing the tremendous implications of high-speed trains for Europe.'
Do you agree with this statement about Britain?

3 How does Britain's transport system compare with the system in your own country? Discuss the following points:
a provision of railways, roads and airports
b level of government subsidy
c future planning to meet growing demand
d solutions to traffic congestion in major cities

Visual interpretation

Study the following graphs. Why might they dissuade you, if you were British, from buying a car?

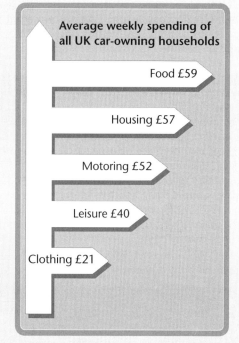

Source: AA/LSE/Family expenditure survey/Department of Environment and Transport

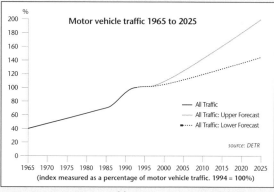

Source: Department of the Environment and Transport

15 *The environment*

The environment and pollution

Like other countries, Britain became more conscious of the degradation of the environment during the 1980s. By the 1990s in almost every sphere of environmental protection the key criterion for policy was the idea of 'sustainability', i.e. the reduction of all forms of environmental degradation to levels that do not cause lasting damage or permanent loss.

National concern has occurred not a moment too soon. With its high population density Britain is more susceptible than most countries to environmental degradation, and thus requires close governmental control and planning in order to protect and regulate all aspects of environment use. Strategic planning is primarily the responsibility of county (or Scottish unitary) councils, while district councils undertake local plans and development control. Nevertheless, central government retains overall authority and overturns county council decisions when it wishes to do so. Inevitably this is an area of tension between national and regional concerns.

Nowhere is the conflict between profitability, or private interest, and public well-being more obvious than in the question of pollution. Britain has been struggling with serious air pollution problems for decades. A century ago it was the sulphur and carbon dioxide from the domestic use of coal that created the notorious mix of smoke and fog popularly known as 'smog'. From the 1950s untreated coal ceased to be used domestically in large cities. Between the 1970s and 1990s a major effort was made to reduce coal-burning for electricity generation, halving sulphur dioxide emissions from 6.2 million tonnes in 1970 to 3 million tonnes in 1994, reducing the poisonous effect of acid rain on forests. Today nitrogen oxide and carbon monoxide emissions, over half of which is derived from motor vehicles, pose the greatest problem to air quality. Each year several thousand people die prematurely on account of poor air quality, while at least 20,000 chronic cases are admitted to hospital. From 1995 the government set standards and introduced a compulsory annual check on the exhaust gas of every vehicle. But the real answer is to reduce the emissions of each vehicle and also to reduce the number of private vehicles on the roads (22 million in 1997). One obvious measure would be to tax carbon fuels. Labour is more reluctant to do this than the Conservatives because it hits the poor hardest. The poorest fifth of the population spend 12 per cent of their income on fuel, while the richest fifth spend only 4 per cent.

The connection between emissions and global warming is now well established. Average temperatures are expected to rise in Britain by 0.2ºC every decade up to 2050. The south will get drier and the north wetter. Another theory is that global warming will destroy the Gulf Stream system. Without the Gulf Stream, most of Britain (and much of northern Europe) will, paradoxically, suffer extreme cold.

Britain is committed to a 30 per cent reduction in carbon dioxide emissions by 2005, and is installing

Sea pollution caused by effluent washed onto Blackpool beach, the North of England's most popular seaside resort.

Tree death from air pollution caused by a nearby power station.

flue gas desulphurisation equipment at every power station. It also intends to generate 3 per cent of its energy requirements from renewable sources. In 1997 it began constructing the world's largest offshore wind farm off the Essex coast. Its 40 turbines will generate sufficient power for a town of 70,000 people. Sixty-five other wind turbine projects are planned.

Water quality is also a major problem. Rivers are still insufficiently protected against polluters: farmers using high levels of nitrates as fertiliser, and industries flushing harmful chemicals into water courses. In 1989 an independent survey estimated that 10 per cent of Britain's rivers were so polluted that they could no longer sustain fish. Furthermore, the actual quantity of water used, particularly in dry periods, adversely affects river flow and river life. Britain must be more economical with its water, but no substantive measures have yet been taken to achieve this.

On land, too, pollutants are a major problem. Britain produces 500 million tonnes of material waste each year, almost 9 tonnes of waste per person. 'Landfill' facilities are limited. Already a substantial quantity of glass, metal and paper is recycled. In 1995 local authorities were set targets:

to recycle or compost 25 per cent of household waste by 2000, and to reduce the amount of waste going to landfill by 40 per cent by 2005. In 1996 the government introduced a landfill tax at two levels, one for inactive waste like bricks and rubble, and a much higher one on waste that contaminates or decays.

Country and town planning

A major concern has been to protect the countryside. Broadly speaking, there have been two major threats. The first comes from agriculture and land use. Chemical fertilisers and pesticides have been destructive of wildlife. More damaging, however, has been the destruction of Britain's hedgerows. Britain, Ireland and northern France have a unique inheritance of hedgerows. England, with only 7.5 per cent of its land area still woodland, is about the most deforested country in Europe. Hedgerows, therefore, are particularly important. Most of them are at least 300 years old, some over 1,000 years old, and a few are relics of ancient woodland before humans started clearing forests some 5,000 years ago. They are a crucial haven for both rare flora and fauna. Some hedgerows have been grubbed up over the past 10 years by farmers wishing to enlarge their fields for highly mechanised wheat production. Even more have perished as a result of neglect. It is estimated that 110,000 miles (177,000 km) of hedgerow, over 20 per cent of the total, have been destroyed since 1986. The government vowed in 1986 to legislate to protect hedgerows but no effective measures have yet been taken.

Rape seed is an example of the tendency towards monoculture in modern farming. A variety of plant and animals species is essential for a vibrant ecology.

Tree-top 'eco-warriors' obstructing the felling of trees. They often attract press coverage and popular admiration.

The other threat comes from urbanisation. At least 40 per cent of 4.4 million new dwellings needed over the next 20 years will be built on 'greenfield' sites in the countryside. While the countryside no longer provides gainful employment, there are still many people who wish to live in the countryside but work in town. On average, 300 people go to live in the countryside every day. That, and growing dependence on private cars for travel, puts pressure on roads in the country. A report in 1996 concluded that while only 17 per cent of England was urbanised, 50 per cent was now seriously disturbed by noise and other forms of pollution generated by traffic. No fewer than 5,000 country lanes that were quiet only 25 years ago, now carry between 2,000 and 5,000 vehicles a day. An area the size of Wales has lost its tranquillity since the mid-1960s. As more people move to or travel across the countryside more roads are built.

One of the strongest indicators of community mobilisation in Britain is the way in which protesters have organised and effectively lobbied against many road or housing development plans. In the 1980s such protesters were frequently derided with a brand new word, 'nimby', an acronym meaning 'not in my back yard'. But in the early 1990s a new kind of protester emerged. 'Eco-warriors' as they were called, were not interested in 'public consultation' because they had no confidence their protests would be effective. Instead, they took every physical measure short of violence to thwart construction workers laying roads or airfields (see p.188). Their protests changed the climate of opinion in the country, dramatically reminding the population of what was being lost through enlargement of the transport system.

In growing recognition of the fragility of the environment, the government commissioned the biggest single survey of England's countryside since the Domesday survey, carried out 900 years earlier, in 1086. Its first step was to produce a map of 157 distinct natural areas, based upon the geology and flora that characterised each. It was hoped the exercise would provide a base line for deciding where new housing would cause minimal damage, and where, for example, to site new woodlands.

In the period 1981–94 no fewer than 1.25 million people left Britain's largest metropolitan areas to live in the countryside. London alone lost over 630,000 people, and the West Midlands conurbation centred on Birmingham lost almost 250,000. Although the process has slowed down, persuading people to return to the city has not been easy. The only sizeable group showing any interest in living centrally in cities are 16–29 year-olds without children. Britain, unlike other European countries has tended to use buildings for only one purpose, either as shops, offices or dwellings. During the 1990s there was an increasing trend among planners to encourage multi-use buildings that would include flats as well as shops or offices, as a means of bringing people back into the city.

Successive governments established entirely new urban areas after the Second World War. Thirty-two new towns have been built since 1946, housing two million people. In contrast, other urban areas have been allowed to decline. In 1990 it was estimated that the number of derelict urban sites in all Britain was equivalent to the area of Greater London. In the 1980s the most dramatic redevelopment of such dereliction was in London's old docklands. Old wharves, or warehouses, were refurbished as luxury flats, in an attempt to revive the local community with a wealthier stratum, and also to draw more economic activity into the area. The most famous and controversial part of the plan involved Canary Wharf on the Isle of Dogs. This site, almost 300,000 square metres, was the biggest ever business development in Europe up to that time. Twenty-six buildings under construction were to provide over one million square metres of office space for up to 60,000 workers. At the centre of Canary Wharf a tower 244 metres high was constructed.

Developments of this kind require confidence as well as finance. In 1990 London Docklands was in crisis with falling land prices and 42 per cent of office space vacant. The Canary Wharf project went bankrupt on completion in 1992.
The revitalisation of Britain's cities depends upon people wishing to live in them, for it is only a resident community which provides cities with culture and colour. In some cases local people have rescued derelict areas. In 1989 in Finsbury Park in north London, for example, local residents helped set up a development company to redevelop an area of old railway sidings, 36,000 square metres, which had been derelict for 20 years. The project, involving £30 million, created an estate of attractive low-cost housing. The idea of community intervention – usually initiated by a handful of angry local people – has started a growing movement of popular action to reclaim such sites, where local government has proved ineffectual.

Urban reclamation is an important issue in Britain if its cities are not to follow in the footsteps of North American ones, where the core of the city dies, and people live and work around the periphery. It is too important to be left to unsupported local community action. The need is for government intervention to provide attractive urban amenities and a highly efficient transport system. This means reducing the number of vehicles in urban areas by making it quicker and cheaper to travel by public transport, and planning those arterial routes which are necessary in a way which does not destroy local life. It also means reversing the trend towards shopping by car at superstores, and reinvigorating the high street, the traditional focus for each local community. By 1997 there was growing concern that central

Peterborough's cathedral precinct acts like a lung in the city centre, providing open space and beauty.

government was not acting vigorously enough to protect the community.

The success of new towns has been uneven. In general those closest to the south east, have been the most successful. Peterborough is a good example. In 1960 it was a dismal and dirty city in decline. Thirty years later it was a bustling cathedral city, with 50,000 more inhabitants and 30,000 more jobs. It is the centre of modern automated engineering with a broad-based service economy. It is also, perhaps less healthily, a commuter town for London. According to the planners who revived Peterborough's fortunes, there were three vital ideas running through the city's redevelopment: an eighteenth-century English idea of bringing the countryside right into the heart of the city (as Regent's Park and Hyde Park do for London); a nineteenth-century industrial utopianism that produced model factories and worker housing; and finally a determination to create a coherent new town within clear confines rather than a sprawling area of random development.

Housing

Britain has an unusually high proportion of owner-occupied dwellings. This is a late twentieth-century phenomenon. In 1914 less than 10 per cent of the population lived in their own homes and 90 per cent of dwellings were privately rented. The real change took place after 1945. By 1960 the proportion of owner-occupied dwellings had risen to 44 per cent, and by 1995 to 67 per cent. This is true even of young single people. For example, 54 per cent of single people under the age of 40 in England are home owners, compared with only 14 per cent in France. For a highly urbanised country, Britain is also distinctive because of its 24.6 million dwellings barely 5 million are flats, or apartments. The rest are houses. Depending on size and also location, there is a hierarchy of desirability. 'Detached' houses, ones that stand on their own, are the most desirable, followed in descending order by 'semi-detached', ones joined to another house, 'terraced', ones joined in a row of more than two, followed by flats, with those in tower blocks at the bottom of the scale.

During the 1980s the Conservatives encouraged home ownership. They believed that state-owned housing failed to cultivate local pride and responsibility. Public housing had become important after 1918 and even more so with the establishment of the welfare state after 1945. In the 1980s the Conservatives obliged local authorities to allow purchase of public housing by

The backs of nineteenth-century terrace housing. Such housing now provides a strong sense of community often lacking in the more contemporary high-rise blocks.

tenants. Many dwellings were sold. Local authorities were also encouraged to hand over the management of the rest of their houses to private housing associations, non-profit organisations which, the government believed, would maintain them more efficiently on a commercial basis. Some councils resisted the wholesale discarding of their housing stock, but central government applied budgetary pressures to ensure that rents were increased, becoming closer to commercial ones in the private sector.

Also in line with its belief in free-market forces, the government largely abandoned the construction of public housing. In the 1970s approximately 100,000 publicly-funded homes were built each year. By 1987 the annual figure was 15,000, and by 1990 less than 10,000. The government looked to the private sector to build new homes, but the number of homes built fell dramatically. Anyway, private builders built the type of home they believed would be most profitable, for upwardly mobile, professional people. In 1995 only 812 local authority owned and 30,000 housing association dwellings were built.

By the end of the 1980s there was a severe shortage of low-cost housing. As mentioned earlier, over 4 million new dwellings will be required nationally by 2016 to meet the growing demand. A substantial proportion must be low cost, and for single people. In 1987 22 per cent of dwellings were occupied by single people, a proportion that will rise to 30 per cent by 2016. The rural sector is particularly affected. Because of a steep increase in house prices caused by the purchase of country cottages by commuters and city dwellers wanting second homes, by 1995 12 low-cost homes were, on average, needed in each village in order to keep pace with the need, six times greater than the planned housing increase. In an attempt to meet the great backlog of demand there was a major increase in house-building in the mid-1990s.

A major reason for housing difficulties has been fluctuations of the market. When demand outstrips supply, as it did during most of the 1980s, prices are forced upwards, making it difficult for young, first-time buyers. Although this makes things harder for everyone, it is the lower-income groups which suffer most. During the past 30 years almost everyone has borrowed money to buy their home. From 1989 growing recession changed the tendency towards home ownership. House prices ceased rising and began to fall, a trend which brought about a major slump in the housing market and the construction industry. Rising

interest rates meant that an increasing number of those who had purchased property in the 1980s could no longer keep up with their mortgage repayments. By 1992 this had reached crisis proportions, with 140,000 repossessions by lending institutions in 1991, 120,000 in 1992 and 100,000 in 1993. It cast doubt on Conservative enthusiasm for property ownership and revived interest in public and private rented accommodation.

This terrace housing is owned by a housing association, providing good quality housing to low-income families.

Conservative housing policies also contributed to the rising number of homeless people which doubled during the 1980s, probably exceeding 350,000 people. In theory by law each local authority must provide accommodation for the homeless of the borough or district. But the 1977 law was modified in 1983 to disqualify those who have intentionally left homes 'where it would have been reasonable' for them to stay, giving local authorities considerable freedom to refuse to accommodate people. This significantly reduced the number of officially homeless people. Nevertheless, more than 40,000 families, let alone individuals, were homeless and in temporary accommodation in 1997.

The vast majority of homeless people flock to London, where they hope to find some way of earning a living. Most are young school-leavers who may have been thrown out of home or been the victims of domestic violence or sexual abuse. In London they find a new difficulty. In order to rent a room they must pay a deposit. It is impossible to raise the money without having a job. It is extremely difficult to get a job without a home address. Even government job training is refused to people without an address.

Many homeless people sleeping 'rough' are only teenagers, like this girl.

As a result of government policy to return as many psychiatric patients as possible to the community, a growing number of mentally-ill people have ended up on the streets. Some stay in cheap and badly equipped hotels or hostels.

Many local authority dwellings in London remain empty and derelict, while there are over 6,000 families housed in bed-and-breakfast hotels. The reason for this strange situation is simple. Local authorities either have inadequate housing stock or have insufficient funds to refurbish derelict accommodation, but they can obtain central government funding for temporary accommodation. The financial waste and human suffering involved is a product of a belief that the state should reduce the provision of state-owned housing in order to make people more self-reliant. By 1997 this policy was clearly a failure, and Labour promised to ensure enough publicly and privately financed dwellings to deal with the problem.

In addition to those living in hostels or hotels, by 1998 there were still almost 400 people sleeping rough in central London each night, approximately one-fifth of the total estimated to be sleeping rough in England. Known as 'dossers', they are embarrassingly visible evidence of the underclass, a sharp reminder to the more fortunate, as they leave the theatre or concert hall, of the proximity of human pain and misery.

Further information

WEBSITES

Environment policy, etc. www.open.gov.uk
(functional index 'environme
Conservation Foundation www.gn.apc.org
(& website index)
Ecologist Magazine   "   "
Ecosystem   "   "
Green Alliance   "   "

PRINTED MATERIAL

Adonis, Andrew and Pollard, Stephen 1997
A Class Act: The Myth of Britain's Classless Society
Chapter 7 Hamish Hamilton
Coxall, Bill and Robins, Lynton 1994
Contemporary British Politics Chapters 23 (housing) and 28 (the environment) Macmillan
Harvey, Graham 1998 *The Killing of the Countryside* Vintage
Malpass, P. 1990 *Reshaping Housing Policy* Routledge
Robinson, M. 1992 *The Greening of British Party Polit.* Manchester University Press

QUESTIONS

Section analysis

1 **The environment and pollution** What are the major causes of pollution in Britain?

2 **Country and town planning** What is meant by 'urban reclamation'? Why is it important?

3 **Country and town planning** Explain the emergence of 'eco-warriors' and what they have achieved.

4 **Housing** Under the Conservative government, 1979–97, a free market approach to housing brought about major changes. What problems have those changes caused? Who has benefited from them? Who has suffered?

5 **Housing** What proportion of people in Britain own their own homes? How many dwellings In Britain are flats, and how many are houses? How do these statistics compare with your country?

Chapter analysis and discussion

1 Has government action
   a helped to protect the environment?
   b succeeded in controlling pollution?
   c promoted successful town planning?

2 Compare Britain's environmental problems with those of your country under the following headings:
   a river pollution
   b acid rain and the production of 'greenhouse' gases
   c preservation of the countryside
   d urban reclamation

3 Discuss the impact on the environment of the following:
   a out-of-town shopping centres
   b privatisation of water authorities
   c intensive agriculture
   d an efficient urban transport system
   e the purchase by town dwellers of weekend country cottages

Visual interpretation

1 Consider the following two maps of England and the table of information indicating the erosion of tranquillity over a 30-year period. What regional conclusions can you draw, and how do these conclusions relate to concepts such as north–south and core–periphery?

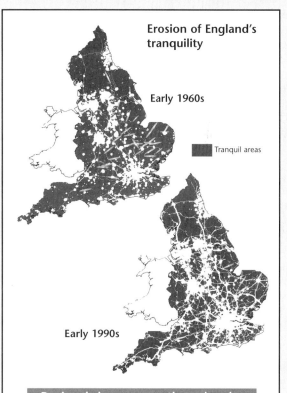

Erosion of England's tranquility

Early 1960s

Tranquil areas

Early 1990s

Regional changes over three decades			
	1960s tranquil areas	1990s tranquil areas	change
East Anglia	72%	64%	-8%
East Midlands	70%	56%	-14%
North East	75%	68%	-7%
North West	67%	55%	-12%
South East	58%	38%	-20%
South West	83%	66%	-17%
West Midlands	70%	55%	-15%
Yorkshire & Humberside	74%	60%	-14%
ENGLAND	**70%**	**56%**	**-14%**

Source: CPRE

16 *The nation's health and well-being*

For most of the century the state in Britain has recognised it has a responsibility to ensure that nobody should be without the basic necessities of life as a result of poverty, unemployment, old age or sickness. After the Second World War the government created health and welfare services which have been the core of 'the welfare state'. The system has grown over the years, funded mainly by tax, but also through National Insurance contributions, compulsory payments made by all earners and their employers. These contributions guarantee a small pension on retirement (now fixed at the age of 65, except for women born before April 1950, who still qualify at the age of 60), a period of income support after becoming unemployed, and a pension if unable to work because of sickness.

By the end of the 1970s these services were becoming increasingly costly and bureaucratic. During the 1980s the Conservatives decided upon major reforms, to use less money but to use it with more discrimination. Reforming the welfare system has proved more complex than expected, and it still suffers from serious problems, some arising from the very attempts at reform.

The National Health Service

The National Health Service (NHS) was established in 1948 to provide high-quality free medical treatment in hospital and outside. Its fundamental principle was equitable access for all, regardless of wealth.

The system rests on a network of family doctors, or 'GPs' (general practitioners) as they are usually known, with attached nurses and other community-based staff. People may register with any GP they choose, as long as the GP is willing to register them. A GP with a full register might refuse extra patients. Beyond the group practice lies the whole arrangement of hospitals and community health services, for example health visitors who monitor the health of vulnerable categories of people, such as mothers and newborn babies, or the old and infirm.

GPs remain the backbone of the NHS, dealing with the vast majority of ailments, and referring those requiring more specialist diagnosis to a hospital, or notifying the health visitor of those who need to be monitored at home. (Many other industrialised countries lost their 'first line' of generalist 'family' doctors during the post-war years.) Except in an emergency, it is normally the GP who refers a patient to hospital for more specialist care, or for an operation. Most GPs have about 2,000 people on their register, some of whom will hardly ever visit the GP's surgery. Others may be regular callers. A GP is often expected to offer pastoral guidance as well as medical skill. On a normal day a GP might see about 35 patients in surgery, and make up to 10 home visits to those who feel too ill to attend surgery. The strength of the system lies in a good working knowledge of the families and individuals in the catchment area, their housing, lifestyle and employment conditions. Good GPs build up an intimate knowledge of their 'parish', and take into account not merely the specific complaint of a patient but also the patient's general conditions of life. Almost all GPs now operate in small groups of perhaps three or more, employing nurses and other professionals such as physiotherapists or dieticians, so that they can share the administrative load and also offer a wider service.

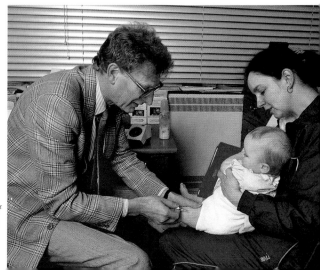

General practitioners provide the front-line of Britain's health services.

A physiotherapist treating a disabled person.

The NHS is the responsibility of the Secretary of State for Health. Until 1995 England was divided administratively into 14 regional health authorities, usually based upon a university medical school, each authority was subdivided into between 10 and 15 districts, and each district was based on one large hospital but also included other hospitals. Since 1996 the regional health authorities have been reduced to eight. Similar authorities or boards exist in Wales, Scotland and Northern Ireland.

The entire system is free, with the exception of prescribed drugs, dental treatment, sight tests and spectacles, for which there are standard charges, except for old age pensioners, children under 16 and some other categories for whom some of these items are free. Anyone entering hospital for surgery will receive all their treatment while in hospital, including drugs, free of charge. Over 80 per cent of the costs of the NHS are funded out of the income tax system. The balance is paid for out of National Insurance contributions and from the prescription charges mentioned above.

On the whole the system has worked extremely well, providing care at lower per capita cost than almost any other industrialised country. Foreign health economists admire the NHS above all for its GP system. GPs control referrals to hospital, and therefore costs, and also provide a local register of the population whereby one may engage in all sorts of targeted health measurements, including vaccination and immunisation. They also admire the NHS for its treatment for all, regardless of the ability to pay; a tax-based funding relating the service to need rather than to income. Finally, they admire its relative efficiency – a characteristic that

would surprise the patients in most British hospital waiting rooms. They have been critical of its lack of consumer choice, and believe that British doctors should delegate more tasks to nurses, and nurses more tasks to order lies.

The cost of providing a service that employs just under one million staff has always been enormous. By the late 1980s, the health and linked social services budget reached one-fifth of all public spending, two-thirds allocated to hospital and community services and one-third to family practitioner services: the GPs, dentists and pharmacists. There is little flexibility for reformers, since over 70 per cent of the budget goes on staff costs.

During the 1980s the government tried to improve efficiency and cut costs. Hospitals reduced the average patient stay by 20 per cent, and increased the number of 'in' and 'day' patients by a quarter. For the NHS such stringency was uncomfortable, for Britain already spent proportionately less on its health service than any other of the main 20 industrialised countries, with the exception of New Zealand, Greece, Portugal and Spain.

By the mid-1980s the annual financial demand on the NHS was growing by 2 per cent above inflation. One factor was the ageing population, possibly accounting for an annual 1 per cent increase in costs. There will be over half a million people aged over 90 by 2001. Every person over the age of 75 costs the NHS seven times more than one of working age. In addition, medical advances were adding about 0.5 per cent annually onto NHS costs. In the winter of 1987–8 the NHS moved into a state of crisis with the sudden closure of 4,000 beds all over the country.

So the Conservative government carried out the most fundamental reforms of the NHS since its foundation. In keeping with its free-market philosophy, it sought a 'demand-led' system which would get as close as possible to consumer choice, and would compel health practitioners to account for the cost of the treatments they prescribed. As long as doctors did not have to face the financial cost of their own work, it was argued, they would not make the hard choices necessary for maximum efficiency. Consequently two categories of 'purchaser' were created: the local health authorities and volunteer GP group practices. They purchased hospital services according to which hospitals seemed to offer the best value for money. It was believed that such a competitive regime would force hospitals to be ultra-efficient in order to attract custom. Purchasers were free to choose contract providers outside their own health authority area. Furthermore, hospitals were free to opt out of local health authority control to become 'NHS Trusts', autonomous and directly funded hospitals selling their services to GPs and health authorities.

The internal-market philosophy had two inexorable effects. First, it was inevitable that a competitive market would produce both winners and losers, and that the winners would tend to be the best-equipped or best-located hospitals that were not overwhelmed with high local levels of sickness. Also, not every GP practice was given purchasing powers, and by 1996 only about 50 per cent had become 'fundholders'. In order to qualify for fundholding status, a GP needed to have a register of 3,000 patients, except in certain rural areas. Fundholding proved controversial. Some doctors welcomed the powers it offered, both for their patients and themselves. Others regretted the greatly increased administrative burden. Meanwhile those GPs without fundholding powers were unable to exercise choice. They found themselves compelled to belong to a market system but with the health authority determining where their patients would get treatment. Where health authorities were under acute financial pressure it was inevitable that the cheapest hospital treatment was the most attractive. Thus a 'two-tier' system, one tier superior to the other, was unmistakably emerging, contradicting the original NHS ethic.

Another area for concern was the loss of public accountability. The government created a Health Executive to manage the new service. This quango was answerable only to the Secretary of State for Health. This loss of accountability was also true at a local level, where elected representatives of the community were no longer part of the local health authority. The other obvious defects were the burgeoning of a health bureaucracy to deal with the new internal market at all levels, the huge transaction costs of running a contract market, and the severely reduced ability of health authorities to plan strategy when their own powers were largely limited to that of purchasers.

Yet there were also gains. One of the main observable achievements of the new system was to halve the waiting times for hospital operations in its first five years. GP practices were also encouraged to widen the services that they were able to perform, including minor surgery, as a more effective primary health care service that could significantly reduce the number of referrals to hospital.

By 1996 the NHS was again in crisis, partly because of inadequate funding. The annual budget by 1996 was in the order of £42,000 million, but tight funding once again led to the closure of wards, and waiting lists again began to grow. One of the problems was that the new system reduced the flexibility of the health authorities to switch money between one need and another. The creation of self-governing trusts, for example, locked up capital investment in relatively small pockets. But it was also true that the annual increase in the cost of the NHS had risen to almost 3 per cent before inflation, by 1996.

A Private Finance Initiative to attract commercial enterprises to build and own new hospitals which could then be leased to the local health authority for periods of 25 or even 60 years, shows little sign of working. The scheme was intended to alleviate the government's short term difficulties. But health authorities feared being locked into long-term contracts from which they had no escape. Moreover, no private investor was likely to put the health of the community before its own commercial interest.

By 1996 the NHS faced a serious staffing crisis. This was the result of several factors: a miscalculation over medical school enrolment in the 1980s that led to a 15 per cent fall in trainee doctors between 1988 and 1994; a greater proportion of women health professionals and of these an unexpectedly high number wishing to work part- rather than full-time; low morale among GPs, leading to many older ones taking early retirement. Finally, there was the quite unforeseen impact of stricter immigration laws

A health visitor, part of community nursing, visits a mother and new-born baby.

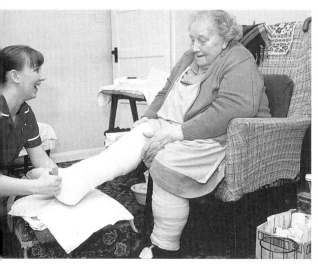
A district nurse, part of the cadre of community nurses, helping a patient at home.

introduced in 1985. Twenty-five per cent of GPs and many junior hospital doctors are from abroad. The change of law in 1985 brought this source of expertise to a halt.

It conveys an idea of the difficulties Labour inherited in 1997 that two-thirds of the health authorities entered the new financial year (which always starts on 6 April), four weeks before Labour's victory, already in debt. Labour faced the immediate task of finding sufficient money to resolve the crisis it inherited. It also had to decide what to do with the internal market to which it was opposed. Rather than subject the NHS to yet more revolutionary changes, Labour decided to modify the system in the hope of retaining its virtues but eliminating its defects. It therefore proposed increasing and restructuring the purchasing power of general practice. It proposed to abandon fundholding by individual group practices, and to group up to approximately 50 GPs serving up to 100,000 people, and to give them about 90 per cent of the NHS budget. These groups would choose the best local balance between community nursing (which keeps people out of hospital), direct primary care including the subsidy for prescribed medicines, and referral to hospital (the least cost effective option). It was hoped this would achieve a real shift from institution-centred to person-centred care, and foster strategic planning at the local level. Each group would still make service agreements with local hospitals. The reduced number of health authorities would receive less than 10 per cent of the NHS budget, and use it for highly specialist treatments like heart transplants. Labour hopes that this will achieve yet more administrative savings while making the NHS more responsive to community needs.

Britain has one of the highest levels of coronary disease and strokes in the industrialised world, particularly among those under 65 years of age. Between 1990 and 1994 the NHS was able to achieve a reduction of 19 per cent in deaths from these causes. But there is a long way to go to bring it into line with other industrialised countries. The British rate of premature deaths from this cause is, for example, three times higher than that in France. It has also been a priority to reduce the mortality rate due to cancers. The NHS has been less successful in some other areas. Take smoking, which accounts for 110,000 premature deaths and 50 million lost working days each year, and costs the NHS £610 million annually in treatment. The level of adult smoking currently is about 33 per cent. While smoking among the adult population is slowly falling, it is increasing among 11–15 year-olds, particularly among girls. The level in this age band in 1994 stood at 13 per cent of girls and 10 per cent of boys.

Like much of the industrialised world, obesity is a growing problem. Despite health warnings and advice on diet, obesity in Britain has doubled in the decade 1986–96, with 17 per cent of men and 13 per cent of women now clinically obese.

Excessive drinking is also a concern, with an increase in alcohol consumption among women, a symptom of the growing part played by women outside the home and the greater stress this implies. One million people have a serious drink problem, but the disturbing feature is that it has become a young addiction. Twenty is the peak age for alcoholic consumption, in contrast with half a century ago when few young men drank.

Britain also lives with a potential time bomb caused by 'mad cow disease', Bovine Spongiform Encephalopathy (BSE). The future incidence of the human form of BSE, a strain of Creutzfeldt Jakob Disease (CJD) cannot be predicted, and 15 years may pass before the scale of human infection is fully known.

Social security and social services

Although 'the welfare state' was created after the Second World War, its origins are a good deal older. In 1907 a reforming Liberal government provided free school meals in its schools. The following year it introduced an old age pension scheme, implicitly accepting responsibility to protect the old from destitution. In 1909 it opened 'labour exchanges' where the unemployed could look for jobs. Two years later it made all working people pay 'national insurance' to provide a fund for those unable to earn either through sickness or unemployment. Thus the crucial principle of the state's obligation to assist the weak in society was firmly established.

The cost of that principle, however, is potentially enormous. The number of people dependent upon social security rose sharply during the 1980s. This was mainly because of the rapid increase in the proportion of the population over the age of 65, who consumed 44 per cent of social security expenditure. But there was also an increase in the unemployed and in dependent single-parent families, partly the result of Conservative policy. Ironically, its idea of 'minimum government' created maximum dependency as the government ceased to protect jobs in what it saw as inefficient or obsolete industries. A ruthless free-market

A 'home-help' assists an old man to dress. Such help ensures that thousands of old people can continue to live relatively independently.

economy led many middle-aged people to take early retirement, either willingly or unwillingly. By the 1990s barely half the males aged 60–64 years old were still in work compared with 90 per cent in the 1960s. Furthermore, 25 per cent of males and 50 per cent of females aged 55–59 no longer worked. This reduced the number of contributors to social security and added to its consumers.

Repeated attempts were made during the 1980s and 1990s to reduce the government burden. The Social Security Act of 1986 sought to reduce costs and target assistance more effectively. It encouraged people to move away from the State Earnings-Related Pension Scheme (SERPS) into private pension schemes. Because of the progressive increase in the proportion of elderly people, the government feared the state would be unable to honour its commitments. The Social Security Act also tried to slim down its system of help to particular categories of people. It refused to recognise those under 25 as homeless, since it argued that people under this age were still the responsibility of their parents. This contradicted the government argument that people should be willing to leave home in order to find work. It also ignored the fact that a substantial number of young homeless were fleeing family conflict, or had been brought up in council care. Sixteen year-old school-leavers became particularly vulnerable since they were not eligible for unemployment benefit until they became eighteen. A growing number ended up sleeping rough.

The reduction of income support or housing benefit undoubtedly put pressure on some to seek employment more actively, as the government intended. The legislation was supposed to end forever the idea that some people could be better off without a job than they would be by going to work. 'Family credit', which sought to 'top up' low pay, was meant to fulfil this intention, but failed to rescue many people from the 'poverty trap'. This is well described by one opponent of family credit: 'Family credit is bad news, I'm afraid … . Many families will be getting more benefit, but you will be trapping them in poverty because each time they earn an extra pound in net income they will lose 70p in family credit and, taking housing benefit into account, they will lose up to 97p in the pound.'

On the other hand, from 1993 the Conservative government provided help for those who were not institutionalised but cared for by their families at home. The new policy placed responsibility on local authorities to assess the needs of dependent categories and to provide appropriate assistance in a flexible way. This proved better for the invalid, better for the carer (many of whom in the past suffered great stress), and better for government, since it led to a long-term saving on institutional care.

Labour inherited a major unresolved problem. By the mid-1990s half the households in Britain were on some kind of means-tested benefit. It wanted to avoid raising taxes for extra funding, and adopted a fresh approach, based on the principle of a twin responsibility, that of the community to help those 'who fall on hard times', and the responsibility of all individuals to make their own provision for foreseeable extra costs, for example pensions, social and nursing care for the elderly. That implied a mixture of public (community) and private (individual) funding provision. When it took office it examined ways to make private provision compulsory. Besides wishing to reduce the community burden, Labour also wished to end the enormous waste of young lives through unemployment. In the words of Frank Field MP, Labour's leading expert on social security, 'Unemployment is both destroying self-respect and teaching that the only way to survive is to cheat. Means-tested benefits paralyse self-help, discourage self-improvement and tax honesty. It destroys social solidarity and polarises society between rich and poor.' Labour began to assist some of the one million young single parents to find work that would guarantee substantially extra money each week.

Social security is provided by central government, but social services are almost entirely the responsibility of local government. The local authorities are responsible for services to the elderly, for example institutional accommodation (only about 5 per cent of those over 65 live in institutional accommodation) and support services to encourage them to continue to live at home. Such support includes the home delivery of hot meals ('meals on wheels'), domestic help, laundry services and adaptations in the home, for example fixing handrails in the bathroom. Most of these services are either free or heavily subsidised. Many of the 6.5 million who are physically and mentally disabled enjoy similar support, and also counselling on the personal and social problems arising from their disability. Residential accommodation is available for the severely disabled, and for the mentally ill. A fundamental principle, however, has been to encourage, wherever possible, the disabled or ill to stay within the community, rather than enter institutions. Although this sounds self-evidently sensible, in practice it has proved controversial since many of

those mentally ill actually needed the care of an institution, and ended up sleeping on the streets as the ultimate result of this policy.

The local authority also has social welfare responsibilities for those with particular problems, such as single parents and children at risk of injury, neglect or abuse at home. During the 1980s, for example, local authorities became much more aware of the sexual abuse of children, something which had previously been thought of as a rarity. It slowly recognised that possibly 8 per cent of children suffer some kind of sexual abuse, and that physical violence to children and sexual abuse were related. In certain cases the local authority is empowered to remove children from home if they are considered to be at risk. Local authorities are also required to provide child day-care facilities.

The local authorities could not possibly carry out these responsibilities without the help of voluntary social services. In fact, over 65,000 registered voluntary organisations exist to provide particular forms of help. A few are known nationally, serving, for example, the blind, or those with cerebral palsy and other specific problems. The vast majority, however, operate on a local level, supported by volunteers.

A residential home for old people. Many people will only enter residential homes once they suffer mental degeneration.

In the London Borough of Richmond, for example, the Vineyard Project provides a day centre in a church basement, with activities for a wide range of people who require community support. Some have had mental illness, others are homeless or feel alienated in some way. They have somewhere to go where they are welcome. Nearby the Single

Community service: young offenders working on an ecological project.

Persons' Emergency Accommodation in Richmond (SPEAR), provides accommodation for up to three weeks for those stranded without a home. It can accommodate 12 people, providing them with a base from which to seek a job and to seek somewhere to rent. Its wardens assist in the search for long-term accommodation. Such is its success, that many of those who pass through SPEAR continue to use it afterwards as a social centre in the evenings. Voluntary support on a daily basis is provided by the churches of the locality. Both the Vineyard Project, and its daughter project, SPEAR, only began as a result of the concern and determination of local people. Each year they must find the money and the volunteers to keep them going. This is the kind of thing being done all over Britain by many of these 65,000 voluntary organisations.

During the 1980s such voluntary efforts came under greatly increased pressure. The government believed the community, i.e. the churches and voluntary organisations, should shoulder more of the welfare burden, while its social security policy also resulted in increased homelessness and poverty for certain categories. Organisations like SPEAR came into being to respond to a growing need. It remains to be seen whether Labour will be able to meet the demands of the needy more effectively.

Further information

WEBSITES

Department of Health   www.open.gov.uk
(functional index 'health')

PRINTED MATERIAL

Adonis, Andrew and Pollard, Stephen 1997
A Class Act: The Myth of Britain's Classless Society
Chapter 6 Hamish Hamilton
Coxall, Bill and Robins, Lynton 1994
Contemporary British Politics Chapter 22 Macmillan
Wood, B. 1992 *The Politics of Health* Politics Associati

QUESTIONS

Section analysis

1 The National Health Service What are the strengths of the GP system?

2 The National Health Service What are the main reasons for the steep rise in the cost of the NHS?

3 The National Health Service What reforms did the Conservative government introduce for hospitals, GPs and regional health authorities, and what do you think were the virtues and defects of these reforms?

4 Social security and services Why did the number of people dependent on social security rise sharply during the period of Conservative government, 1979–97?

5 Social security and services In what ways did the 1986 Social Security Act reduce help provided for young people? What problems resulted?

6 Social security and services How did the Social Security Act of 1986 attempt to reduce the government's social security burden?

Chapter analysis and discussion

1 Policies on health care and social security have changed since the 1970s. In what ways have the following developments affected these changes?
a the huge increase in the number of elderly people
b the growing number of unemployed people
c the desire of government to spend less on health and social security

2 The 65,000 voluntary organisations in Britain provide many forms of help. Do you think that voluntary organisations
a allow the government to avoid its responsibilities?
b put pressure on the government to meet its responsibilities?
c should provide more free help for those in need?

3 Compare the situation in Britain with that in your own country under the following headings:
a Availability of free medical treatment
b Incidence of alcoholism
c Provision of residential accommodation for the elderly, disabled and mentally ill

Visual interpretation

1 Consider the inpatient waiting list graph and the table of comparative expenditure on health by different countries through public and private funding below. Based upon what you have read and on this graphic information, give your opinion in answer to the following questions.
a Do the British probably get best value for money?
b Is Britain underfunding its health service?
c Should it encourage a larger private sector based on ability to pay, as in most other countries, or provide more public funds?

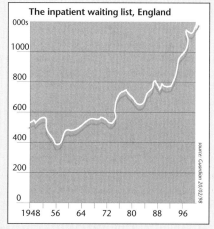

Source: *The Guardian*

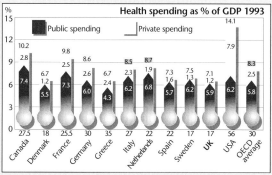

Source: OECD

17 Time for a drink: the British pub

It is appropriate that any book on Britain should end where many British people relax at the end of the working day, in that most popular of places for relaxation, the pub. The British pub exercises a special fascination for foreigners. In fact it is so popular that many imitations exist around the world, some relatively successful, others less so.

Public houses date back to the inns and taverns of the Middle Ages, places where local people met and where travellers stayed. They have always been characterised by conviviality, intimacy and an egalitarian atmosphere. They have always been immensely popular, as Dr Samuel Johnson, the eighteenth-century writer, remarked: 'No, Sir, there is nothing which has yet been contrived by man, by which so much happiness is produced, as by a good tavern or inn.'

For many British that feeling persists, but standards vary considerably. They still like to walk into their 'local' and be sure they will meet someone they know. 'In a good pub,' according to *The Good Beer Guide*,

the greatest attention is given to the drink, and in particular to the beer. Sociability, on both sides of the bar, comes a close second. A good pub encourages social intercourse, and is not dominated by cliques … . In a good pub, whatever further services are offered, there is always one bar (and preferably two) to accommodate those people who simply want to drink and chat without distraction or inhibition induced by overbearing decor, noisy entertainment, or intrusive dining.

This succinct verdict sums up characteristics that should be present but are frequently missing in some of the 80,000 British pubs today. The reasons are manifold, but are largely to do with the integration and growing homogeneity of British society. During the 1960s half a dozen major beer breweries began to buy both small local breweries and local pubs. By the 1980s only a handful of small breweries and barely a quarter of all pubs remained independent. The big breweries bought the pubs in order to market their own beer as effectively as possible.

Traditional English ale or beer rapidly disappeared from most pubs during the 1960s and 1970s. This 'real ale' required special care, for it remained alive and continued to ferment in its wooden cask in the pub cellar, beneath the bar. It was made from barley, hops and pure water and required storage at a constant cool temperature. It was not refrigerated and contained no carbon dioxide gas. To those used to drinking refrigerated lager, real ale can taste flat, warm and weak. To many British, it is the only beer with real taste. The big breweries found it easier to produce 'keg' beer, a pasteurised brew, containing carbon dioxide, that required no special care. It was stored in metal barrels under pressure. It was easier for the manufacturer and for the publican who served the beer to the customer. But it did not compare with the real thing.

The big breweries, in fierce competition with each other, each tried to create their own 'house' style by ripping out the interiors of old pubs and refurbishing them according to a standard appearance which they believed would attract most customers. In so doing they destroyed an essential appeal of many pubs, their individuality. They also tried to improve efficiency and reduce the number of staff required to serve drinks. Most pubs had at least two different rooms for drinking, the public bar and a smarter and slightly more expensive 'saloon' bar.

It was only to saloon bars that women were taken until the greater social liberalisation of the 1960s. Pubs, it should be noted, are still essentially male preserves. Although the days are long past when a woman entering a pub alone was disapproved of, there are still a few pubs particularly in socially conservative areas where women are not welcome, and it is still true that men use pubs far more than do women.

The impact of big brewery control, therefore, is primarily twofold. The quality of the beer has gone down, and large open rooms have replaced two or three less efficient but more cosy rooms, thereby destroying the intimacy which made pubs attractive. The pubs owned by big breweries have also tried to concentrate on a particular clientele. In particular they have tried to appeal to younger people in their twenties. This was not a new development. Many pubs were known for their special character. For example in socially mixed parts of town one pub might be proudly working class and another might attract middle-class people. In Kilburn in London where a large Irish community exists a number of pubs had a strong Irish character. But by the mid-1990s 'Irish' pubs had become widespread, with the popularity of all things Irish. Some pubs have become favoured by particular sub-cultures: motorbikers, students, and so forth.

The warmth and conviviality of a pub will often vary across cities, towns or villages. This is a city pub.

Yet the increased 'specialisation' of pubs has undermined an essential feature of pubs as local community centres where young and old, men and women may meet to relax. In particular, the absence of older men and also of women in many 'specialist' pubs, and the creation of large open rooms in place of more intimate nooks removes some of the restraining influences which discourage young men from drinking too much and misbehaving.

During the 1980s there was a revolt against the power of the big breweries. The Campaign for Real Ale (CAMRA) gained much popular support and a growing number of pubs began to stock real old-fashioned beer as well as keg beer. The big breweries began to allow their tenant publicans to develop the character of their pub as they chose, and to stock a wider variety of beer than merely one brand. In part this was because the big breweries found that pubs were now more profitable than the drink they produced, and that diversification in pubs was desirable.

Today an increasing number of pubs serve food, and coffee or tea as well as alcoholic drinks. Food, which accounted for only 10 per cent of profits in 1980 now accounts for more like 30 per cent. Providing good cheap food is now an important source of profit. The best pubs produce excellent homemade food and welcome families. The best also, even if they attract people from far and wide, still rely on a reliable local clientele who give the pub its basic atmosphere. The worst pubs remain impersonal and only serve mass-produced food, which is often more expensive and less tasty than homemade fare. The greatest threat to pub quality by the mid-1990s was arguably the noise of loud music, making conversation harder with a counterfeit atmosphere of conviviality.

In 1988 the government relaxed the previously strict opening hours, to allow pubs to remain open all day. Fewer than expected have used the opportunity, except to stay open on Saturday afternoons or to remain open for an extra hour on Sunday afternoons. In 1994 pubs were also allowed a certificate to allow children to enter the premises, on condition a separate area could be designated for family use.

Pubs will continue to vary greatly, between the delightful and the ghastly. But in some ways they reflect more accurately than anything else the strengths and weaknesses of British society – strong community feeling in one pub, for example, and the bland tasteless homogeneity of modern society in another. It is also in the pub that people are usually unafraid to express their views, whether these conform to traditional British characteristics of understatement and moderation or whether they reflect a new stridency. For anyone interested in understanding Britain better, the pub is not a bad place to start.

Glossary

Compiled with the help of the *Longman Dictionary of Contemporary English* and the *Longman Dictionary of the English Language*

appeal a formal request to a higher law court to change the decision of a lower court

audit an official examination of the accounts of a business

baby boom a period of high birth rate

backbone the part of a group that provides the main support

balance the books to show or make sure that the money that has been spent is equal to the money that is available

ballot (v) to find out the views of a group by holding a vote

black economy business activity that is carried on unofficially, especially to avoid taxation

bobby on the beat a policeman on duty walking his regular route

boom town a town where wealth and population are growing very fast

break the mould transform the pattern

bring into line with make something work or happen according to a particular system or set of rules

bring to heel force into obedience

Broad Scots the dialect of English spoken in Lowland Scotland

buck to oppose in a direct manner

buzz a very pleasant stimulation

by-election a special election held to replace a politician who has left parliament or died

cadre an inner group of highly trained people in society or an organisation

caste a group of people set apart from the rest of society on the basis of differences in wealth/rank/profession

caution a spoken warning given by a police officer, when the person has broken the law but when the crime is not serious

charter a signed statement from a government, giving rights, freedoms, etc. to the people

claptrap nonsense, stupid talk or writing

clique a closely united (small) group of people who do not allow others to join their group easily

clubland the world of nightclubs

code, criminal/civil/of practice a collection of laws/rules

constituency area or body of voters electing a representative member, more loosely a particular category of support

conurbation a group of towns that have spread and joined together to form an area of high population

cream-off to remove the best people or things

custom-built made especially for an individual or group of people

decency threshold the lowest socially acceptable level

dissolve Parliament disband the present composition of Parliament, thus requiring election to a new Parliament

dodge to avoid responsibility in some dishonest way

dogged by to be relentlessly pursued by someone or something

electoral roll the official list of people who have the right to vote

establishment (adj) supportive of the established order of society

estate, country a (large) piece of land in the country, usually with one large house on it and one owner

estate, housing a piece of land on which houses have all been built together in a planned way

flagship the finest product in a set of things made by a company/industry

freeze to fix prices or income officially at a particular level

fringe (theatre) alternative, unconventional or innovative

gerrymander manipulate an electoral district in such a way as to give one party a particular advantage

grassroots the basic or fundamental level, of society for example

hand in the till embezzlement or other misappropriation of money

harness to use something to produce power

hinterland an area far from urban centres

hipster a person who has a keen awareness of or interest in the newest (cultural) developments

house style the style adopted by a particular company

hub the centre of activity/importance

hung, of a parliament evenly divided between opposing parties, so that decisions cannot be made

jackpot accumulated top prize of money

lip service insincere support

lobby a group of people who are for or against a planned action, in an attempt to persuade those in power to change their minds

local (n) a pub near where one lives, where one often drinks

market forces the free operation of business/trade without any controls by government

melting pot a situation in which different groups or cultures mingle to form a new whole

nerve centre a place from which a system is controlled

off the record given/made unofficially and not to be publicly attributed

old boy a former pupil of a school

peer a member of any five noble ranks: baron, viscount, earl, marquis, duke

peer, life a peer who cannot pass on his/her rank to a son/ daughter after death

plant to hide something on someone, so it will be found out and the person seem guilty

power-house a place which produces things with great forcefulness

revamp to give a new and better form to something

quirky with a particular, possibly eccentric, trait of character or style

rosy giving hope, especially without good reason

rough-and-ready simple

rubber stamp something which acts only to make official the decisions already made by another

run-down in bad condition

seat, marginal a seat which may be lost or won by a small number of votes

seat, safe a seat which is certain to be won in an election by the present holder

self-made having gained success and wealth by one's own efforts alone

shadow (v) to watch closely

shopping arcade a covered passageway or avenue between shops

slapstick boisterous farcical comedy

sleep rough to sleep without proper lodging

splinter group a breakaway group

stalemate a situation in which neither side in a quarrel can get an advantage

stand (v) to compete for an office in an election

subculture a religious, economic, ideological, etc., group distinguishable by a shared pattern of behaviour, attitudes or dress from the surrounding culture

test (match, cricket) any of a series of international sports matches, especially cricket matches

tightly knit closely united by social/political/religious beliefs/ activities

twist someone's arm to persuade someone forcefully to do what one wants

upwardly mobile able to move into a higher social class and become wealthier

walkabout (n) to mingle informally with ordinary people

wanted column a column of advertisements in a newspaper placed by people wanting things

Winter of Discontent a misquotation from the opening line of Shakespeare's *Richard III*, used as an effective political weapon against Labour in 1979

Index